Stay

STAY

*A History of Suicide
and the Philosophies
Against It*

JENNIFER MICHAEL HECHT

Yale UNIVERSITY PRESS
New Haven and London

Lines from Lucretius, *On the Nature of Things*, are reprinted with permission of The
Johns Hopkins University Press from Lucretius, *On the Nature of Things: De rerum
natura*, pages 26–27, copyright © 1995 by The Johns Hopkins University Press.

Yale University Press books may be purchased in quantity for educational, business,
or promotional use. For information, please e-mail sales.press@yale.edu (U.S. office)
or sales@yaleup.co.uk (U.K. office).

Set in Minion type by Integrated Publishing Solutions, Grand Rapids, Michigan.
Printed in the United States of America.

Library of Congress Cataloging-in-Publication Data
Hecht, Jennifer Michael, 1965–. Stay : a history of suicide and the philosophies
against it / Jennifer Michael Hecht.
pages   cm
Includes bibliographical references and index.
ISBN 978-0-300-18608-6 (cloth : alk. paper)   1. Suicide.   2. Suicide—
Prevention.   3. Communities.   I. Title.
HV6545.H372 2013
179.7—dc23   2013016107

A catalogue record for this book is available from the British Library.

This paper meets the requirements of ANSI/NISO Z39.48-1992
(Permanence of Paper).

10 9 8 7 6 5 4 3 2 1

For you who struggle and hold on

Contents

Preface

It was through my scholarly work that I first grew interested in the subject of what people live for in difficult situations, especially when they have no religion, as was the case with many of the people I wrote about in my book *Doubt: A History*. It was through my personal life that I became interested in suicide. In 2007 an old friend and successful poet, Sarah Hannah, whom I had known from graduate school at Columbia University, took her own life. Had she not told me about her sadness, I wouldn't have guessed: she had good friends and a teaching job she loved, she was young and beautiful, and she was writing whip-smart, psychologically rich poetry. At the time I had been going through some frighteningly dark emotional times myself, and so while her death was not incomprehensible to me, it was intensely shocking nonetheless. Our mutual friend from graduate school, Rachel Wetzsteon, another poet, felt that same shock and expressed it in an afterword to Sarah's posthumous poetry book. Then in 2009, just after becoming the poetry editor at the *New Republic* and completing another highly praised semester of teaching, Rachel took her own life as well. These events knocked me around, forced me to confront how we today think about our lives and deaths, and drew

me to ask questions of history and philosophy, the realms I
always turn to seeking understanding. A year or so after Sarah
died I was planning a scholarly essay about the conclusions I
had reached. Before I could write it, I found myself trying to
take in the fact that Rachel was gone too.

A few weeks after I heard that Rachel killed herself, I
wrote an open-letter essay about it for a website I blog for,
The Best American Poetry. I began by stating plainly that I
was feeling rattled by the death. My husband had recently run
into Rachel on the High Line, the Manhattan park built on
old elevated train tracks; I related the encounter, he with our
kids, she with her boyfriend, all walking around, looking at the
flowers, looking down at the city. Then I addressed the reader
with a bold imperative: "So I want to say this, and forgive me
the strangeness of it. Don't kill yourself. Life has always been
almost too hard to bear, for a lot of the people, a lot of the
time. It's awful. But it isn't too hard to bear, it's only almost
too hard to bear." In the West, I wrote, the dominant religions
had told people suicide was against the rules, they must not do
it; if they did they would be punished in the afterlife. "People
killed themselves anyway, of course, but the strict injunction
must have helped keep a billion moments of anguish from
turning into calamity. These days we encourage people to stay
alive and not kill themselves, but we say it for the person's own
sake. It's illegal, sure, but no one actually insists that suicide is
wrong." I announced: "I'm issuing a rule. You are not allowed
to kill yourself. When a person kills himself, he does wrench-
ing damage to the community. One of the best predictors of
suicide is knowing a suicide. That means that suicide is also
delayed homicide. You have to stay."

I told my readers that I was grateful to everyone who
remained alive. I was thinking of specific poets I know who

I thought might stumble upon my post or find it in searching for information on Rachel. I imagined these men and women on the edge of doing what she had done, and I knew many other people unknown to me were struggling; I hoped that they might read my plea, might heed my plea. They were out there, maybe at their desks, and I was inside, at my desk; I was moved to support them, and with a little effort I could feel them supporting me. I claimed that some part of them doesn't want to end it all, and said to that part, "I'm throwing you a rope, you don't have to explain it to the monster in you, just tell the monster it can do whatever it wants, but not that. Later we'll get rid of the monster, for now just hang on to the rope. I know that this means a struggle from one second to the next, let alone one day at a time." I said, "Sobbing and useless is great! Sobbing and useless is a million times better than dead. A billion times. Thank you for choosing sobbing and useless over dead." The essay ended: "Don't kill yourself. Suffer here with us instead. We need you with us, we have not forgotten you, you are our hero. Stay."

The essay drew a large response on the Internet, prompting an editor of the Ideas section at the *Boston Globe* to contact me and ask to publish it in the Sunday paper. The *Globe* printed it on a lovely blue background over a half-page. In the days and months that followed I received a lot of email from people who had read the essay. I heard from men and women who had lost parents to suicide, and several who had lost a child. I heard from people who had once been suicidal and people who were suicidal now. I remember a woman worried for her teenaged son and a husband in despair for his suicidal wife. They thanked me for saying what they hadn't been able to say: "Stay." They had not known how to ask.

I was, and still am, especially moved by people who tell

me that my word and ideas got them through a bad time. The urgency of this made me dedicate myself to the present project, difficult though it has been to think so deeply and constantly on such a painful topic.

After I'd written this manifesto in the heat of emotion, and gotten a significant positive response, it became necessary to recheck all the claims that held the argument together. Did religion take a stand against suicide across most of Western history? How and why? Even more important, how true was the claim that suicide influences others to suicide? Is it demonstrably true that "one of the key predictors of suicide is knowing a suicide"? What about this idea of "a monster in you" that needed to be outsmarted until it could be chased away—does this metaphor imply that no one is fully in his or her "right mind" when ending it all? Then I went looking for philosophers and other writers who had declared that human beings contribute just by continuing to persist in life and rejecting suicide despite anguish. I also surveyed what had been said about the consistent nature of the self over time in relation to such a final act as suicide. The results of these investigations surprised me. The only idea that I had presented that I did not find in my studies was the notion that we owe each other gratitude for staying alive. This book contains what I have learned in my historical and sociological research into these matters and my thoughts on what all of this may mean to us today.

Acknowledgments

Many thanks to my editor at Yale University Press, Jennifer Banks, for her help and insight; and to Dan Heaton, who copy-edited the book with great care. Thanks also go to my agent, John Loudon, for helping me find the right home for this book. Bob and Blaikie Worth have my gratitude for their support of the project.

As always, I am grateful to my husband, John, and our son and daughter, Maxwell and Jessie, for their love.

Stay

Introduction

Ancient Roman history begins with a suicide. The virtuous and lovely Lucretia lived in the late sixth century B.C.E. A married woman and the daughter of a man of distinction, she was known for her industry and faithfulness. The boot of Italy was ruled in ancient times by Etruscan kings, but its people already called themselves Roman. Noble Roman families supported Etruscan kings, but there were considerable tensions. Then one night, as the story is told, a group of Etruscan and Roman men were drinking and got into a discussion comparing the character of their wives. Lucretia's husband boasted about her virtue, and when the men sent someone to check on her, indeed Lucretia was at home weaving and supervising her servants' work. The son of the Etruscan king, Tarquin, was among the drinking party, and he grew obsessed with Lucretia. Waiting until she was alone, he went to her, told her he wanted her, and offered to make her his queen. He told her that if she resisted he would rape and kill her, then cover up the deed by killing a male slave and telling everyone that he had chanced upon them having sex and had

killed them for it. To avoid ruining her reputation, she gave
in to her attacker. He left believing that to defend her life
and her good name, she would guard the secret of what had
happened.

It is an awful story, of course, but for the Romans who told
it, it is Lucretia who triumphs. She dresses herself in black and
runs to her highborn kinsmen, calling together her husband,
father, brothers, and friends, and tells them what the Etruscan
prince did. She demands revenge against the man who did this
to her, but also on the entire political system that allowed it.
Then she takes out a dagger and kills herself. Having told her
own story, she protects her own honor. As she breathes her last,
the gathered men pass around the dagger that killed her and
swear on it an oath that begins, "By this blood—most pure before the outrage wrought by the king's son . . ." and ends "I will
not suffer them or anyone else to reign in Rome." The story
then usually takes the spotlight off Lucretia's corpse and follows
instead the men as they storm off to overthrow the Etruscans.
Thus begins the story of Roman self-governance.

Lucretia's death took place at the very commencement
of Roman history in 508 B.C.E., and it remained an article of
Roman faith that the outrages that led to her death spurred
her countrymen to overthrow their foreign king and to establish not another kingdom but the Roman Republic. The
story emphasizes how highly honor was prized in the ancient
Roman and Greek world, even unto death. Across the next six
centuries Lucretia was celebrated with increasing fervor. Suicides accent the ancient Greek and Roman worlds: Socrates,
Cato, Seneca, and Cleopatra. Socrates in particular showed
how to dispatch oneself with benign calm. Sentenced to death
for atheism and corrupting the youth, he accepted his cup of
hemlock, soothed his friends, and contentedly downed the

poison. The Stoics especially came to regard death lightly; accepting death without emotion was a sign of philosophical maturity. Lucretia's heroic death ensured her cultural immortality. Centuries later she was painted by such celebrated European artists as Titian and Botticelli, as well as by the most renowned woman painter of the Renaissance, Artemisia Gentileschi. Lucretia's image was rendered by the acclaimed engraver Marcantonio Raimondi, and by such lights as Dürer, Raphael, and Rembrandt. Lucretia's story was also told in Chaucer's *Canterbury Tales*, in Dante's *Inferno*, and in Shakespeare's long poem *The Rape of Lucrece*.

In this book we shall follow Lucretia through history, scrutinize several other key suicides—some more famous today, like Samson's under his ceiling and Cleopatra's with her asp—and track self-murder's strange, sometimes eerie, and always instructive guises. These historical travels will reveal a fascinating story about the meaning of suicide across history. It is a compelling story in its own right. It also helps us understand the way people think about suicide in our time. It is a tremendous issue.

In the United States over the past twenty years more than 30,000 people have taken their own lives per year. In the latest documented data from the Centers for Disease Control and Prevention, from 2010, the number was up to 38,364.[1] Consistently, historically and now, more people die of suicide than are murdered.[2] Worldwide, more die of suicide every year than by drowning, or fire, or maternal hemorrhage. Worldwide, for both men and women between the ages of fifteen and forty-four, more die of suicide than in war. In the first half of 2012, active-duty U.S. troops killed themselves at a rate averaging one a day; in 2010 (the latest year for which statistics are available) the rate among U.S. military veterans reached one every sixty-five minutes—about twenty-two a day.[3] For American men under thirty-five, suicide has killed more than AIDS in all but three years since the disease first appeared.[4] Suicide is among Americans' top ten causes of death, and for adults under forty-five, it is among the top three. Between the ages of twenty-five and thirty-four, a death is more likely to be by suicide than by anything but accident; more die of suicide than of AIDS, cancer, heart disease, or liver disease. The rate of increase has been higher among the young, but in sheer numbers suicide is most common between ages thirty-five and sixty-four.[5]

Worse yet, the rates are rising. According to the World Health Organization, in the past forty-five years suicide rates have increased by 60 percent worldwide.[6] In the past ten years the rise has been shocking: in 2001 the number of suicides per year in the United States was 30,622 compared with more than 38,000 in 2010. Between 2008 and 2009 alone, the suicide rate in the United States rose by 2.4 percent.[7] Some of the dramatic increase in this most recent period has been among the young, middle-aged white women, and soldiers and veterans—but the increase is felt across most groups that have been examined. Why are we not responding to this tragedy? Unlike so many other dangers to public health and safety, suicide can seem like a crime without a real victim. But the person who commits suicide is, in fact, a real victim. Additionally, the friends, family, and community of those who die suffer mightily, even fatally, and are likewise victims. The whole of humanity suffers when someone opts out. The suicide is also a real victim because he or she had a future self that may not have wanted this.

As I examine the history of how, in the West, we have understood self-killing, I also will put forward what might seem to be a contrarian position, a nonreligious argument against suicide. It is a philosophical argument but parts of it can or even must be told in terms of history, and parts must be demonstrated through modern statistics. One of the arguments I hope to bring to light is that suicidal influence is strong enough that a suicide might also be considered a homicide. Whether you call it contagion, suicidal clusters, or sociocultural modeling, our social sciences demonstrate that suicide causes more suicide, both among those who knew the person and among the strangers who somehow identified with the victim. If suicide has a pernicious influence on others, then staying alive has the opposite influence: it helps keep people alive. By staying alive, we are contributing something precious to the world.

Another main argument that I hope to rescue from history is that the suicidal person owes something to his or her future self; a future self who might feel better and be grateful that the person who he or she once was fought through the terrible times to make it to something better.

We tend to think that as modern people we should be able to live our lives with less delusion than people in the past. Yet by looking at ourselves from a fresh historical perspective, we see that our arguments with the old beliefs of our culture have led us into some ideological dead ends. In this book I show that history set us up for an unwinnable battle—there is no triumph in having argued people into the grave—and offer the reader another way of seeing our historical path and our possibilities for ourselves and for the future.

When I looked into history to find whether philosophers had articulated this idea before, I was surprised to find two excellent arguments against suicide widely commented upon in history, but still relatively unknown. The first is that we owe it to society at large, and especially to our personal communities, to stay alive. The second is that we owe it to our other selves, especially, as I have mentioned, to our future selves. Both religious and philosophical writers have written marvelous things about both these ideas, but they are often in the background. The reason is that a foreground argument has gotten all the press: Religious people have tended to lean heavily on the argument that God forbids suicide. Meanwhile, in response, secular, philosophical people have insisted that we are free to take our own lives. In my experience, outside the idea that God forbids it, our society today has no coherent argument against suicide. Instead, many self-described open-minded, rationalist, sophisticated thinkers emphatically defend people's right to do it. How did the secular philosophical worldview come to claim people's right to suicide? How did those in the modern world—who fight death so fiercely elsewhere—come to accept or at least leave unchallenged an ideology that kills? The answer is a fascinating story of a reaction against religion that somewhat accidentally led to a dark fatalism.

Historically there have been some great minds, religious and secular, who have argued for our interdependence and mutual need. More recently, there have been numerous sociological, epidemiological, and psychological studies demonstrating the reality and power of suicidal influence. We also have evidence that intervention can reverse that influence. Schools have been shown to experience a rise in the suicide rate after a single suicide, but "talk-throughs" can change those results. Ideas can take lives and other ideas can save lives.

Throughout the medieval and early modern periods in Europe, suicide was condemned by the major Western religions, Judaism, Christianity, and Islam. Suicide was considered a more damning sin than murder, because you were actually stealing from God; what is more, you were doing so with no time left for repentance. The prohibition did not stop everyone, but we have examples in fiction and nonfiction from across history of people turning away from suicide because of the religious rule against it. It was not only divine justice that a suicidal person had to worry about, though. Throughout the Middle Ages, the Christian Church condemned suicides; commonly the church enforced punishment of the corpses, which might be dragged through the streets, impaled on a fence and left to rot and be eaten by animals, or buried at crossroads with stakes through their hearts. More practically, the suicide's estate could be confiscated, further harming his surviving family. Dante's *Inferno* is but one of many works of literary and figurative art to provide graphic depictions of the hell awaiting the suicide's soul, and these must have been a serious deterrent for some Christians.

Religion took a wrong turn by relying so heavily on divine disapproval of suicide, and on corporal (even postmortem) punishment of the offender, and secular philosophy took a wrong turn when it concluded that without God and religion, man was his own master and thus people should be free to kill themselves. Both religious people and those against or indifferent to religion have written about other reasons to reject suicide, and my intention is to bring those arguments to modern attention.

In the early modern period, Hamlet could not think about suicide without worrying about the possibility that the afterlife might be a horrible dream. Shakespeare wrote the play around 1603, just as ideas about suicide were in flux, with some theatrical description still showing it as evil and some

taking it as a reasonable response to bad fortune. Indeed, it is
worth hearing him mull it over in his own words:

> To die, to sleep;
> To sleep: perchance to dream: ay, there's the rub;
> For in that sleep of death what dreams may come
> When we have shuffled off this mortal coil,
> Must give us pause: there's the respect
> That makes calamity of so long life;
> For who would bear the whips and scorns of time,
> The oppressor's wrong, the proud man's contumely,
> The pangs of despised love, the law's delay,
> The insolence of office and the spurns
> That patient merit of the unworthy takes,
> When he himself might his quietus make
> With a bare bodkin? who would fardels bear,
> To grunt and sweat under a weary life,
> But that the dread of something after death,
> The undiscover'd country . . .

A bodkin is a large needle with a large eye used for pulling
ribbon through a hole or loop in fabric. It will come up several
times in the history of suicide.

"Who would bear" this painful life, Hamlet asks, if he
or she were not kept from suicide by "the dread of something
after death"? Even for those who did not believe in the specifics
of Christian hell, the prospect of some kind of life after death
was full of fears and doubts. For Hamlet, suicide is off the table
because death might be worse than life.

During the Enlightenment, as people questioned church
doctrines, from its attitude toward poverty to sexual mores
and marriage laws, the prohibition of suicide also came under

scrutiny. Philosophers such as David Hume and the Baron d'Holbach launched campaigns defending suicide. The church had long had enormous power over private citizens, and its gruesome suppression of suicides and would-be suicides reflected that imbalance. Secular thinkers now declared that the church had no right to outlaw suicide. Wrote Hume,

> The superstitious man, says Tully, is miserable in every scene, in every incident in life; even sleep itself, which banishes all other cares of unhappy mortals, affords to him matter of new terror; while he examines his dreams, and finds in those visions of the night prognostications of future calamities. I may add that tho' death alone can put a full period to his misery, he dares not fly to this refuge, but still prolongs a miserable existence from a vain fear lest he offend his Maker, by using the power, with which that beneficent being has endowed him.[8]

The Enlightenment enhanced the value of the self above that of community and tradition and made of each man and woman an independent being. As we will see, both Hume and d'Holbach sometimes advocated the right to suicide so vociferously that they can be said to have been recommending suicide. Thus, built right into the world's most momentous revolution about the value of average individual human beings was a mechanism by which they were invited to judge their own lives, possibly to find them without value or worth, and to end them.

The Enlightenment's rationalist defense of suicide grew through particular historical events and conversations, especially between clergy and philosophers. On the one hand, persecution of attempted suicides continued, albeit in much attenuated form, and in some places, the suicide's estate was still liable to seizure. On the other hand, some secular voices rejected the religious condemnation of suicide, even defending it as a positive phenomenon, honorable and emancipating. For the clergy, suicide was wrong because God said it was wrong, and harsh injunctions against it were demanded. For Voltaire and Hume and d'Holbach and other rationalists, God and the church had nothing to say about the matter.

The advance of modernity brought new concern for individual rights and private property, and these, as well as the rise of the scientific medical profession, began to have an effect on government policies. In the seventeenth century suicide had still been seen, in part, as the work of the devil. By the eighteenth, "melancholia" was the dominant term in discussing suicide—and melancholia was the purview of doctors. From the worst sin possible, suicide became relatively value neutral; it could even be seen as virtuous when enacted in protest against an insult to one's ideals. By the twentieth century, there was a general sense among secularists that people had a right to suicide, and a right to make the decision on their own.

Today, millions of people have no religion, and there are millions more whose religious beliefs do not completely rule out suicide. Yet our culture's only systematic argument against suicide is about God. This limitation is untenable because even among believers, some believe that God will forgive the act and provide a blessed afterlife, and even in the absence of that faith, a suicidal person in her darkest hour might not be able to feel the God she otherwise believes in. Those who believe in no god, obviously, will not be dissuaded from suicide by a divine proscription. Generally, we *ask* people not to do it, for their own sake, but we do not say that they must not do it. We have no secular, logical antisuicide consensus. The arguments against suicide that I intend to revivify in public consciousness assert that suicide is wrong, that it harms the community, that it damages humanity, that it unfairly preempts your future self. Throughout history an optimistic cavalcade of people has sidestepped the religious debate and put forward sound reasons to resist suicide based on each of our relationships to humanity, especially friends and family. Today's sociological studies back up the historical claim that we need one another—or, rather, the specific claim that suicide causes suicides. Anti-suicide philosophers, meanwhile, claim that we owe ourselves better, that the self that wants to do us in is not the true self, that something real and potent exists beyond the individual. Furthermore, religion had something right when it emphasized the collateral benefits of surviving through pain. Some brilliant secular minds have also written on the subject. The atheist philosopher Arthur Schopenhauer in particular believed that the very pain we want so much to avoid is the most express path to wisdom. I will also consider some modern dissenting opinions to the idea that suicide is wrong, and offer some responses.

As may be clear already, this book is chiefly about despair suicide, rather than what might be called end-of-life management. People who are fatally ill and in terrible pain are dealing with different issues and may certainly be seen as altering the way that their illness kills them, rather than actually taking their own lives. Of course, ailing people may also be depressed and may struggle with the worry of being a burden, and in this sense the message of this book might be of use to them as well. It is possible to be unkindly permissive to such a person on the subject of hastening death. Still, what I am most particularly addressing is the problem of darkness in the midst of life, and what I want to say is that there are arguments against suicide that ask individuals to hold on. It is also worth mentioning that I am attempting to reach those people sufficiently lucid as to be available to be reached through argument. Camus surmised that he was "only slightly indulging in irony" when he guessed that this population vacillating on the brink of suicide constituted the majority of humanity.

I also want to point out that I do not mean to pass judgment on those who have committed suicide. I mean instead to express to the suicidal person who has rejected suicide that you deserve gratitude from your community and from humanity. I assign no blame to those already lost, I only feel sorrow for them. Instead, I am trying to proselytize to the living in favor of rejecting suicide. The main New York University library has put up a high decorative wall (above the old fencing) around all the precipice walkways that abut an open middle space down to the lobby floor. They did this after losing too many students to suicide there. Writers through history have given us conceptual barriers to suicide with which we ought to be familiar, as a culture.

Some of the stories this book tells of are dark but rich; when read deeply, even desolate stories can help us live. Consider contemporary author Pat Conroy, writing of literary characters who committed suicide but whom he sees as warnings against it. "Let me call on the spirit of Anna Karenina. . . . Let me beckon Madame Bovary to issue me a cursory note of warning whenever I get suicidal or despairing as I live out a life too sad by half."[9] Karenina threw herself under a train; Bovary drank arsenic. Both somehow call us back to ourselves—and, as Conroy attested, back to life. We need to recognize the strange nature of human experience and let it encourage us. We need to share our pain: it is an act of consolation when

Conroy offers a description of his life as "too sad by half." Tolstoy's and Flaubert's heroines had many predecessors. Familiarity with these stories provides a strange solace. In 1621 the scholar Robert Burton wrote, "I write of melancholy by being busy to avoid melancholy."[10] Likewise, reading about depression can lend some peace of mind. It helps to find out that one is really not alone in extreme sadness, but that it has been shared by much of humanity. Many people have contemplated suicide. Many have done it. Many have rejected suicide for one powerful reason or another. In this book I intend to let the arguments against suicide pile up, in the hope of letting these thinkers lobby the reader on behalf of life.

1

The Ancient World

The tale of Samson, in the book of Judges, is one of the most famous biblical stories of someone engineering his own death. Samson was special from before birth. His mother said that during her pregnancy she was visited by an angel and told that as long as the infant followed Nazirite vows he would have special strength from God. These included refraining from all alcohol—the mother-to-be also had to stop drinking—and never cutting his hair. He grew up in an Israel controlled by the Philistines, and when he became an adult, his strength against them was legendary, demonstrated by such feats as killing a thousand armed soldiers using only the jawbone of an ass. Once he was attacked by a lion and killed it with his bare hands. This vignette fits into the story of his engagement to a Philistine woman. On his way to a party for the coming wedding, he visits the site of his dead lion and finds that a swarm of bees has made its hive in the lion's ribcage. He takes some of the honey, shares it with others without telling them where he got it, and teases his in-laws-to-be with a riddle: "Out of the eater something to eat, out of the strong something sweet." It ends in a bloodbath. The Bible says that in the time of the Philistines, Samson ruled Israel for twenty years. It is love for another Philistine woman that topples him. He falls for Delilah, who nags him to expose his secret weakness, until eventually he tells her that he must not cut his hair.

She immediately betrays him, shaving his head as he sleeps. The Philistines capture Samson in this weakened state, and they blind him with a sword. Later they chain him and make the strongman use his residual strength to push the grindstone around a grain mill, like an ox. The Philistines then drag Samson to their temple, where thousands are gathered to celebrate their victory over him. Meanwhile, however, Samson's hair has grown back a bit, and he prays to God for renewed strength. Samson does not ask God for an escape from his captivity and restoration of his reign, though. Rather, he asks for one last burst of power so that he can pull down the ceiling and kill as many Philistines as possible. As for himself, he says, "I will die with the Philistines." Then Samson flexes mightily, and the ceiling comes down on the multitude. It was said that Samson killed more in death than he did in life. The biblical author says nothing of the morality of his action and does not tell the story as a tragedy. Instead, it is framed as the last impressive act of an unusual hero.

Nor did the ancient Hebrews express explicit disdain for the suicides of lesser figures, which occur on a few occasions in the Hebrew Bible and are mentioned as mundane responses to failure. Wounded and defeated, Saul asks his armor bearer to kill him; when the man refuses, Saul falls upon his own sword, which the armor bearer then does as well. A character named Anhithophel tries to overthrow King David, and when he fails, hangs himself; Zimri usurps the throne of Israel, fails, and burns down the palace around him; and Abimelech, wounded in battle and dying of a broken skull, has his armor bearer kill him. Jonah tried several times to kill himself, but God kept saving him, most notably when Jonah jumped overboard on a voyage he was taking to avoid doing God's bidding. God caused him to be swallowed by a whale, which later spat him out. For thousands of years, Samson and Saul and Jonah have remained part of the conversation about suicide.

Overall, the Hebrew Bible has been seen as neutral toward suicide, but there are exceptions. Job, for example, though he is made so miserable that he wishes he had never been born, resists suicide even when his wife suggests that he "curse God, and die" (Job 2:9).[1] Job says, "My soul chooseth strangling, and death rather than my life" (7:15)—seemingly suicidal words, yet he does not do it. For this reason, Job has long been seen as an antisuicide book.

Consider also some of the wisdom of the apocryphal book of Ecclesiasticus, written around the second century B.C.E.

> Give not over thy mind to heaviness, and afflict not thyself in thine own counsel. . . . Love thine own soul, and comfort thy heart, remove sorrow far from thee: for sorrow hath killed many, and there is no profit therein. Envy and wrath shorten the life, and carefulness bringeth age before the time. . . .
>
> For of heaviness cometh death, and the heaviness of the heart breaketh strength. In affliction also sorrow remaineth: and the life of the poor is the curse of the heart. Take no heaviness to heart: drive it away, and member the last end. (Ecclesiasticus 30:21, 22–24; 38:18–20)

"Love thine own soul, and comfort thy heart." We are given a clear directive there: "Sorrow hath killed many, and there is no profit therein." Scripture is thus not as neutral as it might have seemed.

In this chapter I will introduce the major figures of ancient suicide, especially those from stories that keep recurring in Western civilization. Through these portraits, beginning with the mythical and then turning to the historical, we will see a range of motives for self-murder. In the mythical most fall into one of these categories:

- suicide because of great loss,
- altruistic suicide,
- suicide because of shame,
- and suicide because of love gone wrong.

It will become clear that the ancient Jewish and the Greek and Roman worlds were not categorically against suicide; in fact, they sometimes celebrated it. Nonetheless, there is little evidence that suicide was common, at least until the first century B.C.E.

As we will see, suicides of the ancient Greek and Roman worlds do not generally look like our era's despair suicide, the tragic end result of depression. In the ancient world it is very rare to find anything like this diagnosis for any individual, real or fictional. We hear what sounds like despair suicide in negative generalizations—Plato, for instance, praises a suicide as a noble act done for some good reason and adds contrasting disdain for people described as merely having weak characters, unable to face life. But while some figures are specified as noble suicides, the ignoble kind is generally left hypothetical. The ancients considered it suicide even when one was coerced into killing oneself, as was Socrates, a situation which looks, to modern eyes, more like execution.

Another consideration to keep in mind regarding suicide among the ancients is that while families surely lamented a suicide in their midst—wives sometimes followed their husbands' example—suicide in the ancient world was less commonly committed against the family than *for* them. In the past several centuries suicide might lower the status of a family, but in ancient times suicide was often committed in the wake of a shameful event, in order to preserve or repair the family's name or fortune. In the ancient world, legal regulation was limited, and the honor and trustworthiness of the family name was paramount.

We begin with the archaic myths from Homer and Hesiod and later Greco-Roman literature of Sophocles, Ovid, and others. (Many ancient stories have multiple versions, and sometimes a suicide occurs only in some tellings.) Consider the daughters of Erechtheus. Having asked the oracle how Athens could win the war against Eleusis, Erechtheus was told that he must kill one of his daughters. According to one source, "When he slaughtered the youngest, the others also killed themselves, for some say that they had sworn an oath with each other to die together."[2] They could not stand the loss.

Similar is the story of Erigone. When the god of wine, Dionysus, taught viticulture and oenology to one Icarius, the man foolishly shared his newfound love of wine with his neighbors without sufficiently briefing them on the effects. Drunkenness convinced them that they'd been poisoned. Terrified and infuriated, they killed Icarius and buried him under a tree. His daughter, Erigone, "abandoning hope, and overcome with loneliness and poverty, with many tearful lamentations she brings death on herself by hanging from the very tree beneath which her father was buried." As another source tells us, "sorrowful Erigone wept her fill for her slain sire, and already was untying the fatal girdle, and bent on death was fastening it to the sturdy boughs."[3] The sad story of loss does not end there. Erigone's dog Maera led her to her father's grave, and having done so, the little dog threw itself into a well.

Two stories of special powers lost stand out. The Sphinx strangled and devoured anyone unable to answer her riddle, "What creature walks on four legs in the morning, two legs in the afternoon, and three legs in the evening?" But when Oedipus solves the riddle, answering "man," who as a baby crawls on all fours, as an adult walks on two feet, and then in old age walks with a cane, the Sphinx leaps from the acropolis to her death. Similarly, the Sirens kill themselves when Ulysses successfully evades them: "Ulysses proved fatal to them, for when by his cleverness he passed by the rocks where they dwelt, they threw themselves into the sea."[4] They could not accept having their power thwarted, even once. In each case the supernatural beings had one cardinal purpose and, bested, they could not allow themselves to survive.

Iphigenia, the daughter Agamemnon sacrifices so that Artemis will allow the winds to shift and launch the Greek fleet toward Troy, provides an example of death for a community at war. But in some versions of this tale, Iphigenia makes the sacrifice on her own, for love of her country. "I have chosen death: it is my own free choice. I have put cowardice away from me. Honor is mine now."[5] Honor in this world is not only about the family but also about the polis, the city-state in which one lived. That final short sentence makes it clear that Iphigenia sees something positive in dying in this fashion for the sake of her community.

Yet that is not how her mother, Clytemnestra, reads the

situation; when Agamemnon returns from the war, she avenges her daughter's death by killing her husband. Her other daughter, Electra, then persuades her brother Orestes to avenge their father's death by killing their mother. Having done it, he is driven mad by divine spirits. He is later tried and acquitted by an Attic court, with Athena casting the deciding vote. Though a certain equilibrium is restored, Iphigenia's suicide had wide and mortal repercussions, from Agamemnon's House of Atreus to the walls Troy.

Another memorable account from Greek mythology of sacrifice for community is the story of the Coronides, Menippe and Metioche, daughters of Orion. After their father's death, their mother raised them with the help of the gods— Athena tutored them in weaving, and Aphrodite gave them beauty. When all of Ionia was suffering a plague, an oracle declared that two young women must be sacrificed willingly. As one ancient chronicler tells it,

> Of course not one of the maidens in the city complied with the oracle until a servant-woman reported the answer of the oracle to the daughters of Orion. They were at work at their loom, and, as soon as they heard about this, they willingly accepted death on behalf of their fellow citizens before the plague epidemic had smitten them too. They cried out . . . that they were willing sacrifices. They thrust their bodkins into themselves at their shoulders and gashed open their throats.[6]

Other sources have one of the sisters cracking her loom over her skull.

The illustrious Roman poet Ovid (43 B.C.E. to 18 C.E.),

wrote of an artist's depiction of Orion's daughters, pictured in the streets of Thebes, wounding themselves with great courage, "cutting their throats, piercing their brave hearts with swords," and dying "for the sake of their people."[7] Here too, suicide has a laudatory quality to it, frighteningly explicit in the wounds they suffered, but summed up as a self-sacrifice for the community.

A classic suicide of shame in ancient literature is that of Ajax. When Achilles is killed, his armor is to be awarded to the next-greatest Greek hero, and Ajax assumes it should fall to him. When the armor is awarded to Odysseus, Ajax goes mad and seeks revenge against his former comrades. Duped by Athena, Ajax slaughters a herd of sheep, thinking they are the Greek warriors. When he awakens from his stupor and sees what he has done, he is so dishonored that he kills himself with his sword. There is a shimmering irony in the fact that the dispute was over armor: the protective garb has left Ajax vulnerable to the foe no piece of armor could have protected him from: his own jealousy, rage, shame, and regret.

Another suicide of shame is that of Jocasta, Oedipus's mother. The story, told most famously by Sophocles, begins with Laius, king of Thebes, being informed by the oracle at Delphi that any son born to him would kill him. When his queen, Jocasta, gives birth to a son, they set him out to die by exposure, piercing his ankles with a small stake. But a servant saves him and gives him to a shepherd; eventually he is adopted by the childless king and queen of Corinth. As a young man, Oedipus hears a rumor that he is adopted, and he visits the oracle to learn the truth. There he is told that he is fated to kill his father and marry his mother. In an attempt to avoid this destiny, he travels far from those he assumes are his parents, all the way to Thebes. On the road he finds himself blocked by another chariot, that of Laius, his true father, and the two fight over who should pass first. In self-defense Oedipus kills Laius. Continuing his journey, he encounters the Sphinx and answers her riddle, thus bringing about her death. The people of Thebes are so grateful to be free of the Sphinx that they make him king and marry him to the newly widowed Queen Jocasta. Four children later the truth is gradually revealed to Jocasta and Oedipus; she hangs herself in shame, and he blinds himself with a pin from her cloak.

One of the great myths of suicide for love is that of Thisbe, a beautiful Babylonian girl, and Pyramus, the boy she loves but is forbidden to marry. They plan a secret meeting one night, but things go horribly wrong. Arriving at the meeting place early, Thisbe is frightened by a lion and runs away, dropping her shawl. The lion, its mouth still bloody from an earlier meal, chews at the garment. When Pyramus finds the bloodstained shawl he thinks Thisbe has been killed and stabs himself in his anguish. Thisbe returns, finds Pyramus dead, and stabs herself. In Ovid's account she cries out in agony over the loss of him, then picks up the sword, places the point of it beneath her breast, and falls "onto the blade still warm with her lover's blood."[8] This prototypical story of love gone wrong later provided a template for Shakespeare's *Romeo and Juliet*.

The story of Narcissus is a story of self-love. In Ovid's famous account, when Narcissus sees himself in the water's reflection, he is frozen there by his own beauty and dies. In two earlier versions he kills himself. In one attributed to Parthenius of Nicaea and written around 50 B.C.E., Narcissus is so tortured by his own image that he plunges himself into the water and purposefully drowns himself. In a version by the mythographer Conon, a slightly earlier contemporary of Ovid,

Narcissus is said to destroy himself, after which the narcissus flower blooms in the ground soaked with his blood.

Then there is Hercules, who represents a whole different kind of self-enacted death, one that may not even be suicide. His lover yearns to make the straying Hercules love her anew. Tricked by an enemy of the demigod, she soaks his robe in what she believes is a love potion, but when he puts it on, it sears his flesh, and when he tries to take it off, it pulls out his organs. He asks his friend to build a pyre, and he throws himself on it and dies. A suicide might be called Herculean when it simply hastens an inevitable and otherwise painful end.

Euripides, who lived from around 480 to 406 B.C.E., was the most modern of the three ancient Greek playwrights whose work survives to this day. In his play *Iphigeneia in Aulis* he writes: "Ill life o'er passeth gracious death"—that is, even a bad life is better than a good death.[9] In *The Madness of Hercules,* Euripides' hero says: "Yet, thus I have mused—how deep soe'er in ills—shall I quit life and haply prove me craven? Or, . . . I will be strong to await death."[10] Euripides values life and seems to disapprove of suicide.

These ancient suicides of myth and literature are all marked by considerable passion. But historical suicides in the ancient world are characterized less by passion than by philosophical calm. The prominent Greek and Roman suicides were typically people who were being told—often by legal authority—to kill themselves. Though our modern definition of suicide doesn't generally include forced self-murder, the protagonists in these historical events are included because they killed themselves with a display of bravery and even indifference to death. Such deaths were celebrated as a prime feature of the philosophical approach to life. We will also look at some commentaries on suicide from the ancient Greek and Roman era.

It should be noted before we look at these deaths that they were understood to be final—ancient Greek culture did not imagine an eternal afterlife for ordinary people. The gods were immortal, and in some stories a mortal might return from the dead, usually to seek reparation for some injustice on earth. But even in those rare cases, the return to life after death is always short-lived.

Perhaps our earliest declaration of a theory of antisuicide was by the pre-Socratic philosopher Pythagoras, who lived between about 570 and 495 B.C.E. One of the greatest philosophers and mathematicians in ancient Greece, he founded the Pythagorean school, which was active until the early Christian era. Pythagorean philosophers deprecated a voluntary end to life because, to them, life is sacred. Pythagoras taught that each of us is stationed at a guard post, responsible for attending to it until we are dismissed. Plato would borrow the idea, which remained a cogent metaphor for centuries.

One of the earliest chronicles of an ostensible real-life suicide recorded in ancient Greece is also one of the few to refer to madness. Cleomenes I, one of two kings of Sparta from 519 B.C.E. until his death in 491, was a remarkably belligerent ruler. His suicide is of particular interest because he would be cited in the coming centuries by such figures as the Renaissance philosopher Michel Montaigne and the Enlightenment philosopher David Hume. The first- and second-century Roman historian and essayist Plutarch wrote Cleomenes' story, and the tale has been remembered as much for its rejection of suicide as for its eventual suicide. Cleomenes had engineered the ousting of the other Spartan king, Demaratus, by bribing the Delphic oracle, but his actions were discovered and he had to flee. When all seemed lost, his friend and fellow warrior Therycion passionately argued that they should kill them-

selves rather than risk falling into enemy hands. Cleomenes
rejected the appeal, declaring that suicide would be weakness,
not courage, and said he would stay alive as long as he could
for others, "For it is an ungenerous thing either to live or die
for ourselves."[11] Eventually, he was imprisoned, went mad, and
killed himself, by slashing at his legs and belly with a knife. The
women in his family were later killed, and they died with such
poise that they were remembered as models of sublime grace
in the face of death.

Another of the earliest historical records of suicide is
what we would today call a suicide cluster. As Plutarch described it several hundred years after the story was supposed
to have occurred:

> Once upon a time a dire and strange trouble took
> possession of the young women in Miletus for
> some unknown cause. The most popular conjec-
> ture was that the air had acquired a distracting and
> infectious constitution, and that this operated to
> produce in them an alteration and derangement of
> mind. At any rate, a yearning for death and an in-
> sane impulse toward hanging suddenly fell upon all
> of them, and many managed to steal away and hang
> themselves. Arguments and tears of parents and
> comforting words of friends availed nothing, but
> they circumvented every device and cunning effort
> of their watchers in making away with themselves.[12]

Finally someone proposed an ordinance that in the funeral processions of the women who hanged themselves, they
would be carried naked through the marketplace. This worked.
Protective of their reputations, "the women who were not

afraid of the most dreadful of all possibilities, death and suffering," could not bear the thought of the disgrace that would
come to them after their deaths and this ended the epidemic.
These events have been remembered as a mysterious and disturbing phenomenon throughout history.

More understandable was Socrates' death in 399 B.C.E.
It is easily the great suicide of ancient Greek history, and like
many suicides of the ancient world, it was enforced. Socrates
left no writings, believing that philosophy was best done in
conversation, so almost all we know of his ideas comes from
his student Plato. Socrates questioned every aspect of life in
his contemporary world of ancient Greece, especially the hunger for power, envy of riches, and competition—all distrac-
tions, in his view, from what was real in life. He famously said
that he knew nothing but had more wisdom than most because at least he knew that he knew nothing. Eventually, he
was charged with corrupting youth. His death, described by
Plato in the *Phaedo,* has been remembered as a model of poise
and resignation. To save the women the trouble of washing
his corpse, he bathed; then he requested the poison hemlock
before it was forced upon him, and calmly described its action
in his body to the friends and students who stood around him.

Socrates in his jail cell mused to his listeners that there
might be a kind of philosopher's heaven where life's intellectual conversations and convivial drinking continue, but this
afterlife is suggested as only one possible outcome. It adds a
critical dimension to the famous coerced suicides that the victims had been, on some level, willing or even glad to go. A
second written account of the death of Socrates, by Xenophon,
shows a world-weary philosopher not just resigned but almost
eager to die and avoid the humiliations of old age. Xenophon's
Socrates proclaims himself "better off dead." Socrates is de-

picted as somewhat indifferent to the outcome of his trial, paying more attention to discussing ideas than to winning, and he does not plead for his life.

The two accounts agree that Socrates' friends would have been able to bribe the guards to allow his escape. But he rejects flight, saying that he must live by the laws of his polis and accept his community's dictates. Moreover, he said, wherever he might run, he would always be his same questioning self and thus would eventually infuriate someone else and get into similar trouble. To escape would just be putting off the inevitable.

Still, in his famous dying scene recorded by Plato, Socrates tells his followers that suicide is wrong. The gods put us here, he contends, and only they should be allowed to tell us when to go. He encourages others to live, to reject suicide. He borrows the formulation of Pythagoras, asserting that each of us has been put in life the way a sentry is assigned a guard post; suicide is a terrible abandonment of that calling. Absent a compulsion such as that which Socrates' own sentence carries, everyone must stand at his post. We will take a closer look at responsibility and community as bars to suicide in Chapter 5.

Plato, who lived from around 424 to 348 B.C.E., wrote about society, government, and morality but also thought about the true nature of the world—conceiving, for example, the theory of ideals, wherein everything in the visible world has somewhere an ideal form that represents its true reality. Plato described the hidden nature of reality in his telling, in the *Republic,* of Socrates' Parable of the Cave. In it, people are chained to face the far wall of a cave on which shadows of objects pass by, cast by representations of the objects in front of a fire. When a person is freed from the chains and turns around, he is blinded, first by the fire, then by the light outside. Gradually he begins to see the real world, including, eventu-

ally, the sun that illuminates everything. The lesson is that
what passes for "knowledge" is merely a shadow; true knowledge comes in stages of understanding that are painful and
disorienting at first.

Given this penchant for otherworldliness and extended
metaphor, on suicide Plato was relatively straightforward. In
his *Laws* Plato listed the types of suicide and the circumstances
that might excuse suicide. To kill oneself when compelled by
the state, like Socrates, Plato wrote, was not contemptible, and
suicide was also forgivable for someone who had experienced
a truly extraordinary loss or intense shame: for one so dishonored as to be beyond redemption, suicide could be the right
path, assuming it did not add further disgrace. In the end the
only proscribed suicide was killing oneself out of "weakness to
the vicissitudes of life," which we may take as plain sadness.

Plato's student Aristotle was the more practical-minded
of the two, the inventor of many sciences and disciplines from
marine biology to logic, ethics to psychology. He rejected suicide as an injustice to society, since a person cannot steal from
himself but can steal himself from others. It is a concept we
will revisit in coming chapters. By contrast, he allowed self-
sacrifice for the sake of the country. Aristotle made it clear that
suicide was wrong, and yet giving up one's life for the community was to be lauded. In practice, such distinctions are rarely
so easy to make, as young people in particular can be swayed
by such ideas to put themselves in harm's way.

Likewise, medical opinion on suicide is rarely as straightforward in practice as it is in conception. Here too the ancients
provide an express rejection of suicide. Hippocrates, one of
the founders of scientific medicine, lived from around 460 to
377 B.C.E. As is well known even today, his byword for doctors was "First, do no harm." This principle included a rejec-

tion of helping healthy people commit suicide. Indeed, part of the Hippocratic Oath specifies, "I will neither give a deadly drug to anybody if asked for it, nor will I make any suggestion to this effect." That said, however, for Hippocrates, passive euthanasia was another matter. Here he suggests that doctors not try to treat patients who are being "overmastered by their disease."[13] These matters may seem more salient for us than for the ancient world because we have more effective treatments, so withholding them is really equivalent to bringing on premature death. Yet practitioners of ancient medicine were often as convinced of its efficacy as are our medical personnel today, and they saw the decision to treat or not to treat as of great consequence. We do not know exactly where Hippocrates drew the line, but it is significant that he was not willing to give a fatal drug to someone who wanted to die; "First, do no harm" was not only a warning against excessively invasive medical practices but also a guide for the physician faced with a suicidal patient.

That medicine took such a firm stance is especially important when we come to the era of the Stoics, who might otherwise convince us that the ancient world had no objection to suicide. Stoicism, which began late in the Greek period, was a dominant philosophy throughout the Roman period. It was founded in the third century B.C.E., by Zeno of Citium, and thrived until 529 C.E., when the Byzantine emperor Justinian closed all the philosophical schools in deference to Christianity. At the heart of Stoicism was the idea of accepting life as it is. When you are suffering you have a choice, Stoics said, of either achieving your desire or conquering your desire so that you are at peace. Stoics called for doing one's duty, so faced even with death, they encouraged one another to accept the situation calmly. This came to mean a willingness to die even if

it was not necessary. Stoics counseled one another to stay alive
so long as life was pleasing. One should leave life as one leaves
a room that has become too smoky. The Stoics considered this
to be strength, but from our perspective, such a suicide might
seem rather to indicate weakness, a choice not to bear the difficulty of life. With the Stoics, the weight was never on actually
committing suicide but rather on not fearing death. Nevertheless, Stoicism has been famously connected to the tolerance of
suicide.

Like the ancient Greeks, the ancient Romans, with some
exceptions, thought of death in naturalist terms. The idea of
an afterlife for ordinary people, distinct from gods, begins to
emerge, vaguely, in the Judaism of the eighth and seventh centuries B.C.E., starting with the prophet Isaiah. Centuries later
the author of Ecclesiastes dismisses the notion of an afterlife,
thus providing evidence that some believed in one:

> For that which befalleth the sons of men befalleth
> beasts; even one thing befalleth them: as the one
> dieth, so dieth the other; yea, they have all one breath;
> so that a man hath no preeminence above a beast: for
> all is vanity. All go unto one place; all are of the
> dust, and all turn to dust again. Who knoweth the
> spirit of man that goeth upward, and the spirit of
> the beast that goeth downward to the earth? (Eccle-
> siastes 3:19–21)

Elsewhere the eponymous Preacher writes:

> For to him that is joined to all the living there is
> hope: for a living dog is better than a dead lion. For
> the living know that they shall die: but the dead

know not any thing, neither have they any more a reward; for the memory of them is forgotten. Also their love, and their hatred, and their envy, is now perished; neither have they any more a portion for ever in any thing that is done under the sun. (Ecclesiastes 9:4–6)

Romans had considerable contact with the Jews and knew of the beliefs about the afterlife against which Ecclesiastes was arguing.

Reinforcing the idea of an afterlife, a range of "mystery religions" came to prominence in the Hellenistic age, dating from the death of Alexander the Great in 323 B.C.E., and some spread throughout the vast Roman Empire. The cult of Isis was one of the largest of them, and one of its central tenets was that if you took part in the mysterious rites, Isis would protect you and give you life after death. Other prominent mystery religions were the Eleusian mysteries and, later, the Mithraic mysteries. Most devotees of the mystery religions were sophisticated, cosmopolitan people, who passed them on from generation to generation over many centuries. The "mysteries" at the center of these cults were well-kept secrets, known only in part by the general membership; typically they included nighttime rituals, special foods, dancing, sacrifices, purifications, theatrical symbolism, and general drinking and revelry. These members-only cults claimed they could offer their initiates protection in life and a kind of life after death. We do not know exactly how many people participated in the mystery religions, but we do know that they were a major counterpoint to the pre-Christian imperial cult, devoted to worshiping the emperor and the state. The imperial religion, mandated across the Roman Empire, offered little in the way of warmth, comfort, or promises for the future. The expansion of the mystery religions at this time seems to have been an answer to that cold religion of the state. In the time of Christian Rome the mysteries were persecuted and outlawed. The emperor Theodosius I banned the Eleusian mysteries in 392 C.E.

Aside from the mystery religions and the monotheism of the Jews, pre-Christian Romans rarely encountered the notion of an afterlife. The value of one's life was to be measured while one lived, for the sake of the world of the living. The Romans, especially as the Empire expanded, lacked the compact unity of the ancient Greek polis, a community meaningful enough to hold a place at the center of its members' lives. Instead, honor was due to the state at large. In some ways that meant death was meaningless; many suggested that allegiance to the values and virtues of the culture was the main way to secure purpose and inner peace. One of those virtues was to train oneself to be calm in the face of death, even to sacrifice oneself if necessary for the greater good.

Like Stoicism, the Epicurean movement spanned the Hellenistic period and the early Roman era, and like the Stoics, the Epicureans were thought of as tolerant toward suicide. Epicurus established a sort of school, called the Garden, where people got together to talk philosophy and share friendship. It was mostly men, but there were a few women adherents as well. Little of Epicurus's writing survives, but the fragments are informative. What is clear is that Epicurus, who lived from 341 to 270 B.C.E., considered few things as important for a happy life as making peace with the fact of death. Epicurus was devoted to saving people from their fears, especially fear of death, fear of the gods, and fear of pain. Life, he argued, was basically benign. Our worries about the gods are silly, he explained, because the gods are only shadows living between universes, oblivious to our existence. He counseled ways of meditating on its absoluteness so that it would appear less frightening. Why, for example, should we fear something about which we will be utterly ignorant when the time comes?

Whatsoever causes no annoyance when it is present causes only a groundless pain in the expectation. Death, therefore, the most awful of evils, is nothing to us, seeing that, when we are, death is not come, and when death is come, we are not. It is nothing then, either to the living or to the dead, for with the living it is not and the dead exist no longer.[14]

Still, despite his counsel that we not fear death, Epicurus was adamant that suicide was unreasonable, even a kind of weakness.[15] He was certain that the motives that lead to self-murder are not physiological. He suggested that people who choose suicide do so because they grow tired of the vicissitudes and tedium of life, and weary of their fear of dying. Epicurus does make allowances for people in dire pain and insupportable illness.

The Roman poet and philosopher Lucretius was the great bard of Epicureanism and is said to have taken his own life at age forty-five, in 55 B.C.E. The report of Lucretius's death by suicide comes to us, however, in a text written four hundred years afterward, by the Christian chronicler Jerome, who decried the views of Epicurus and Lucretius and the huge movement they represented. Since Lucretius wrote a great deal about how to be happy and at peace, Jerome's account could have been mere slander. But Jerome was a lot closer to events than we are today, so neither can we automatically dismiss his testimony. After all, Lucretius wrote about how to alleviate pain, but it was from a rather dark emotional perspective, so suicide would not be inconsistent with what we know of his temperament.

Because we have so little of Epicurus's own writing today, we get a lot more detailed information from Lucretius's book-length poem *On the Nature of Things*. Following Epicurus, Lucretius dispenses with worry about death by attempting to get his reader to face it, to see that everyone dies and that the length of one's life is a trivial matter:

> Death, then, is nothing to us, no concern,
> Once we grant that the soul will also die.
> Just as we felt no pain in ages past
> When the Carthaginians swarmed to the attack,
> *
> So too, when we no longer are, when our
> Union of body and soul is put asunder,
> Hardly shall anything then, when we are not,
> Happen to us at all and stir the senses,
> Not if the earth were embroiled with the sea and
>   the sea with heaven!
>   * * * * * * * * * * * * *
> Now if you happen to see someone resent
> That after death he'll be put down to stink
> Or be picked apart by beasts or burnt on the pyre,
> You know that he doesn't ring true, that something
>   hidden
> Rankles his heart—no matter how often he says
> He trusts that there's no feeling after death.[16]

The reason for this resistance, Lucretius suggests, is that "he posits, unknowing, a bit of himself left over." As Epicurus argued and Lucretius expanded and put into verse, since there are no gods intervening for us or watching us, nothing is required of us other than that we get along with others. Pain doesn't last long, and when it does it is usually bearable.

We do not know much about Lucretius, but in contrast to Epicurus, who exalted friendship and his conversation garden, Lucretius seems to have been a solitary figure. He expounds the same philosophy that Epicurus describes in his letters, but Lucretius counsels his reader from a stance that feels more like existential nihilism. He encourages his fellows to think often about the multitude of those already dead and how little it now matters how long they lived. He deals with self-criticism and embarrassment with the same pointing toward death; in this context, he observes, such things do not matter. While friendship and a basic joy in the small things in life were key to Epicurus's system, Lucretius seems to have been a more pessimistic fellow.

Lucretius wrote so much about being philosophical about death that his purported suicide is considered to be proof that he "lived by his word" on the subject, rather than evidence of depression. Having written so much about taking death lightly, the thinking goes, he took his own death lightly. But Lucretius may well have been a despair suicide. He wrote compellingly of the sufferings of humanity, especially of the anxiety, worry, and disappointment that oppress us. "Thus," he wrote, "each man tries to flee from himself, but to that self, from which of course he can never escape, he clings against his will, and hates it." According to the unsympathetic Jerome, Lucretius went mad after taking a love potion, remained intermittently mad during the period when he wrote his books, and eventually took his life for this reason. Again, we must remember that this account was written centuries after Lucretius died, by an author with an antagonistic agenda, so we cannot know how true it is.

Also important because it was to be remembered for the next two thousand years is the story of Arria. In the year 42 C.E., Caecina Paetus was accused of disloyalty by the emperor Claudius and ordered to kill himself. When he found himself unable to do it, his good Roman wife, Arria, grabbed the dagger from him and stabbed herself, famously saying, "Non dolet, Paete!"—It doesn't hurt, Paetus!—and handed the dagger back to him for his turn.[17] She became an epitome of noble self-sacrifice and a paragon of the philosophical spirit.

In the late first and early second centuries C.E., there were reports of many Stoic suicides. This was the era of the Pax Romana, but though the Mediterranean was peaceful, expansion of the Roman Empire ensured continuous wars on the frontiers. Stoicism, with its attention to duty and self-discipline, even self-abnegation, was a dominant belief system among the soldiers.

Pliny the Younger (61–c. 112 C.E.) praised several of the era's suicides. Some of these remind us of the praise bestowed on Arria. He told the story of a man suffering so acutely from ulcers that he wanted to take his life but could not bring himself to do it, until his wife helped.[18] Praising her as the equal of Arria, Pliny told how this ulcerous man's wife aided him by tying the two of them together with a rope and then jumping into a lake—achieving both their deaths.

Virgil (70–19 B.C.E.), the great Roman poet who gave us the epic *Aeneid,* tells a story of suicide for love. Dido, the first queen of Carthage (in modern day Tunisia), was in love with Aeneas; in anguish at his leaving Carthage, she stabbed herself to death. Consider this romantic passage on the ancient queen:

"Let me die, I go gladly to the dark.
May the heartless Trojan see my flaming pyre
from far out on the deep

and let it bring him evil omens." She spoke
and then her maidens saw her fall
upon her sword, the red blood spouting
and frothing over her sword
drenching her hands.[19]

There is no apparent condemnation of her action here. By Virgil's time suicide tended to be described as a choice that might be made by anyone so inclined.

For ancient Romans the only people expressly forbidden to kill themselves were soldiers and slaves, because of their respective duties of service to others. (The Stoic army suicides show that this prohibition was not altogether effective.) For no one else was there a religious or legal prohibition against suicide. Yet the culture and philosophy of the age that praised a few famous suicides also encouraged most people to persevere and bear even a difficult life, including one full of inner turmoil and self-hatred. Life, whatever its hardships, was meant to be lived for others, and honor required a person to live as long as life gave him, unless an occasion presented itself by which he could aid his fellow citizens.

We have seen that the story of the Roman Republic begins with the suicide of a woman in the name of family honor. It ends with an equally fascinating and macabre suicide of a man in the name of political honor. The Roman Republic began around 500 B.C.E., underwent centuries of advancement, crisis, revival, and reform, and eventually ended with a dramatic shift to empire in the mid-first century B.C.E. The Republic did not go out quietly, though. After five centuries during which the ideas of honor and duty were employed to manage the chaos of human society, the last pious plea for the sanctity of the Republic came from the strange and famously "incorruptible" Cato the Younger.

Cato was a paragon of moral integrity, a Roman statesman and politician famed for his steely resolve and resistance to the common bribes of the period. He was also a Stoic. Cato was one of the most prominent orators of his time, and he brought all his skills and tenacity to bear in his long struggle against Julius Caesar. In 49 B.C.E. Cato urged the Senate to demand Caesar's return to Rome, stripped of his proconsular command. Instead, Caesar illegally led his army into the city—famously crossing the Rubicon River and committing himself to this risky course of action—and seized power from the Senate. When Caesar's army brushed aside the attempt of Pompey's army to deflect his advance, Cato, rather than face a victorious Caesar and the end of the Republic, took his own life. In fact, he may have taken it twice. In one version Cato stabbed himself, slicing open his belly, and collapsed into a tray that clattered to the ground, thus alerting his family. They rushed into his room to find him on the floor in a pool of blood, alive though disemboweled. A doctor replaced his intestines and stitched up his wound, but when left alone again, Cato ripped out the stitches, eviscerated himself again, and finally died. Caesar is said to have reacted to this news with the words, "Cato, I begrudge you your death, as you would have begrudged me your pardon." Like Lucretia, Cato was enshrined as a Roman hero. It is an amazing commentary on the complexity of real human experience that Cato, credited with a maddeningly calm, steady, single-mindedness, responded to an untenable shift in his world by pulling his guts out.

Thus the Roman Republic opened and closed with dramatic suicides hinged on outrage and a sense of right and wrong,

suicides envisioned as courageous, community oriented, and heroic. In the first, the case of Lucretia, the virtue of purity demands
the creation of the Republic for its own defense; in the second,
the Republic dies, and the virtue of purity opts to die with it.
Another salient commentary on suicide came from the
brilliant Roman orator, philosopher, and statesman Cicero,
who lived from 106 to 43 B.C.E. Among many other works, Cicero was the author of *On the Nature of the Gods,* in which
an Epicurean, a Stoic, and a Skeptic (an adherent to another
major philosophy of the time) debated whether the gods exist
and, if so, what they are like. Cicero had been against Julius
Caesar in defense of the Republic, but when Caesar prevailed
he made peace with the situation and lived with honor in
Rome. Cicero judges suicides according to their situations and
motivations. He finds Cato a model of liberty but also cites
Plato's opinion that we have no right to abandon our posts. Finally, Cicero was impressed by self-sacrifice for the sake of the
greater good, writing, "But noble deaths, sought voluntarily,
for the sake of country, are not only commonly reckoned glorious by rhetoricians but also happy. They go back to Erechtheus, whose daughters sought even with eagerness for death
to save the lives of their fellow-citizens."[20]

Military and political reversal persuaded the senator and
army commander Cassius to kill himself, though he enlisted a
freedman to strike the fatal blow. Brutus, also a politician and
army commander, who famously conspired in the assassina-
tion of Julius Caesar, also took his own life when his army was
defeated. (Actually, he got wrong information and killed himself prematurely, though his side did eventually lose.) Brutus's
wife followed her husband's death by taking her own life. Porcia Catonis was Brutus's first cousin and second wife, and also
Cato's daughter. She is supposed to have swallowed hot coals

or put them in her mouth and suffocated from the fumes; it
is likely that in fact she burned coals in an unventilated room
and died of carbon monoxide poisoning, and history and romance muddled the details.[21] Either way, it is a poignant image
of swallowing what cannot be swallowed. She has been remembered as both a devoted wife and a devoted Republican,
and as either deeply philosophical or a little mad with grief.

Just a bit later in Egypt, Cleopatra responded to Augus-
tus Caesar's triumph in 30 B.C.E. by taking her own life, clutch-
ing two poisonous asps to her breast. Her lover Marc Antony
took his own life as well. Mistakenly thinking that Cleopatra
has already killed herself, he stabs himself with his sword. Still
living, he is brought to Cleopatra and dies in her arms. Of all
the ancient suicides, Marc Antony had the worst reputation
within his own culture, not because he took his life, but because he took his life for love. Like despair suicide, this was
not what the ancients had in mind when they praised a man
for ending his own days.

In the first century C.E., Stoic philosopher Seneca is also
remembered as having taken his own life. He wrote plays and
other literature, often relying on the tenets of Stoicism. Coming after the Golden Age of Latin—the era of Cicero, Lucretius, Virgil, and Ovid—Seneca is one of the most prominent
of the less illustrious Silver Age writers. He was also a political
adviser to the emperor Nero. Seneca wrote that we must not
worry inordinately about our own death, but neither should we
run to it. Seneca committed suicide after being implicated in a
plot to assassinate Nero; he was probably innocent, but Nero
ordered him to kill himself. This might make us think of his
suicide as entirely coerced, but his contemporaries observed
that he had some choice in the matter. Even without our knowing whether he could have avoided his fate, Seneca's writing

about despondency makes him seem like a despair suicide, a
suicide of sadness. Here is how he talks about the bad times:

> Hence the boredom, the disgust for oneself, the tu-
> mult of a soul fixed on nothing, the somber impa-
> tience that our own inaction causes, especially when
> we blush to admit the reasons . . . tightly contained
> in a prison with no exit. . . . As Lucretius says, "Thus
> all continually flee themselves." . . . We follow our-
> selves; we cannot get rid of that intolerable com-
> pany. . . . We lack the strength to bear anything:
> work, pleasure, ourselves, everything in the world
> is a burden to us. There are some whom this leads
> to suicide because their perpetual variations make
> them turn forever in the same circle and because
> they have made all novelty impossible for them-
> selves, they lose their taste for life and the universe.

But Seneca never advocated suicide in his writings. Indeed,
he tells his reader to resist the temptation to die. He writes of
having experienced a time of misery in which he was tempted
to end his life, but consideration of the feelings of his aged
father kept him from doing so. "I saw not my own courage
in dying, but his courage broken by the loss of me. So I said
to myself, 'You must live.' Sometimes even to live is an act of
courage." George Minois, a historian of suicide, wrote in 1995
that the kind of *taedium vitae* that Seneca talks about did not
really take lives; rather, "its most typical manifestation was
floating in a perpetual state of indecision between life and
death."[22] This nagging vacillation between living and dying has
been a major theme of the suicidal through to modern times.
After Socrates' death, Seneca's is one of the most remembered

ancient suicides. When he took his own life, it was by rather gruesomely cutting himself up.

These stories stake a place in one's memory. Socrates and Seneca are the famous coerced suicides. Most others were putting an end to what seemed to be an intolerable situation. Lucretia, Cato, Cassius, Brutus, Porcia, and Cleopatra all refused to let anyone conquer them, but you cannot quite say they "won." Instead, they fashioned exits from difficult situations. Clearly, in the ancient world, for a person who had been defiled or humiliated, or was threatened with the like, killing oneself might sometimes be a praiseworthy response. These suicides were not seen as exacerbating their crime or failure, they were not called cowards for escaping punishment, but rather seemed to be partially absolved, as if the act were a self-punishment that could assuage the stigma of bad luck and redeem earlier wrongs.

It is reasonable to surmise that the same force that took Lucretia's life and the lives of Orion's weaving daughters actually kept a lot of people alive in the ancient world. People were profoundly enmeshed in their families and in their tribes or city-states. Honor before everything means that under normal circumstances one has to stay at one's post. Lucretia is compromised and furious, but she is not killing herself because she is depressed. She is not killing herself in spite of her family's protests. She is enacting the values of the group, which here are about a woman's chastity. She is putting her family first in removing herself from life. Orion's girls, Menippe and Metioche, put their community first in taking arms against themselves. Their deaths have to do with being profoundly connected to their society. This is quite the opposite of the alienation and loneliness often associated with suicide in the modern world.

Before we leave the ancient world, we have to look at one

last development in our story, suicidal martyrdom. As we saw, the Hebrew Bible does not feature many suicides. Yet in the period of history after the five books of Moses, when Jews confront the power of Rome, martyrdom emerges. When Roman soldiers tried to march through town, the ancient Hebrews took offense that there were graven images on their shields, and in the ensuing confrontation, the Romans were surprised by the Hebrews' willingness to die rather than allow any trespass of their laws. Such martyrdom is not technically suicide: though the victim does opt for death, the oppressor does the killing. Still, in a case like the siege of Masada, it is hard to deny that it is suicide in fact as well as intent. The ancient chronicler Josephus tells the gruesome story. After the Romans surrounded and laid siege to the fortress Masada, the Jews had no prospect of escape. To avoid being conquered, the men agreed that each would kill his own wife and children. After tearful goodbyes, they dispatched their families, then drew lots to choose a squad who would kill their comrades, each man to be slain lying down and embracing the corpses of his family. At last a final executioner was chosen, again by lot, and he killed the killers, ultimately running himself through with his own sword.

Only two old women and some children chose to hide and survive; 960 died. The Romans broke through the defense the next day expecting a fight; instead, they entered an eerily quiet place of "terrible solitude" and could not guess what had happened. Even after the hiding women emerged and reported the mass suicide, the Romans did not believe it until they found the bodies. They "could take no pleasure in the fact, though it were done to their enemies." It was just too disturbing.[23] Lucretia had long been a Roman heroine, but those who witnessed this mass suicide found it profoundly unsettling.

2

Religion Rejects Suicide

The ancient Roman world in which Christianity emerged prized manly honor and female purity above all else, certainly above longevity. There was no reason for early Christians, at first a sect of Judaism, to suddenly imagine suicide a sin. Judas is the only suicide in the Christian New Testament—there are conflicting accounts, but in Matthew 27 he hangs himself. Many have claimed that Jesus was a suicide as well, including the early bishop of Hippo, Augustine; the later theologian Thomas Aquinas; and the Elizabethan poet John Donne (about whom more later). Jesus certainly fits the criteria of clearly accepting his coming death and of declining to take any of several courses of action that might have saved his life. Like Socrates, he refuses to plead his own case at trial, even seeming to mock and provoke his judges. In the book of John we find Jesus saying: "No man taketh [my life] from me, but I lay it down of myself" (John 10:18).

Christianity evolved and took shape in the Roman Empire. This, we have seen, was a world that accepted suicide as a

reasonable or even good response to some situations. Our earliest records confirm that Christians did not consider suicide
a sin; indeed, it could be celebrated. For instance, around the
year 300 the scholar Eusebius, soon to be a bishop, wrote a book
collecting the stories of Christian martyrs whose deaths he had
witnessed or heard about. He included the story of a Christian
woman and her two virgin daughters who had been arrested
for their Christianity. Fearing that the soldiers would rape them
and ruin their purity, they instead chose to sneak away and
jump into a river to their deaths. Eusebius's description of the
incident incorporates the assumptions of his cultural moment:

> A certain holy person,—in soul admirable for vir-
> tue, in body a woman,—who was illustrious be-
> yond all in Antioch for wealth and family and repu-
> tation, had brought up in the principles of religion
> her two daughters, who were now in the freshness
> and bloom of life. Since great envy was excited on
> their account, every means was used to find them
> in their concealment; and when it was ascertained
> that they were away, they were summoned deceit-
> fully to Antioch. Thus they were caught in the nets
> of the soldiers. When the woman saw herself and
> her daughters thus helpless, and knew the things
> terrible to speak of that men would do to them,—
> and the most unbearable of all terrible things, the
> threatened violation of their chastity,—she ex-
> horted herself and the maidens that they ought not
> to submit even to hear of this. For, she said, that
> to surrender their souls to the slavery of demons
> was worse than all deaths and destruction; and she
> set before them the only deliverance from all these

things,—escape to Christ. They then listened to her
advice. And after arranging their garments suitably,
they went aside from the middle of the road, having requested of the guards a little time for retire-
ment, and cast themselves into a river which was
flowing by. Thus they destroyed themselves.[1]

The text focuses on the purity of the mother and her ideals, and
the respect her actions merit. Notice that while the daughters
are praised for womanly chastity, the mother gets a uniquely
ungendered dignity for her uncompromising and courageous
act. Eusebius, following one of Christianity's first theologians,
Origen, saw the achievement of the afterlife as a process with
steps, something like Platonic stages toward the ultimate
"good"; progress on these steps could be lost through sin. Thus
for Eusebius it was logical for the women to kill themselves
in order to evade the threat of sexual sin, which would have
set them back on their path to salvation. Eusebius lived in a
dynamic period of ancient Christianity, and the persecutions
that he chronicled stopped suddenly in 313, when the emperor
Constantine lifted the ban on Christianity. Nonetheless, this
episode would be cited in key religious and secular discussions
of suicide over the next two millennia.

The period of Christian martyrdom was a remarkable
era of people walking into death of their own free will. Martyrdom is usually treated as a willingness to die for one's beliefs,
but there have always been questions about whether some
martyrs were actively seeking death for the same reasons that
conventional suicides do.

Kalman J. Kaplan, a psychologist and historian of the
early Christian period, has written about the nature of martyrdom in history. Kaplan holds that the death of Jesus was

voluntary and can be understood as a suicide.[2] Kaplan's bolder statement is that Christians experienced something like a suicide survivor's guilt, confusion, and anger over Jesus's decision to die, which they then took out on themselves and, later, on Jews at large. While acknowledging that for martyrs, death was unavoidable, Kaplan finds also "a desire, and indeed, an active pursuit of death."[3] He points to the Donatist heresy as an extreme manifestation of this impulse: "Whole companies of Donatists, for example, threw themselves from rocks." Donatists would not accept the sacraments from priests who had renounced the faith during the period of persecution. The church accepted such men back into the fold and sanctified sacraments performed even by compromised priests, holding that the office, not the man, conferred their sacredness. The Donatists disagreed and in many cases were more than willing to die in support of their beliefs.

Kaplan does not use this terminology, but he implies that the martyrs were a "suicide cluster" that started with Jesus: "What are the potential responses of the Christian survivor to the death of Jesus?" According to Kaplan, "He may choose to die as a martyr-suicide himself. This brings him close to Jesus Christ in two ways: 1) through imitation of the death of his savior and 2) through offering a reunion with Jesus Christ in the next world."[4] Martyrs' zeal for death can be easily shown— "I am yearning for death with all the passion of a lover," wrote Ignatius of Antioch—but the idea of an immediate and blissful afterlife provides a radically different context for the question of imitation.[5] Still, it is something to consider in our analysis of the ripple-effect repercussions of suicide.

The death of Jesus may have reverberated in the death of the martyrs, yet even in the early days of Christianity, suicidal martyrdom was not recommended as a path by the key figures of the religion. Even Paul, who was fixated on the afterlife, did not advise suicide. He wrote, "For I am in a strait betwixt two, having a desire to depart, and to be with Christ; which is far better: Nevertheless to abide in the flesh is more needful for you" (Philippians 1:23–24).

Despite Paul's choice of life, the rage for martyrdom in Christianity, or sects of it, continued after adherents were no longer being persecuted. In fact, the popularity of martyrdom outlasted its usefulness for the movement. As Christianity became more established, martyrdom stopped seeming like a valiant defense of the religion and started to seem like an unnecessary tragedy. Losing its members this way no longer made sense for the church. Efforts to quell the popularity of martyrdom resulted in the first general bans on suicide. In 305 the Council of Guadix amended its list of martyrs by deleting the names of all those who had died by their own hand. The 348 Council of Carthage went farther than the church had before, actively condemning all those who had chosen suicide under the pretext of piety but in fact for personal reasons.

One of the outstanding theologians of this early period of Christianity was Augustine of Hippo, North Africa, whom the church canonized. Saint Augustine made a point of asserting that Jesus' death was voluntary, writing, "His soul did not leave his body constrained, but because he would and where he would and how he would." Yet Augustine deprecated other suicides. Writing around the year 400, Augustine considered Eusebius's story about the pretty virgin girls killing themselves and decided that Eusebius was wrong in his judgment. For Augustine, the sexual act would not have been the girls' sin. He held that they should not have killed themselves. With that reversal we leave behind the classically inflected sense that honor—or even virtue, or purity, or the absence of sin—ought to decide the matter of guilt. We have arrived at a morality dependent on individual intention.

In his *City of God* Augustine has no tolerance for suicide, calling it a "detestable crime and a damnable sin." Augustine's approach to morality is based on the afterlife, and his ideas about suicide are squarely prohibitive. Consider his certainty and his proclaimed reasons: "This we affirm, this we maintain . . . that no man ought to inflict on himself voluntary death . . . that no man ought to do so on account of another man's sins, for this were to escape a guilt which could not pollute him, by incurring great guilt of his own; that no man ought to do so on account of his own past sins, for he has all the more need of this life that these sins may be healed by repentance. . . . Those who die by their own hand have no better life after death."[6] It is fascinating that Augustine makes this rather generous plea to the suicidal person who feels guilt and self-revulsion: you must stay here to redeem past sins. Still, for Augustine's judgment such arguments are secondary; God had issued a command that one must not kill oneself, within the commandment "Thou shalt not kill."

> It is not without significance, that in no passage of the holy canonical books there can be found either divine precept or permission to take away our own life, whether for the sake of entering on the enjoyment of immortality, or of shunning, or ridding ourselves of anything whatever. Nay, the law, rightly interpreted, even prohibits suicide, where it says, "Thou shall not kill." This is proved especially by the omission of the words "thy neighbor," which are inserted when false witness is forbidden: "Thou shall not bear false witness against thy neighbor."

... The commandment is, Thou shall not kill man; therefore neither another nor thyself, for he who kills himself still kills nothing else than man.

Augustine finds this injunction so strong that he must hypothesize that Samson had received special orders from God. "Samson ... who drew down the house on himself and his foes together, is justified only on this ground, that the Spirit who wrought wonders by him had given him secret instructions to do this."

He even speaks of the purity of Lucretia:

> But all know how loudly they extol the purity of Lucretia, that noble matron of ancient Rome. When King Tarquin's son had violated her body, she made known the wickedness of this young profligate to her husband Collatinus, and to Brutus her kinsman, men of high rank and full of courage, and bound them by an oath to avenge it. Then, heart-sick, and unable to bear the shame, she put an end to her life. What shall we call her? An adulteress, or chaste? There is no question which she was. Not more happily than truly did a declaimer say of this sad occurrence: Here was a marvel: there were two, and only one committed adultery. Most forcibly and truly spoken.

Even though her body had been violated, Lucretia was chaste, according to Augustine, and no adulteress. Furthermore, in a wonderful turn of phrase: "This crime was committed by Lucretia; that Lucretia so celebrated and lauded slew the innocent, chaste, outraged Lucretia." The only crime of this celebrated, highly praised woman was that she killed an innocent, pure, and furious woman—herself. He continues:

> Pronounce sentence. But if you cannot, because there does not appear any one whom you can punish, why do you extol with such unmeasured laudation her who slew an innocent and chaste woman.
> ... She is among those
> Who guiltless sent themselves to doom,
> And all for loathing of the day,
> In madness threw their lives away.[7]

Since rape and incest are strong predictors of women's suicides in our own time, it is useful to know the story of Lucretia and that centuries of thinkers have insisted that what happened to her was not her fault. In his disdain for suicide Augustine was a man of his times—the Christian proscription against self-murder had its philosophical roots in the early Middle Ages—but his reasoning was original.

In the wake of the movement led by Augustine and other church fathers to end voluntary martyrdom, the first legislation in canon law to rule against suicide was passed at the Council of Arles in 452. The logic was similar to the ancient Roman law against slaves committing suicide—that it was a kind of theft—but now the injunction applied to everyone. The Council of Angers reiterated the injunction in 453. The second Council of Orleans in 533 denied funeral rites to suicides who had been accused of crimes. This was generalized by the Council of Braga to all suicides in 563. The Council of Antisidor ruled against churches taking offerings for the souls of suicides in 590.[8] Over the succeeding centuries, suicide came to be thought of as the worst sin possible because it stole specifically and entirely from God, and because it left no time for repentance. Interestingly, along with these ideas that suicide was a crime against God, theologians also often mentioned that it was wrong because it was the opposite of perseverance and hope. In some places Christian postmortem punishments were consistent with older practices. Pre-Christian local belief systems regarding suicide had included rites of purification and maiming of the corpse, steps taken to avoid the deceased's return. This is also the period when suicide becomes firmly connected with the devil.

Islam arose in the seventh century c.e. and was, in its origins, fiercely against suicide. Endurance of an unbearable life was explicitly prized. This point is made clearly in the Koran:

> Nor kill (or destroy) yourselves: for verily God hath
> been to you most merciful! If any do that in rancor
> and injustice, soon shall we cast them into the fire:
> And easy it is for God.[9]

The Sahih al-Bukhari, one of the six major hadiths of Sunni Islam (and considered by many to be the most authentic book after the Koran), states that "whoever commits suicide with something, will be punished with the same thing in the [hell] fire."[10] As the founding sociologist Emile Durkheim wrote, "Nothing, in fact, is more contrary to the general spirit of Mahometan civilization than suicide, for the virtue set above all others is absolute submission to the divine will, the docile resignation 'which makes one endure all patiently.'"[11] Modern mainstream Islam remains squarely antisuicide. An article on the Muslim Public Affairs Council website provides a snapshot of contemporary attitudes: suicide is "ugly, anti-Islam, anti-nature, and anti-life."[12] The author of another website declares that, even in the case of severe depression, "suicide is a major sin."[13] That essay also draws on the idea above, that Allah will punish the sinner with an endless reprise of the method used to commit suicide. "Whoever drinks poison and kills himself," for instance, "will be sipping it in the Fire of Hell for ever and ever." Believers are told to be patient and to remember that they are not the only ones experiencing hardships and calamities. It is ironic that violent and highly visible suicides in the name of Islam have come to be associated with a religion that so emphatically legislates in favor of life, consistent with prizing submission to the will of God.

The medieval period was marked by increasing hostility toward suicide. One reason for this was the decline in Stoicism. More generally, Christian thought on suicide was in part a reaction against ancient paganism. The Greek and Roman heritage was increasingly forgotten and misremembered and distorted, but its examples of those suicides considered noble had been preserved. Throughout the Middle Ages, church leadership took Aristotle and Ptolemy as authorities on cosmology and other sciences, but Greek and Roman thought on moral issues was summarily dismissed. Moral authority was the business of church fathers, councils, theologians, and, above all, the papacy.[14] Early medieval punishments were mild enough, forbidding burial rites and the like, but constraints became much more stringent in the high Middle Ages of the eleventh, twelfth, and thirteenth centuries. This is when most western European governments promulgated laws mandating the forfeiture of at least some part of the suicide's estate, and in various regions the practice of desecrating the suicide's corpse gained increased state sanction.

The style of desecration varied widely from place to place, in part because of the cult roots of the practice, but a common thread was the idea that the suicide's soul was a danger to the living and had to be ritually disposed of. The self-murderer had to be ostracized from the community in order to prevent a kind of pollution. At Metz and Strasburg, suicides were set adrift on a river. In other areas of France and in Germany, suicides were dragged to a place of execution, hung on chains, and left to rot. In England and elsewhere, suicides were buried at crossroads with stakes through them to help keep their souls from wandering around and harassing the living. The Council of Hertford promulgated a canon in 672 denying self-murderers normal funerals; in 693 the Council of Toledo decided that those who attempted suicide would be excommunicated; and a canon attributed to King Edgar around the year 1000 repeated the prohibition, exempting the mad.[15]

The next big change in how suicide was discussed in Christianity came in 1271, when the medieval Christian theologian Thomas Aquinas expanded on Augustine's rule. Aquinas agreed that Jesus had essentially taken his own life, but Christians were not permitted to follow this example.[16] Aquinas championed a prohibition of suicide for three reasons: 1) it injures the community of which an individual is a part; 2) it is contrary to natural self-love, whose aim is to preserve us; and 3) it "violates our duty to God": since he gave us life, only he should be allowed to end it. Aquinas's first two concerns, for community and for the self, are powerful secular arguments as well, and we will return to them in later chapters to see how they might be applied outside of a religious context. His last argument was so strong in the Christian context that over the years the other two reasons were marginalized. Over time, the idea that God requires one to bear up under one's burdens and stay alive—no matter what—grew into a significant part of Christian theology. Obedience to God meant that the believer must simply stay and do her part, whatever that part may be. After Aquinas, throughout Christendom, suicide was regularly understood as sinful. It was not something you could do to escape a sinful life, or to avoid having to succumb to sinful circumstances. In the 1300s, Dante gave enough weight to Aquinas to put (most) suicides in one of the worst circles of hell. Dante has compassion for Dido, the queen of Carthage abandoned in love, and places her in a gentler outer circle. But the devil is at the center of Dante's hell, and the three-faced devil has a trio of famous suicides in his mouths: Cassius, Brutus, and Judas. Each was condemned for his fatal betrayal, but it is also true that for Dante, suicide was very wrong indeed.

Dante's devil was huge and had wings (unfeathered, "like a bat") and chewed on all three of these sinners, crunching them so that they suffered horrendously and constantly. It clawed at them to such a degree that much of their skin was removed. Judas was said to suffer the worst, for his head was in the devil's mouth, with his legs dangling out. Cassius and Brutus did not have it much better: they were held by their legs with their heads hanging upside-down from the devil's maw.

In life as well as literature, Christian religious practice in the high Middle Ages was to condemn suicides. Records show families of suicides arguing for leniency for a father or sister, and the pleas of the highborn were sometimes granted. Regardless of rank, though, suicides were increasingly punished.

The ferocity of the response to suicide can seem unbelievable, but examples from across Europe span several centuries. The records of Paris are uniquely comprehensive. When a Parisian man killed himself by plunging into the Seine in 1257, his body was fished out and his case tried. He was found guilty, and his body was sentenced to torture; most commonly, that meant being drawn and quartered, or eviscerated and hanged by the neck before the community and left there until birds and maggots consumed the corpse.[17] In 1288 a man committed suicide near the Church of Sainte-Geneviève in Paris, and the abbey hanged his body. It was later decided that they had neglected the important rite of dragging his body through the streets behind a horse, so the entire "execution" was repeated, this time with the grisly detail enacted. In 1299 the miller Jean Cliot drowned himself in a river and the abbey ordered his hands to be pierced with wooden stakes before his body was drawn and quartered.

When reasons for these suicides are mentioned, they are generally deep sadness, suddenly dire circumstances, or the devil's influence. The evidently "mad" were much more likely to be forgiven and given minimal censure. Self-murder was often the recourse of women facing poverty after having lost their husbands, for instance, and of men facing criminal punishment. In the 1300s the idea of despair appears more specifically, as when in 1394 Jean Masstoier threw himself in a river, was saved, and later—still in an anguish of "melancholy of the head"—he drowned himself in a well. In the 1400s, chronicles were likely to add to any reason for a suicide that the person was "tempted by the enemy," that is, lured by the devil. In 1421, Denisot Sensogot, a Paris baker, hanged himself, and the reason reported was that he did it "by the temptation of the enemy and on the occasion of his madness and illness." There were odd exceptions: Jeannette Mayard, a shoemaker's wife and "good Catholic," in 1426 hanged herself because she was "given to drink and jealousy," but she was not much blamed for it.[18] By and large, sane suicides were discussed as sinners and religious criminals; they were tried, and when found guilty, their bodies were violated, then buried in such places as a "cemetery of the damned," or, at the very least, just outside the churchyard.

The idea of the devil tempting people to suicide was deeply ingrained and widespread. It had some conceptual advantages in that it allowed people to externalize their most self-destructive impulses, and in a form that they were already conditioned to think of as something to be resisted and rejected. Consider the testimony of one troubled woman:

> Then Satan tempted me again and I resisted him again. Then he tempted me a third time, and I yielded unto him and I pulled out my knife and put it near my throat. Then God of his goodness caused me to consider what would follow if I should do so. . . . With that I fell out a weeping and I flung away my knife.[19]

Judaism was not as extreme in its punishment of suicide as the Christian Church, but in the Middle Ages, temples too refused suicides burial in Jewish cemeteries. There were (imperfect) Latin versions of the work of Josephus in circulation in the Middle Ages (a better version in Greek was discovered in 1544) and Jews were aware of Josephus's words against suicide: "It is equally cowardly not to wish to die when one ought to do so, and to wish to die when one ought not. . . . 'It is noble to destroy oneself,' another will say. Not so, I retort, but most ignoble; in my opinion there could be no more arrant coward than the pilot who, for fear of a tempest, deliberately sinks his ship before the storm. No; suicide is alike repugnant to that nature which all creatures share, and an act of impiety toward God who created us. Among the animals there is not one that deliberately seeks death or kills itself, so rooted in all is nature's law."[20] Also, from at least as early as the tenth century Jews annually studied *The Ethics of the Fathers*, which dates from between 200 B.C.E. and 200 C.E., and contains such admonitions as this:

> Let not your heart convince you that the grave is your escape; for against your will you are formed, against your will you are born, against your will you live, against your will you die, and against your will you are destined to give a judgement and accounting before the king, king of all kings, the Holy One, blessed be He.[21]

In the Middle Ages and into the early modern age (from the fifteenth through the seventeenth centuries) the idea of "rites of reversal" arose. Like the long-administered stake through the body of a suicide, the rites of reversal were intended as a hindrance to resurrection. Following these rites, the cadaver of a suicide would be placed in the ground face down, lying north-south, opposite to the normal burial practices. The standard ritual of the stake was also further elaborated during this period: in 1590 the coroner of London ordered that the top of the stake pinning down the corpse of Amy Stokes be left exposed to provide deterrence to other would-be suicides.[22] Corpses were hanged by their feet or dragged head down, satisfying the terms both of rites of reversal and of postmortem torture.

The Protestant Reformation spread across Europe beginning in the early 1500s, but as Martin Luther and John Calvin wrought revolutionary changes in worship and policy, both followed the medieval Catholic Church's teachings on suicide. Both held that whatever their suffering, people ought to respect God enough to endure his torments. Rather than soften strictures, the Reformation ramped up religious hostility to suicide. A macabre policy of threats and violent punishments continued for centuries. Calvinist city leaders had bodies of suicides disemboweled and placed naked in the public square. Again, the idea of torture and exposure was punishment for the crime, but was also intended as a deterrent to others, which is why the torture was as visibly repugnant as possible.

Martin Luther saw suicide as the consequence of the devil's temptation. In 1544, writing about a woman who had killed herself, Luther speculated that she had been possessed and that she might be considered a victim of the devil:

> I have known many cases of this kind, and I have
> reason to think in most of them, that the parties
> were killed, directly and immediately killed by the
> devil, in the same way that a traveller is killed by
> a brigand. . . . Yet still the civil magistrate is quite
> right in punishing this offence without exception,
> lest the devil should make more and more way in
> this respect. The world merits such warnings, now
> that it has taken to epicurising, and setting down
> the devil as nothing.[23]

So though the devil was the one responsible, people were also responsible because the world had been dismissing God and the devil with him—"epicurising" elegantly laying the blame to that ancient pagan philosophy.

Thus suicide was condemned in the Reformation, but there were complex factors. The anguish suicide brought on the family and the community drew it into sectarian disputes that were rife in the Reformation. Deaths of this manner were used as propaganda between the sects from the beginning of the Reformation and through the sixteenth and seventeenth centuries. The Geneva Bible glossed the biblical suicide of Ahithophel to invoke "God's just vengeance even in this life [which] is powered on . . . enemies, traitors, or persecutors of his Church."[24] The English historian John Foxe's *Acts and Monuments of the Christian Church*, later known as the *Book of Martyrs* (1563), was a wildly popular and gory depiction of the suffering Protestants had undergone at the hands of Catholics. It also told of some "punishments" that befell English Catholics. Many, he wrote, were driven to suicide. For instance, Foxe told of a student of law, Henry Smith who had been raised well by a pious Protestant father, but who, while studying, "was induced to profess Catholicism." He visited France and returned "with pardons, crucifixes, and a great freight of popish toys." "Not content with these things he openly reviled the gospel religion he had been brought up in; but conscience one night reproached him so dreadfully, that in a fit of despair he hung himself in his garters." Foxe held that true believing Protestants never succumbed to despair or suicide.[25]

Anti-Calvinist writers, on the other hand, charged that the Puritan doctrine of predestination drove the pious into despair and self-destruction. In England's environment of Puritans versus anti-Puritans, the conversation about suicide began to focus on the pressure of this predestinary doctrine. Especially in early Protestantism, the idea was that from before birth some people were destined to be saved and some damned—since God knew all—and that people could intuit whether they were among the saved. This challenge could be maddening for those who tried to behave as if they were predestined for heaven, and it could be crushing for those who found themselves behaving in ways that made them feel pre-

destined for hell. Within the church and among the lay population, anti-Calvinists blamed predestination for a spate of
self-murders.

While the behavior was barbarous, it must be said that
the intention may not have been cruel insult to the deceased,
but rather just what the authorities were claiming. People
across history speak of being haunted by suicides and tempted
by them toward the grave. The harsh practices surely would
help to make the mind feel sure the person is gone, and would
also be a deterrent to further suicides. Postmortem torture
and exposure of the corpse has often been explained as expressing supernatural beliefs, but the reasons for some of it
may be closer to the ancient Greek story of the virgin suicide
cluster and how it was stopped by the threat of a different kind
of postmortem exposure.

The macabre abuse of corpses was eventually ended for
the same reasons that the practice of torturing live bodies of
criminals before their execution came to be seen as barbarous,
in part to civilize public space and in part because individual
people's crimes and punishments were increasingly seen as
matters belonging to them personally rather than to the community in general. It no longer seemed reasonable to attack a
man or woman's body for the purpose of teaching other people
a lesson. Lynn Hunt, in *Inventing Human Rights,* outlines this
process, as a cornucopia of corporal punishments for living
and dead dwindle down, over less than a century, to incarcera-
tion for the living, with the dead finally escaping further mortification. With the rise of modernity in the sixteenth century,
suicides' corpses were increasingly left in peace.[26]

3

To Be or Not to Be
New Questions in the Rise of Modernism

The Middle Ages have traditionally been characterized as a period of religious domination, when the arts, science, philosophy, and politics largely stagnated. That assessment has undergone a number of revisions as historians have discovered innovation in those years and connections between the period and the one that followed it, the Renaissance. Still, the Renaissance represents a dramatic efflorescence in almost every aspect of human ingenuity. The painter Giorgio Vasari, looking back in 1550 at the previous two hundred years of Italian art, first termed the period a "rebirth" of culture and of ancient ways of thinking, writing, and making art. The Italian Renaissance is generally dated, as Vasari dated it, from around 1350 to 1550, with the rest of Europe starting later and taking the movement into the seventeenth century.

The Renaissance is best remembered for its changes in art, in the development of perspective and other new artistic techniques, and in the proliferation of superb artists, most

notably Michelangelo and Leonardo da Vinci. Literature also
was revolutionized during the era, as authors began writing
in the language of their own countries, rather than in Latin,
and subject matter became more inclusive and more personal
than it had been since ancient times. Francesco Petrarch, seen
by contemporaries as the leader in this change, searched old
monasteries and libraries for ancient texts and took as one of
his heroes the Roman writer Cicero. Like Cicero's speeches
and writings, Petrarch's letters and poems were conversational
and witty, unlike the stark style of the Middle Ages. Petrarch
was also among the first of his age to reject medieval philosophy and to base his philosophical thinking on the views of the
ancient world.

As we have seen, medieval punishment for suicide had
been intensely cruel, and it became even crueler during the
rise of the Protestants. In the late Renaissance, those who took
their own lives continued to suffer nasty treatment, but these
practices began to be sharply contrasted by philosophical and
literary investigation of suicide. In fact, several writers and
thinkers of the Renaissance and the early modern period that
followed it were fascinated with suicide and looked at it from
different angles. Most still came out against suicide, but the
reasoning now was based less on church doctrine and more on
independent assessment of the situation. The Renaissance was
also a time of innovation in diplomacy, economics, and social
mores, so it is not surprising to see changes in every aspect
of culture, and the new way of looking at suicide was part of
these larger cultural and political changes. Petrarch led the
way in philosophy and literature: his hero Cicero, we have
seen, was at least tolerant and sometimes admiring of certain
ancient suicides. Moreover, the printing press, which fueled
the Renaissance's dissemination of knowledge, churned out its

first book, the Bible, in 1453, and by 1473 it had printed *On the Nature of Things,* by Lucretius, named by some as a suicide himself.

The Renaissance brought a revival of many classical authors, whose works had been hard to find for centuries. Through new editions of Plutarch, Livy, and Pliny, the reading public learned of Epicureanism and Stoicism, of Lucretius, Cato, Brutus, and Seneca. Petrarch in 1366 made use of classical texts to write a polemic against suicide. He reprises the classical arguments against suicide, including the ideas that it is not proper to abandon one's post and that killing oneself is against human nature. Moreover, he adds, in a Christian context, suicide is against God's will. Of Cato and Seneca he writes, "I grieve to condemn such great men; but I have strangely wondered indeed, how so cruel an opinion could enter into the heart of so worthy a man as Seneca, who does indeed say I will leap out of this ruinous building of my body—but O Seneca, though sayst not well!" Cato, he observes, has been commended by some and "sharply reprehended" by others; he sides with those who see him dying not to defend the Republic but out of envy of Caesar. Petrarch even suggests that perhaps "Cato sought occasion to die, not so much to escape Caesar's hands as to follow the principles of the Stoics; and by some notable deed to give his name to posterity."[1] Thus are dismissed the heroes of ancient suicides. Petrarch also writes that suicides are caused by anger, disdain, impatience, and "a kind of furious forgetfulness of what thou art." Of those who procured their own deaths, "how glad would they now be to return into this world again, to abide poverty and all adversity."[2] For Petrarch, suicide is an unmitigated evil.

This attitude was not monolithic. Ten years later, Chaucer's poem *The Legend of Good Women* included long sections dedicated to the suicides of Lucretia, Dido, Cleopatra, and Pyramus and Thisbe. Chaucer praises them all. He describes Lucretia after she has told her kinsman what happened to her:

> She seide, that, for her gilt ne for her blame,
> Her husbond sholde nat have the foule name,
> That would she nat suffer, by no wey
> And they aswereden all upon hir fey,
> That they foryeve hit her, for hit was right;
> Hit was no gilt, hit lay nat in her might
> And seiden her ensamples many oon.
> But al for noght; for thus she seide anoon
> "Be as be may," quod she, "of forgiving,
> I wol nat have no forgift for no-thing."
> But prively she caught forth a knyf,
> And therwith-al she rafte re-self her lyf
> And as she fel adoun, she caste her look
> And of her clothes yit she hede took;
> For in falling yit she hadde care
> Lest that her feet or swiche thing lay bare
> So wel she loved clennesse and eek trouthe.

There is forgiveness for Lucretia here, for the crime committed against her, but her final act is taken as the pinnacle of being a "good woman."

In the late 1500s, there begin to be more suicides in literature, and suicide is often depicted in a positive way.[3] For example, in an anonymous English manuscript of 1578, Saul is put on trial for killing himself. Saul boldly defends himself by calling upon the examples of Samson, the Christian martyrs, Socrates, and Cato.

Another somewhat positive take on suicide was written by John Harington, one of the favorite courtiers of Queen Elizabeth I. Harington imagines a dialogue between Samuel, Saul, and Solomon on the question of "Whether it be damnation for a man to kill himself." Samuel submits a strict religious rejection of all suicide, while Saul offers a contrary argument, praising both Cato and Samson for having avoided abuse by their enemies. As Saul puts it, "Was it not better for me to kill myself, seeing that I see death present before mine eyes, than suffer mine enemies to abuse me ignominiously, to triumph over me despitefully, and to revile me contumeliously? If a man be condemned to die is it any matter whether he or the hangman shall tie the halter about his neck and cast him off the ladder?"[4] Then Saul asks, "Did not the martyrs of Queen Mary's days willingly offer themselves to the flames?" Harington praises Samson, whom God himself gave the prodigious strength necessary to kill himself in his circumstances. He also mentions Socrates as a suicide worthy of praise. Solomon, a symbol of justice, decides the matter without abandoning the notion of religion but with much more sympathy for the idea of suicide. He does not condemn suicide outright. Instead, he says that we must "leave all to the secret judgment of God, referring all to his mercy." Paintings and literary depictions of suicide also began to change at this time. No longer was the suicidal person being tempted by demons to disobey the word of God. In God's most secret mind, the judgment, we are told, is likely to be one of mercy.

Cultural sympathies changed as the modern era evolved. In the political realm, individuals gained more rights and more say in government. In the religious realm, chiefly with the rise of Protestantism, there was increased emphasis on the individual's experience. No longer was the priest the intermediary between a believer and God; now individuals were encouraged to read the Bible for themselves and to personally assess their relationship with God. The individual was appearing for the first time as a human being without a polis, without a household god, without a priest and interceding saints, but with a God of his own, albeit one whose crucial attributes are invisibility and unknowability.

One product of the revival of interest in the ancient world during the sixteenth and seventeenth centuries was the appearance of many paintings of Lucretia, her suicide, and the founding of the Roman Republic. The earliest of these paintings we will consider is Sandro Botticelli's *Tragedy of Lucretia*, which dates from 1500. Botticelli depicts the heroic suicide already dead, surrounded by a crowd of soldiers, large figures who are themselves dwarfed by the Roman architecture in the background. The imposing scene represents the importance of the state and the citizen's dedication to it. The woman herself is small, slightly splayed on her funereal slab, neck arched backward in a pose of utter surrender, the dagger that killed her still protruding from her chest. The men around her, all in the partial armor of the Roman soldier, are in an array of poses, but somehow geometrical, as stiff as the architecture around them. This painting has often been interpreted as a portrayal of the pain and beauty of sacrifice to the state. The woman is tiny, the men are large, the buildings of the state are imposing. Lucretia's ancient story here reminds its viewers of the powerful states that ruled in the late Renaissance. Then things changed.

Botticelli's work is unusual for showing Lucretia after her suicide, a small part of her context. Many of the later paintings zoom in on the figure of the woman herself, still alive. Often the context is sparse, and the painting or drawing is less about Lucretia's story than about Lucretia herself. By focusing on her eyes and posture they hint at her inner life, and we now begin to see her as an individual suffering a grave problem, ascertaining the value and meaning of her own life. She is often holding a long dagger and sometimes has already stabbed herself in the belly, or is about to do so. Raphael drew her with spread arms depicted in such vibrant lines that she seemed to be dancing with the knife, barely pointed at her. For this graceful pose she is dressed in a toga, which falls in disarray over her body, one breast exposed, her head back and eyes closed, the emotion of the moment almost lifting her up off the courtyard stones. Raphael drew his Lucretia for a collaboration with printmaker Marcantonio Raimondi, and it became one of the most famous prints of the Renaissance. This Lucretia does not make one think of the state, or even of sacrifice. Instead it is all about the woman pictured, who seems miserable and as yet uncommitted to death.

Alternatively, Lucretia was sometimes imagined as the epitome of calm, virtuous and reasonable, as in the work of an unknown Dutch painter of the early sixteenth century. Sometimes she is angry, as in Albrecht Dürer's 1518 *Suicide of Lucretia,* which shows her naked and frowning monstrously at the sky. She has already stabbed herself here, and blood spurts out of the wound, but she is still standing and practically growling, a powerful figure seemingly still full of life. This picture has been generally dismissed as Dürer's worst. The art critic Fedja Anzelewsky has written that Dürer "tried in vain to convey something of the tragic greatness of the Roman heroine through her expression."[5] It is true that she is not beautiful here, but it can be argued that if you approach the picture with an interest in the woman herself in this terrible decision, her anger and her ugliness become singularly appropriate as representations of her inner state.

Titian's 1517 *Tarquinius and Lucretia* portrays her earlier in the story, fighting off her attacker. Tarquin is dressed
in princely finery—red stockings, red velvet pantaloons—and
she is naked save for a wisp of bedsheet across her thigh. Sur-
prisingly, he has a dagger, and she is doing everything she can
to keep it away from herself: the image of the archetypical
suicidal woman here fights for her life. She is adorned with
a bracelet on each wrist, big earrings, a ring, and a necklace
of pearls. She has a pretty face, a complex blond hairdo, and a
curvaceous body, all of which represent a powerful woman of
considerable status, and full of life.

In the 1630s Lucas Cranach the Elder, the preeminent
German painter of his age, painted a whole gallery of Lucretias. All are in some stage of undress, most look directly at the
viewer, and while each held a dagger to her waist or breast,
no one seems hurt. The Flemish artist Joos van Cleve showed
Lucretia in Flemish finery, breast exposed, and having already
plunged the dagger into her chest. The look on her face is
misery. The Italian Baroque painter Guido Cagnacci also has
Lucretia alluring in her bare-breasted disrobe, dark of feature
and demeanor, having already taken the knife into her side.
Cagnacci also painted a poignant *Death of Cleopatra,* another
famous ancient suicide.

Nowhere is Lucretia more powerful and more dreamily
contemplative than in Rembrandt's *Lucretia* of 1664. For him
she is fully dressed and looking European in a noblewoman's
gown and jewels, her blade threatening herself from a good
distance. She seems more commanding than vanquished. She
is not exactly killing herself anymore, and she seems to be a
new, stronger vision of the self. These pictures, by Dürer, Titian, Cranach, van Cleve, Cagnacci, and Rembrandt, provide
evidence of a fascination with Lucretia that transcended a

range of political and social differences across these historical moments. Taken together—imagined as a composite—they seem to show European culture as a woman tapping on her chest with a tapered dagger, drifting in and out of her clothes, thinking about what she wants to be and how she can wrangle that reality for herself through life and death. This era was not sure whether it liked Lucretia better wounded and dying or still unharmed and very much alive. It was not just Lucretia's problem but everyone's. For some it seemed best to die, but for others a kind of resolute determination was the more important character trait.

When the ancients told the story of Lucretia, she always died; they did not pause to capture the moment when she considers killing herself. Indeed, her death had to happen for the real action to get going, the agony of the sacrifice felt by those standing around her; the oath to take power away from their foreign king, and indeed from any king; and then, of course, the fighting and the establishment of a government. But the Renaissance revival of interest in Lucretia was very different. After Botticelli's, in none of these most famous depictions does Lucretia die. Even when already stabbed, she is yet living. Interestingly, there is a statue in Vienna by the artist Ignaz Platzer called *Junius Brutus, Swearing Revenge at Lucretia's Corpse.* Lucretia stands next to Brutus. The conceit is that he is holding her up in one arm while he gives most of his attention to the dagger he is about to swear by, but we cannot help notice that Lucretia even here seems to be standing on her own. Instead of the ancient emphasis only on what comes after, Renaissance sensibilities cannot ignore the live woman contemplating her suicide.

Obsession with Lucretia in this age was not limited to the visual arts. One of the two long poems Shakespeare wrote was

The Rape of Lucrece (1594), a rich and beautiful philosophical work wrought in musical language, and full of wrenched
emotion. After Lucrece has killed herself, and her father and
husband have fallen on her in anguished mourning, Brutus,
long known as a joker, a buffoon, in this moment matures and
worries that the men will likewise do themselves in. "Seeing
such emulation in their woe," he plucks the knife from Lucrece's side and then declaims against their prospective suicides and also against Lucrece's:

> "Thou wronged lord of Rome," quoth he, "arise!
>   Let my unsounded self, suppos'd a fool,
>   Now set thy long-experience'd wit to school.

> "Why, Collatine, is woe the cure for woe?
> Do wounds help wounds, or grief help grievous
>   deeds?
> Is it revenge to give thyself a blow
> For his foul act by whom thy fair wife bleeds?
> Such childish humor from weak minds proceeds;
>   Thy wretched wife mistook the matter so,
>   To slay herself, that should have slain her foe."[6]

This is not at all what the ancient Roman men and women
had thought, of course, when the story was first told. The men
gathered in the story were not said to be in danger of responding to her suicide with their own, whereas in Shakespeare's
era it was possible to imagine romance and heartache forcing
a man's hand against himself. Beyond the threat of the men
killing themselves, Brutus does not approve of Lucrece's act;
indeed, he calls it mistaken. Shakespeare's characters counsel
that we must meet our psychological and political problems
by externalizing our rage, not internalizing it. One element for

which Shakespeare is praised is that his works generally incorporate several strong competing perspectives. Often enough, the wisest of perspectives is voiced by a court fool, or someone used to playing the fool. This fool-gone-wise, Brutus, says Lucrece mistook the matter. As we have seen, Chaucer also thought that those around Lucretia would have forgiven her, but her act was elevated as a sign of extreme purity and honor. In Shakespeare's telling of it, she did the wrong thing, and he exhorts all to eschew her example.

Of course, Lucretia's story is not Shakespeare's most famous meditation on self-slaughter. *Hamlet* was written only a few years later, about 1601, and exquisitely expresses the growing uncertainty about suicide. Early in the play Hamlet declares the wish that "the Everlasting had not fix'd / his canon 'gainst self-slaughter," but his deeper meditation on the subject comes later. It is among the most beautiful, sad, and intellectually quixotic passages in the English language.

> To be, or not to be, that is the question:
> Whether 'tis nobler in the mind to suffer
> The slings and arrows of outrageous fortune
> Or to take arms against a sea of troubles,
> And by opposing end them? To die—to sleep,
> No more; and by a sleep to say we end
> The heart-ache and the thousand natural shocks
> That flesh is heir to: 'tis a consummation
> Devoutly to be wish'd. To die, to sleep;
> To sleep: perchance to dream: ay, there's the rub;
> For in that sleep of death what dreams may come,
> When we have shuffled off this mortal coil,
> Must give us pause—there's the respect
> That makes calamity of so long life;

For who would bear the whips and scorns of time,
The oppressor's wrong, the proud man's contumely,
The pangs of despised love, the law's delay,
The insolence of office, and the spurns
That patient merit of the unworthy takes,
When he himself might his quietus make
With a bare bodkin? Who would fardels bear,
To grunt and sweat under a weary life,
But that the dread of something after death,
The undiscover'd country, from whose bourn
No traveller returns, puzzles the will,
And makes us rather bear those ills we have
Than fly to others that we know not of?[7]

He is not just asking whether he is too tired and miserable to go on, and he dismisses the question of whether he has something to live for after all. Life is pain, it is slings and arrows. What he asks is: which is more noble, which is more sensible? Fate and fortune are outrageous and batter us and pierce our flesh. Heartache and a thousand normal human shocks are wretched. Yet when he says that death is an ending "devoutly to be wished," it does sound like he is still trying to convince himself. Even the vibrant line about taking up arms against a sea of troubles shows a kind of severe ambivalence, for swords are not the best way to fight the sea. Hamlet does not kill himself. His answer in that deep but narrow question is "to be." But in this pivotal moment he does not say that he has to stay here, alive, for any specific reason. He just does not see immediate death as a decisively inviting alternative. Beyond those immortal lines, the Lucretia poem is a better place to go for Shakespeare's wisdom against suicide. What is certainly clear here is that attitudes were changing, and the church's argument that God alone is allowed to take a life is given no role in the deliberation.

Note, however, that after Hamlet's erstwhile love interest Ophelia kills herself, her survivors plead against her being judged a suicide and punished for it. Of Ophelia, one of the gravediggers says, "Will you ha' the truth on't? If this had not been a gentlewoman, she should have been buried out o' the Christian burial."

Interestingly, in Shakespeare's *Cymbeline*, Imogen is kept from stabbing herself because of the notion that suicide is forbidden by God.

> Against self-slaughter
> There is a prohibition so divine
> That cravens my weak hand.[8]

Different characters are given different responses to this complex question. Here, religion's claim that God rejected suicide clearly had influence on people.

For another of Shakespeare's meditations on the topic, we turn to Cleopatra. In Shakespeare's depiction, the queen makes this speech before she presses first one and then another poisonous asp to her breast:

> Give me my robe. Put on my crown. I have
> Immortal longings in me. Now no more
> The juice of Egypt's grape shall moist this lip:
> Yare, yare, good Iras! Quick! Methinks I hear
> Antony call. I see him rouse himself
> To praise my noble act. I hear him mock
> The luck of Caesar, which the gods give men
> To excuse their after wrath. Husband, I come!

Now to that name my courage prove my title!
I am fire and air; my other elements
I give to baser life.[9]

Consider her "immortal longings" and the image of her
already dead lover Marc Antony—recall that he has errone-
ously thought Cleopatra already dead and killed himself—
rousing himself from lounging in the afterlife to praise her
"noble act." The mistake of Marc Antony's death haunts all
suicides, with its reminder that we do not always know where
we really are in our story. Consider also Cleopatra's understanding of the act as one of courage equal to a queen. In the
final line we feel we are hearing more from the Elizabethan
Englishman than from the ancient Egyptian, for Shakespeare's
beautiful phrase "I am fire and air; my other elements I give to
baser life," sings of a more modern poetry of death.

Suicide sometimes seems acceptable or even noble in
Shakespeare's works. He lived in a time when people were
beginning to question religious intolerance of suicide. Religion's proscription of suicide surely saved lives, but punishment not only of those who attempted suicide but of even the
survivors of suicides struck many as unfair. As we have seen
in the Lucretia paintings, suicide was becoming more visible
and more tolerated in the early modern period, and literature
followed suit: Shakespeare's works include no fewer than fifty-
two suicides.

Still, many of Shakespeare's suicides are foolish, mistaken,
or wrongheaded. *King Lear*'s Gloucester is another noble character who seeks to end his life. Gloucester's world has come
down around him in the treachery and infighting that has
followed Lear's unwise division of his kingdom. Gloucester,

blinded, miserable, and without hope, asks his beggar friend (his son Edgar in disguise) to lead him to Dover:

> There is a cliff, whose high and bending head
> Looks fearfully in the confined deep:
> Bring me but to the very brim of it,
> And I'll repair the misery thou dost bear
> With something rich about me: from that place
> I shall no leading need.[10]

But Edgar tricks him, taking him on a trek to some fields near Dover, where he describes a little rise as if it were a precipice. After sending his friend away, Gloucester takes what he thinks will be a fatal leap and falls flat on his face to the ground. At this point Edgar, no longer disguising his voice, pretends that Gloucester's leap was real, and that they are at the bottom of the colossal cliffs now; he feigns shock the man is still alive. Edgar suggests that something otherworldly had preserved Gloucester, who vows: "henceforth I'll bear / Affliction till it do cry out itself / 'Enough, enough,' and die." The false fall reforms him. It also gives him an opportunity to express the insight that the pain that would inspire suicide will fade if we can wait it out.

A profoundly mistaken pair of suicides in Shakespeare is that of Romeo and Juliet, a reworking, as we have seen, of the ancient story of Thisbe and Pyramus. The underlying cause of the tragedy is the enmity between the young lovers' families, which puts Romeo and Juliet in an impossible situation in the first place. Yet the immediate cause of their death is brash impatience. If Romeo could have waited just a few minutes more, Juliet would have awakened from her potion-induced sleep, and their world would have changed. Even if one's beloved is not temporarily in a deathlike trance, waiting can sometimes dull the urgency for suicide.

If Hamlet's "to be or not to be" soliloquy is the best-known example of someone weighing suicide, *Romeo and Juliet* is easily the most famous dramatization of the actual act. For that reason alone, it is worth really considering the extent of the error. Not only was the final moment of each life based on a horrible mistake, but there is also a more encompassing error. At the start of the play, Romeo is pining for a different girl, as certain that she is his true love as he will later be of Juliet. What if he had killed himself over that lost love? As many of us know from experience, when one love is thwarted, another often blossoms in its wake—especially in cases of young love and young lovers.

Shakespeare seems to be warning us that we can misinterpret our situations just as his characters do. Even if your life is not fodder for farce, replete with disguises and secret pacts, even if does not rise to the exalted level of tragedy, your reading of its twists may itself be somehow twisted. In the plays, many characters see their lives through a distorted lens, making it hard to know what course of action is best; Shakespeare, we may surmise, is asking us whether our own lenses give any truer a view.

Another interesting development of this period is the association of the biblical Jonah with suicide. Historian Paul S. Seaver tells us that a future bishop of London, John King, linked Jonah and the sin of suicide in a 1594 sermon. A few years hence the future archbishop George Abbot also preached on Jonah and the sixth commandment, though he speculated that when Jonah threw himself into the sea, he did so with prophetic knowledge of God's intention to save him, an example that "may not be followed by us."[11]

The ingenious author Michel Montaigne (1533–92), who invented the genre of the essay, left us with a legacy on suicide similar to Shakespeare's. "Essai" means "try" in French, and Montaigne's essays represent attempts to interpret his own psychology as well as the nature of the world around him. In his most extensive discussion of suicide, he begins by listing quotations from the ancient world in support of the right to take one's own life. However, he does not let this list pass unchallenged.

> For many hold that we cannot abandon this garrison of the world without the express command of him who had placed us in it; and that it is for God who has sent us here not for ourselves alone, but for his glory and the service to others, to give us leave when he pleases, not for us to take it. We are not born for ourselves, it is said, but also for our country; the laws demand of us, for their interest, an accounting of ourselves. . . . Otherwise as deserters from our posts, we are punished in both this and the other world.[12]

Montaigne then goes even farther, claiming that "virtue, if energetic, never turns its back under any circumstances; it seeks out evils and pain for nourishment." Not every person in distress can claim an "energetic" quality of virtue capable of finding nourishment in pain, but Montaigne believes that suffering can be salutary for any person, over time. For Montaigne, as for some other great minds, pain tempers a person's character, leaving one wiser and often happier for having endured it.

In Montaigne's time the world was in a turbulent state of

change. Whole new worlds had been revealed to Europeans, and in those worlds were new plants, new animals, and new peoples with entirely different cultures. The thinking of the ancient world had been rediscovered as an alternative to the theories and styles of more recent times. Politics, too, was in a state of upheaval. Wars of religion pitted Catholics against Huguenots during the latter half of Montaigne's life, and across the English Channel, the official government and religion of England had changed several times in his lifetime. Montaigne himself was raised Catholic, but his mother was "New Christian"—her parents had been forced to convert from Judaism. The cultured world was also coming to know of the Copernican model of the solar system, to take it seriously, and to absorb the profound shock that it entailed. Earth had been the presumptive center of the universe, the other planets and the stars lining up in concentric circles around it; now Earth was just one planet among several, orbiting a star. With so many assumptions being reexamined, it was not surprising that people were finding new means of expression and new ways to imagine their lives, and their deaths. In this sense Montaigne was a man of his times, but he was also an original mind of the first order. New, secular ideas about suicide were beginning to emerge, and his strong words reflected and advanced those changes. He made contributions both in his respect for some ancient suicides and in his secular critique of others. For contemporaries, his tolerant retelling of certain ancient suicides was the more striking characteristic of his writing. For our purposes it is most important to note that on balance he rejected suicide and that in his critique of some ancient suicides his displeasure was not about their having sinned but about their having failed to rise to the challenges of life. Contrasting an exemplum of classical suicide with a defeated general who had endured torture and death at the hands of his enemies, he proclaimed: "There is much more fortitude in wearing out the chain that binds us than in breaking it, and more proof of strength in Regulus than in Cato. It is lack of judgment and of patience that hastens our pace."[13] Later in the same text he makes the point again, in memorable terms. "It is an act of cowardice, not of virtue, to go and hide in a hole, under a massive tomb, in order to avoid the blows of fortune. Virtue does not stop on the road or slow its pace for any storm that blows."

Montaigne enlists Plato in support, writing, "Plato, in his *Laws* ordains an ignominious burial for the man who had deprived his closest and best friend, namely himself, of life and of his destined course when constrained not by public judgment . . . but by the cowardice and weakness of a timorous soul." Montaigne also says it is against nature for one to despise oneself—a sickness peculiar to man and not seen in any other creature.

Montaigne thinks of this self-hatred as a kind of vanity and writes that it is by a similar vanity that we wish to become something other than we are, in this case, he writes, "the desire contradicts." "A man who wishes to be made into an angel does nothing for himself; he would never benefit from the change. For when he is no more, who will feel and rejoice in this improvement from him?"[14] Montaigne then quotes Lucretius on the impossibility of feeling or knowing anything after death, then observes: "The security, the freedom from pain and suffering, the exemption from the ills of this life, that we purchase at the price of death, bring us no advantage. To no purpose does the man avoid war who cannot enjoy peace, and to no purpose does the man flee from trouble who does not have what it takes to relish repose."[15] Thus Montaigne, though he cited God's disapproval in his list of reasons not to kill oneself, imagines no afterlife and gives this as a reason for a depressed person to eschew suicide. Death is final, bringing no comforting rest, so suicide is a bad idea.

Asking straight out, "What occasions are sufficient to justify a man's decision to kill himself?" Montaigne muses on the philosophical idea that trivial reasons keep us living so trivial reasons might lead us to death; "still," he writes, "some moderation is necessary." "Fantastic and irrational humors" have driven some people to suicide, such as the virgins of Miletus, who in "a mad conspiracy" hanged themselves until threatened with being shown naked to the whole city after death.

Then Montaigne gives a wonderful retelling of the Cleomenes story we encountered in Chapter 1. Here we are told that Cleomenes has fled from an honorable death in a battle he had just lost and Therycion urges him to kill himself to at least prevent his enemies from subjecting him to further shame and probable death. But Cleomenes refuses. With wry humor Montaigne writes that "with Spartan and Stoic courage" Cleomenes refuses this counsel as cowardly. Says Cleomenes, "That is a remedy . . . which must not be used as long as there is an inch of hope remaining."[16] For Cleomenes, Montaigne tells us, sometimes it is steadiness and valor to live.

"And Cassius and Brutus, on the contrary," Montaigne declares, demolished the last remnants of Roman liberty, of which they were the protectors, by the rash haste with which they killed themselves." One of the famous stories Montaigne recounts is of the Island of Cea. There Sextus Pompeius met a ninety-year-old woman who calmly told her fellow citizens that she was ready to die and, having bequeathed her goods and said her goodbyes, was permitted to take her own life. She did so by drinking poison, and "she entertained the company with an account of its progress," not unlike Socrates. Montaigne was willing to consider the respect that the ancients sometimes afforded suicides, but in his own personal opinion he seems resolutely attached to life. None of his keen awareness of the pain of existence seems equal to his sense that life is worthwhile and worth seeing through. As the Montaigne scholar Hugo Friedrich put it, "Montaigne lets nothing dissuade him from the urgency of thinking about death (not even when later he deliberately transforms this thinking into forgetting), and he lets nothing convince him that death, which annihilates life, therefore makes life worthless."[17]

Montaigne even seems to tease some of the famous ancient suicides as not exactly the grand models of calm in the face of death that they were known for being. Of Cato, writes Montaigne, "When I see him dying and tearing out his entrails," the Roman is enjoying his final drama "more than any other action of his life." In fact, Montaigne suggests, he might even believe that the ancient Roman "was grateful to fortune for having put his virtue to so beautiful a test and for having favored that brigand in treading underfoot the ancient liberty of his country."[18] Even Socrates is examined in this light. Montaigne asks, "And who that has a mind howsoever little tinctured with true philosophy can be satisfied with imagining Socrates as merely free from fear and passion in the incident of his imprisonment, his fetters, and his condemnation? And who does not recognize in him not only firmness and constancy (that was his ordinary attitude), but also I know not what new contentment, and a blithe cheerfulness in his last words and actions?"[19] Socrates was not just accepting his situation, Montaigne suggests; rather, "does he not betray a . . . sweetness and joy in his soul at being unfettered by past discomforts?" For Montaigne, suicide is never as brave as it may look.

Overall, the impression one takes from Montaigne is that suicide is a wrong choice. He makes a strong case in pointing out that the nothingness death offers is not peace, and by citing the impossibility of knowing what your future holds. Still, as Shakespeare had done in his plays and his poem on Lucretia, Montaigne opens up the question. Montaigne's investigation was rationalist rather than religious, praising many of the ancient suicides, mocking others. Still, his granting suicide any tolerance at all was revolutionary. Montaigne's popularizer Pierre Charron summarized the essayist's thoughts in a 1601 book called *Of Wisdom,* which reinforced the idea that rationalism included a shocking tolerance for suicide. In part, *Of Wisdom* accomplishes this in its keen description of depression: "When once despair takes possession of us, the soul is perfectly put upon the rack; and the thought that we shall never be able to obtain what we aim at, is so torturing and violent, that it bears down all before it; and we lose what we stand actually possessed of for the sake of somewhat which we apprehend impossible to be possessed."[20] Like Montaigne, Charron insists that custom makes most things right or wrong, and that had we lived elsewhere—on the Island of Cea, for instance—we would act according to the customs of that environment.

Around this same time, in 1610, the theologian and poet John Donne wrote *Biathanatos,* a defense of suicide from a religious perspective. Donne is probably most famous for his *Holy Sonnets,* especially the one that begins "Death, be not proud," in which he asserts that death should be humbled by the fact of the afterlife. His *Biathanatos,* published posthumously, was quite an anomaly. Donne was not cavalier about suicide but did not think that it ought to be subject to the cruel laws of the religious and governmental judgments. Donne left the manuscript to his son, who later confessed that his father's wishes had "forbid both the press and the fire." In his preface, Donne admits that he often considered suicide and he was not kept from it by any belief that it was sinful. He insists, "I have the keys to my prison in my own hand, and no remedy presents itself so soon to my heart as mine own sword."[21] For Donne, this was not an irreligious stance, especially because he saw Jesus as a suicide. "It is a heroic act of fortitude, if a man when an urgent occasion is presented exposes himself to a certain and assured death as he did."[22] Donne saw Jesus as having willingly given his life to redeem humanity, a self-sacrifice that made him a model for the martyr suicides that followed. "Apollonia and others who prevented the fury of the fire, did therein imitate this act of our Savior, of giving up his soul, before he was constrained to do it."

In 1621 there was another momentous development in the reconceiving of suicide: the publication of the English scholar Robert Burton's *The Anatomy of Melancholy*. Burton takes a decidedly and unprecedentedly medical view of self-murder. According to Burton, melancholy is due to an excess of black bile and to circumstances in which susceptible persons find themselves. He writes that the experience of melancholy can leave a person with an exceptional mental profundity, and that for this reason we might compare it to women's pain in childbirth: stunningly intense, yet not avoided, because of the astonishing good it brings.[23] Burton also observes that melancholy characterizes the obsessive ruminations of serious people and that his own melancholy inspired him to write about the subject. "I write of Melancholy," he explains, "by being busy to avoid melancholy."[24] What with black bile and another of his pet theories, the influence of Saturn, Burton's ideas do not strike us as scientific today, but his attempt to describe what happened to desperate people represented an advance over theories of demonic possession or the devil's temptations. Burton takes what had been a religious battle and categorizes it within terms that implied the medical model.

Indeed, Burton includes a classification for what he called "religious melancholy," to which he devotes a section of his book long enough to have been a book of its own. Burton sees religious melancholy created by excesses of both overpassionate Catholics and overpassionate Protestants. He fulminates against priests who scare their parishioners, adding, "But above all others the dam of that monstrous and superstitious brood, the bull-bellowing Pope which now rageth in the West, that three headed Cerebrus hath played his part." Meanwhile due to terrifying Protestant preachers, Burton sees many patients who are suicidal because "thinking they are already damned, they suffer the pains of hell and more than possibly can be expressed." Many had killed themselves, thinking they "hath offended God"; he tells of a woman who threw herself from a window, breaking her neck, some who hanged themselves, some who cut their throats. Burton asks whether such deaths are necessary and answers: "Experience teaches us that though many die obstinate and willful in their malady, yet multitudes again are able to resist and overcome, seek for help and find comfort, are taken from the chops of hell." He offers much advice, but above all Burton counsels those suffering from religious melancholy to stay away from tracts and sermons that excite these concerns, and for all melancholies he insists, "Give not way to solitariness and idleness. Be not solitary, be not idle." Burton ends his book with the stirring words: "Hope, ye miserable. Ye happy, take heed."[25]

Some kind of deep religious despair was clearly widespread, because, by the turn of the sixteenth century, Calvinist leaders had begun to recognize suicidal crises and to shape a scheme of conversion and redemption protective to the men and women affected. Burton describes such crises as a kind of illness, which the church's cure only exacerbated. The ministers "making every small fault and thing indifferent an irremissible offence, they so rent, tear, and wound men's consciences that they are almost mad and at their wit's ends."[26]

Suicide can seem like it is a private matter respondent only to a given person's internal experience, but historical investigation exposes trends. People hear about ways of responding to their pain and act on them. Before leaving this historical period, we must consider one more variant: suicidal murder, similar to what we today call "suicide by cop." The phenomenon is examined in historian Vera Lind's essay "The Suicidal Mind and Body."[27] Suicidal murder describes the actions of a person who seeks to end his or her days by killing someone else in order to be punished by death. Lind, writing about Germanic territories, tells us that the idea attracted people because suicide was considered a worse crime than murder, but also because this method allowed time for penance and repentance, the comfort of a clergyman, and the chance to be forgiven by God and go to heaven. A servant killed a boy in 1752 for no reason other than that the servant himself wanted to die. "Thus he had the chance to die as a 'poor sinner'—and he wanted to die anyway—because he would have time to show remorse and be comforted by a pastor before his execution. In this way the servant could be sure of dying a 'good' Christian death, something that he never could achieve by committing suicide."[28] The problem of suicidal murder was so extensive that in 1767 a law was put into effect that denied the death penalty to people who committed murder with the sole purpose of ending their own life. The rather cruel alternative punishment was life imprisonment.

Details of such trends show us that they were connected to a given age, gender, and life-circumstance of the victims. Historian Arne Jansson's essay "Suicidal Murders in Stockholm" looks at the early modern period in Sweden's capital and tells us that while researching violent deaths in Stockholm, he was surprised to find a considerable number of confessed suicidal murderers.[29] In the time he studied he found sixty-five such people. Ample evidence suggests a real increase in Sweden's suicides starting in the late seventeenth century. As in Lind's essay, we find a rise in a particular idea influencing individuals to arrange their own deaths. In Jansson's studies, suicidal murder was a method mostly used by women, fifty-three of the sixty-five. Social isolation and poverty seemed to contribute to the phenomenon: of the fifty-three women, only seven were married, and three of those were separated from their husbands at the time of the murder. Some women invented murders by claiming to have given birth and done away with the baby. The courts came to doubt such confessions. Jansson tells us that for men an alternative path to indirect suicide was to falsely confess to bestiality; in the sixteenth and seventeenth centuries at least six hundred people were executed in Sweden for this crime. A considerable number of men apparently confessed without having been accused, and while some may have done so out of guilty feelings for having actually committed the act, others were surely seeking death. Courts had no way of knowing. Jansson adds, "But confessing to a crime that one has not committed came to be popularly known as 'lying oneself out of life' and judges became increasingly skeptical of such unsolicited confessions."

Jansson offers some explanations for the rise of suicidal murders:

> Most notably, why did the far northern regions of Europe show a special penchant for such indirect suicides? One factor was surely that of imitation. After committing murder, Christina Johansdotter, for example, had confessed that she was following the example of others in seeking the death penalty for herself. In the years under study, one can speak of clusters of cases of suicidal murder. There were three cases in 1689, five in 1706 and nine in 1709–1710, all of which suggests that imitation was a contributing factor in Stockholm's plethora of indirect suicides.[30]

Suicidal murders declined in the eighteenth century. Jansson believes that the Enlightenment helped reduce the fear of old religious arguments, including the anger of God and the fear of hell. Suicide was now more likely to be interpreted through the lenses of mental illness and personal hardship.

Even as art, theater, government, and public opinion began to treat suicide in these complex new ways, most Christian authors still raged at the offense it posed to God. Corpses were still tortured and could not be buried in church grounds. Assets were still seized. The Enlightenment rejection of religion's prohibition of suicide is the next great change in the story, and it is to that drama that we now turn.

4

Secular Philosophy
Defends Suicide

One of the main points of this book is to tell the story of how philosophy in Western culture got its reputation for tolerating suicide. We have seen that ancient philosophers wrote against suicide, but that some celebrated suicides nonetheless were praised as having been virtuous and philosophically sound. We have seen that in the Middle Ages, religion regulated against suicide and Christian thinkers like Augustine and Dante condemned the celebrated "philosophical" suicides of antiquity. Because religion set itself so firmly against suicide, and because it did so expressly in opposition to these renowned ancient suicides, from early on Western culture considered philosophy itself as relatively tolerant of suicide. This association was increased in the early modern era, when art and literature created some fascinating portraits of ancient suicides. Again, because of religion's harsh judgment against suicides, any sympathetic look at a famous suicide might be associated with the new rationalist thinking. Religion and philosophy thus squared off over suicide. At first it was a somewhat one-sided fight (in public at least) as few philosophical voices were openly and explicitly defending suicide. Tolerance of suicide was a legacy of the ancient world, and that legacy was reflected in some secular art and literature, but early modern religion was uncompromising in its condemnation. In this chapter I will show that initially religious sources accused contemporary philosophers and philosophical clubs of being in favor of suicide. Then, with the advent of the Enlightenment and its overt skepticism toward religious and traditional ideas, we find some philosophers directly proclaiming a secular philosophy tolerant of suicide.

A new age of critical examination of religion was key to the philosophical rehabilitation of suicide, but other factors influenced the changing attitudes as well. One of the most important was the rise of scientific medicine, which influenced people to think of suicide less as sinful than as a morally neutral result of a nervous disease. Political and economic pressures also reinforced the new philosophy and learning. A signal tenet of the nascent ideology of capitalism was respect for private property, which made it more difficult for governing bodies to confiscate the estates of suicides. With a decline in punishment came a decline in judgment, as individual suicides became less likely to be considered guilty of crime.

In different places, over different periods of time, the patterns of change had their own logic. As Michael MacDonald and Terence R. Murphy argue in their *Sleepless Souls: Suicide in Early Modern England,* English culture of the early modern period underwent two phases of change regarding suicide. During the first phase, the Reformation tightened moral strictures of all kinds, including those against suicide, while governments drew revenue from fines and forfeitures levied for crimes, including suicide. The second phase encompassed a much more complicated softening of response. MacDonald and Murphy detail the complexity of the rise of tolerance toward suicide with nods to the changing economic, judicial, and intellectual currents, including

> local hostility to the forfeiture of self-murderers' goods, the abolition of the prerogative courts during the English revolution, the governing elite's intensified reverence for private property, the reactions against religious enthusiasm, the rise of the new science, Enlightenment philosophy, the increase in literacy among the middling classes, the vast expansion of the periodical press, and the gradual absorption of empirical epistemology into the mentality of the upper and middle classes.[1]

Rationalist, progressive thinking was one of many forces that conspired to make attitudes toward suicide more neutral. Perhaps partly as a result came a general impression among contemporaries that suicide was on the increase. Already in 1702 the English diarist John Evelyn wrote that it was "sad to consider how many of this nation have murdered themselves of late years."[2]

Our story in this chapter begins just before the Enlightenment, generally thought of as extending from 1750 to 1850. Already reports can be found of contemporary people described as intellectually open to suicide. When the Oxford scholar Thomas Creech took his own life, in 1700, some contemporaries connected the act with Creech's having translated Lucretius. Educated people knew that Lucretius had written in favor of a "philosophical," dispassionate approach to the idea of death, and were familiar with the possibility that he had killed himself. Thus Creech was seen as having committed suicide in part because his love of this figure of the ancient world had convinced him that suicide was a positive choice. Other publicly discussed suicides of the period were also seen as being partly based on philosophical argument. In 1704 an aristocrat named George Edwards killed himself by inventing a contraption by which three pistols would go off at once. John Smith, an Anglican minister, published a pamphlet in which he presented Edwards's suicide as a symptom of the terrible lengths to which philosophy and irreligion had progressed in the country, especially the "new Epicureanism." He blamed all those who upheld the principles of Hobbes, Spinoza, and the neo-Epicurean Walter Charleton. He also compared Edwards to the deist Charles Blount, who believed in a creator but rejected most other aspects of religion. Blount had also killed himself, twenty years earlier, and Smith insisted that taking a stance against Christianity deprived men of reason.[3]

In fact, Edwards's story was more complicated than that. He had been famously pious as a young man, but after reading a number of philosophical works, he grew increasingly rationalist in his interpretations of scripture. Finally he came to believe that much of the Bible could not be true. He asked, for example, how all the races of the world could have come from one white Adam. With such scandalous opinions he found himself shunned by former friends, and his wife left him. It was then that he put an end to his days. This death and its public discussion received a great deal of attention. Some saw irreligion and philosophy as the cause of Smith's suicide; others blamed the intolerance Smith encountered among the religious. What was generally agreed upon was that suicide was on the rise, and though John Donne, a religious man, had written a treatise calling for tolerance of suicide, irreligion and philosophy were more closely associated with suicide.

The more that philosophers and philosophical clubs became synonymous with antireligious attitudes and renewed interest in the ancients, the more these people and places were connected to tolerance or encouragement of suicide. Just as religious writing had used the ancient suicides as a counterpoint, the new secular writing used ancient heroes to valorize self-murder. Jonathan Swift published an essay in 1709 in which he praised Cato as the greatest among the ancients. Joseph Addison's popular play *Cato* celebrated the Roman's suicide as a glorious apotheosis. Cato's death is the play's grand climax, featuring solemn exposition by the dying man, including the cry, "Lose not a thought on me, I'm out of danger," painting death as an escape from harm. This play had many memorable lines. Historian David McCullough has pointed out that Nathan Hale's "I only regret that I have but one life to lose for my country" adapts Addison's "What a pity it is / That we can die but once to serve our country."[4] In either phrasing it is a remarkable request for multiple self-initiated deaths. There is evidence that such attitudes mattered to people who saw the play or read of it. We know from a report in *Gentleman's Magazine* that the poet Eustace Budgell threw himself to his death in the Thames, having left behind a note reading, "What Cato did and Addison approved, / Cannot be wrong."[5]

The suicide rate in the English aristocracy in this period was thought of as so high that other nations wrote of the practice as "the English malady." When George Cheyne published *The English Malady* in 1733, he did not have to argue that the English had a particular problem with nervous diseases and, lately, with suicide. He wrote that his friends had

urged him to write the book because of the recent "frequency
and daily increase of wanton and uncommon self-murders."[6]
Cheyne explained that the problem was the melancholy dispo-
sition caused by gloomy weather, but that the immediate cause
was the progress of anti-Christianity and the rise of a secular
philosophical spirit among the English people. The suicide
question became, especially in England and France, one of the
most visible battlegrounds between the secular and the religious. Among the educated classes, books and essays on the
subject were widely read, and lectures brought the matter to
a broad population as well. In George Minois's words, "Cato,
Epicurus, and Lucretius had become heroes once again, and
it was chic to be broadminded about suicide and oppose the
clergy."[7] In this era London and Paris were hotbeds of Liber-
tinism, which represented a philosophy of freethinking and
open-mindedness in religion, politics, and social mores. The
Libertines were frequently devoted to Epicurus. Libertine circles were scandalous for their interest in sex, and they were
also known for their disdain for the religious rejection of suicide. Often secular philosophy was linked to suicide because
of its profound equanimity in the face of death, a stance that
seemed to some the pinnacle of strong-minded maturity. With
the Libertines we see a more playful version of this stance: they
refused to take death seriously and entertained ideas of suicide
alongside ideas of extramarital sex, seeing both as a rejection
of the rigidity of religious morals.

If someone wanted to appear rationalist and secular, and
yet take a stand against suicide, he had to make a point of it.
This is evident in the very origins of the word "suicide," which
dates to this period. The word was invented in England by the
scholar Sir Thomas Browne in his popular *Religio Medici,* in
which he praises the Roman poet Lucan and what he calls his

"Stoic genius," but says he goes too far when he praises self-assassination as with the suicide of Cato. "This is indeed not to fear death, but yet to be afraid of life. It is a brave act of valour to condemn death, but where life is more terrible than death, it is then the truest valour to dare to live. And herein religion has taught us a noble example."[8] ("Suicide" didn't pass into French and then the rest of the European languages until the middle to late eighteenth century.) It adds a measure of importance to these words to note that Browne was himself well known to suffer from bouts of melancholy.

We now come to John Henley, author of the foremost work against suicide of his age. Henley was not a traditional Christian thinker, preferring his own logical arguments to the dogma of the churches, but like conventional Christianity he saw suicide as wrong, and he criticized the lauded suicides of antiquity. In 1730 Henley published the pamphlet *Cato Condemned; or, The Case and History of Self-Murder, Argued and Displayed at Large, on the Principles of Reason, Justice, Law, Religion, Fortitude.* Henley started his career as an English clergyman but transformed his preaching into a kind of one-man-show, inspirational, protoabsurdist theatrical experience and began charging admission. He became popular with freethinkers and said he hoped to "die a rational." Alexander Pope sketched him as the "great restorer of the good old stage / Preacher at once and Zany of thy age." Henley condemned Cato. Henley's rejection of suicide was based on secular grounds, though he also mentioned that God disapproved. As Henley saw it, "Life . . . is made for some purpose, directed to some end. This end has been assigned to be the following of Reason, Virtue, Nature, or God. However it can not have been the aim of life, that it should be destroy'd; the true end of any being must be to act according to the utmost of its Faculties; this is properly, the following of Nature. The Faculties of Man are Knowledge and Free-will." This went much farther than religious decrees that suicide was wrong simply because it went against God's plan. Instead, Henley argued that life intrinsically had purpose and that human beings had to find a way to follow that purpose, whether following reason, virtue, nature, or religion. "Self-murder," he says, is wrong, then, because "it takes away all reason and virtue and all the noble trial and satisfaction of them; so that on Principles of Nature itself, it must be deemed utterly unlawful."[9]

Henley also saw self-murder as "repugnant to the end for which our nature was given us, and to that limited right which we have over our own lives, so it is opposite to the duty of man, considered as a member of civil society." We are all members of society and these connections are to be honored. As for the tedium of life, here is what Henley offers us:

> It is a beaten notion of the Epicureans and Stoics, that life is only a dull narrow circle of the same actions, and therefore is inconsiderable; Lucretius describes this conceit, and Seneca applauds it. But they seem to forget that the life of man is a progress in understanding and goodness; which is not a tasteless round of the same actions, but ever opens a new scene to the mind and to the conduct. The life of sense is indeed a dull circle; but that of reason and virtue improves upon our hands, and makes us every day wiser and happier.[10]

The abiding pleasures of life, Henley explains, renew themselves despite all the repetition of existence. We discover new truths. We find new ways to do good for others, which both make us proud of ourselves and bring the praise of others. He acknowledges that life can be tiresome and hard but believes that as we go through life we gain wisdom and the ability to be the person we want to be.

Despite his title, Henley knows well that the ancients did not uniformly side with Cato's action. Many of them held that suicide is wrong, he writes, and "this the very pagan philosophers expressed in the strongest language," that "no man ought to quit his station."[11] Beyond pointing out that ancient philosophers were antisuicide, Henley criticizes the traditionally celebrated ancient suicides. Cato's death, he writes, was "a mixture of pride and impatience." Brutus and Cassius came to an "immature end." Of the ninety-year-old matron of the Isle of Cea, Henley explains that she pridefully refused to experience a change in her prosperity.[12] He writes that he knows about the misery both of physical pain and mental anguish, which he acknowledges may be equally tormenting, but he still rejects suicide, exhorting sufferers to manage the disorderly troubles of the heart. "Courage," he tells us, "consists in bearing pain" as well as in resplendent deeds and impressive actions.[13] Furthermore, Henley proclaims that if the ghosts of Cato and Brutus were told of a country where men deliberately dispatch themselves in moments of misery born of small disappointments, weariness of life, or a fear of poverty, they would be furious about it and would fiercely abhor being held as a precedent for such behavior.[14]

Henley emphasizes that the celebration of Cato's suicide in antiquity does not mean that all of antiquity was in favor of suicide as a response to the difficulties of life. "And yet this justice must be done the heathen world," writes Henley, "that the laws of their states and the reasonings of their best philosophers, condemned this practice as a rash forsaking of the station in which the providence of the gods place mankind, and their expressions are numerous and strong against it."[15] Henley reminds us that in the work of "the best philosophers" of the ancient world, self-murder is rejected, and that such rejections are plentiful and robust. And he deprecates even the relatively few cases in which pagans were applauded for suicide. These celebrated suicides had been spoken of as examples of courage, honor, and liberty, but for Henley suicide represents not courage but cowardice or desperation, not honor but shame, and not liberty but slavery to one's passions.[16] Henley's work was celebrated by contemporaries. Apparently there was a hunger for a treatise rejecting suicide from a rationalist perspective.

In the history of suicide, Henley is unusual in positing a relatively secular antisuicide philosophy. Christian, Jewish, and Muslim authorities forbade suicide on theological grounds and chided the ancient pagan world for encouraging suicide as a response to difficulties. Henley, in contrast, made energetic and imaginative arguments against suicide independent of church prohibition. He also supplied an unusually nuanced view of ancient ideas about suicide. He recognized that his culture's main image of ancient suicide—that of Cato and the other celebrated deaths of the sort—was incomplete, ignoring the teachings of the great ancient philosophers against suicide. Across the centuries, secular philosophy had been consistently associated with being pro-suicide, so Henley's contribution was to make powerful arguments against suicide that did not depend on church prohibition.

As popular as Henley was, his defense of secular philosophy and antiquity from the conventional charge of support for suicide remained a minority opinion. A much better known figure today, Anglo-Irish philosopher Bishop George Berkeley (1685–1753), rejected suicide from a more conventional perspective. He described a rise of suicide in his time and linked it directly to a rise of irreligious philosophy. Berkeley is most famous for his idea of immaterialism, the concept that all we know of anything is our perception of it and all anything really amounts to is our perception of it. Nothing, in this thinking, is real in its own right. Everything—the chair, the table, the universe—is in our minds and in the mind of God. Everything is an idea. Berkeley was also a strong defender of Christianity against freethinkers and against the acts of suicide which he believed flowed from freethinking. In 1732, Berkeley wrote *Alciphron; or, The Minute Philosophy: An Apology for the Christian Religion Against Those Who Are Called Freethinkers.* Berkeley resisted calling his subjects freethinkers, it being rather too nice an epithet for his liking.[17] He claimed that they reduced the glory of life to something minute, a nub of animality followed by death. A character in the book objects that this was like faulting the mirror for the wrinkles one sees there, but Berkeley gives the stronger voice here to the case against the "Atheist, Libertine, Enthusiast, Scorner, Critic, Metaphysician, Fatalist, and Skeptic." Suicide was not the bishop's primary subject, but he is certain of its origins: "As the Minute Philosophy prevails, we daily see more examples of suicide." A friend had been such a philosopher, he explains, who when wavering in his philosophic certainty "endeavored to fortify his Irreligion by the discourse and opinion of other Minute Philosophers, who were mutually strengthened in their own unbelief by his. After this manner, authority working in a circle, they endeavored to atheize one another."[18] Berkeley was the best-known voice among many who argued that suicide was on the rise because people no longer trusted religion enough to follow its rules.

In the Enlightenment, the attitudes Berkeley described

came to be proclaimed openly by philosophers. Enlightenment philosophers attacked a variety of religious prohibitions
and claimed that many rules of the churches—including the
religious prohibition of suicide—were merely superstition and
custom. The loudest champions of the right to suicide were
two of the greatest upstarts against Christianity, the Enlightenment philosophers David Hume and Baron d'Holbach. When
we examine their philosophical arguments, we find that they
were concerned more with rejecting religious control than specifically with establishing a more liberal attitude toward suicide for individuals and society. It is an important distinction,
because it seems that some people were convinced by these
philosophers and acted on their convictions. According to
contemporaries there was a marked increase in suicides in this
era, and many blamed philosophical arguments in favor of
the right to suicide. When we read those arguments and find
them to be fiery and witty attacks on the religious prohibition
against suicide, not sensitive, empathetic meditations on the
meaning of life, it is fair to wonder whether this philosophical sally against the churches did indeed inspire more negative
consequences than its arguments merited.

David Hume (1711–76), a Scottish philosopher, was one
of the most interesting figures of the Enlightenment. It is un-
clear whether Hume believed in God. He did not call himself
an atheist but often sounded like one. In a chapter of his *Enquiry into Human Understanding* of 1748, a character defends
the beliefs of Epicurus in denying "a divine existence and consequently a providence and a future state."[19] Contemporaries
and readers ever since have seen this as Hume's own argument
against the ideas of his era, couched in an ancient context so
as to deflect criticism. Using a proxy to argue for Epicurus,
Hume could express the idea that there is no God, no justice

built into the world, no afterlife. Elsewhere he writes of the uselessness of the concept of God once we accept that we cannot know anything about him. Theologians, faced with skepticism about the reality of the biblical God, had already begun to read the Bible as allegory and to describe God as unknowable. Hume wrote that if we really could not know anything about this notion of a divinity, we were left with a notion of no divinity. Hume also wrote that we did not need God as a basis of human morality; rather, he observed, doing good brings peace of mind and the high opinion of one's fellows. He even claimed that religious notions of morality grew from this human source.

"On Suicide" is one of several provocative, irreligious essays Hume wrote in the 1750s. It is a defense of our right to end it all that comically dismantles the church fathers' proscriptions. He notes that "modern European superstition" holds suicide to be impious because it is not God's idea for us to die now. But then, he teases, is it not impious "to build houses, cultivate the ground, or sail upon the ocean?" God did not arrange any of these things for us. If the disposal of human life was strictly the province of the Almighty, Hume argues, it would be equally criminal to act for the preservation of life as for its destruction. "If I turn aside a stone which is falling upon my head," he explains, "I disturb the course of nature, and I invade the peculiar province of the Almighty, by lengthening out my life beyond the period which by the general laws of matter and motion he had assigned it."[20] Hume was a bold and original thinker. Throughout history people had argued that we had to stay alive simply because the gods or God had put us in our situations and only such divine authority should be able to remove us from them. Hume here cements the common association of religious skeptics and the defense of suicide.

Furthermore, Hume says, God did not put him into his life as a general puts a soldier at his post; rather, his life occurred because of a series of random events and almost as random human choices. He argues, "When I shall be dead, the principles of which I am composed will still perform their part in the universe, and will be equally useful in the grand fabric, as when they composed this individual creature." Hume also says that the suicide no more steals rights from God than does the magistrate who sentences someone to death; the suicide may even be doing the public as much good, by getting rid of a "pernicious" person. He even says that when our existence becomes a burden we ought to kill ourselves because, "'Tis the only way that we can then be useful to society, by setting an example, which if imitated, would preserve to every one his chance for happiness in life, and would effectually free him from all danger of misery."[21] It is a remarkably uncharitable assessment of what people mean to each other. This is one of the most potent origins of our culture's perception of secular philosophy as pro-suicide, so it is important to note that it does not address much outside the fight with religion. Hume delivers a tirade on the religious arguments against suicide, but his glance at the question on its own terms is an incredibly cold one.

As original as Hume's ideas were, they were matched by those of Baron d'Holbach, a French philosopher born in Germany and one of the key figures of the French Enlightenment. The baron wrote on suicide with his classic cheek; he too laughs at church logic and fumes at religious cruelty, and does not reconceive the question in humanist terms. D'Holbach's support of suicide was so gleeful it was almost a giddy paean to the grave.

D'Holbach published his best-known work, *The System*

of Nature, in 1770. In this materialist treatise he proclaims the world to be a system, utterly materialist, with no God and with the actions of human beings so profoundly determined by other forces—society, culture, biology, physics—that it is nonsense to speak of free will. The baron writes sentences so long you find yourself rather spat out by the end of them, not sure where you have just been, and he hides his occasional brilliance in long pages of rambling thoughts. When he gets to matters that concern us most though, he is quite interesting and relatively concise. On suicide he ruminates on why he thinks people are afraid to die and why these particular fears are laughably wrong. For more than a page he lists great people who have died, pausing now and then to say something like "the universe will not be stopped by thy loss."[22] Death is real, he keeps insisting, and you should think lightly of your own.

D'Holbach encourages his reader to forgive the person who is terminally ill and in dire agony, but he goes much farther. His language seems to support the idea that we might commit suicide for the respect it might garner from others, or for the escape from minor ills. Consider how he describes suicide in other cultures:

> The Greeks, the Romans, and other nations, which every thing conspired to make intrepid, to render courageous, to lead to magnanimity, regarded as heroes, contemplated as Gods, those who voluntarily cut the thread of life. In Hindoostan, the Brahmin yet knows how to inspire even women with sufficient fortitude to burn themselves upon the dead bodies of their husbands. The Japanese, upon the most trifling occasion, takes no kind of difficulty in plunging a dagger into his bosom.[23]

What kind of problems could be legitimate causes for suicide, according to d'Holbach?

> Man can only love his existence on condition of being happy; as soon as the entire of nature refuses him this happiness; as soon as all that surrounds him becomes incommodious to him, as soon as his melancholy ideas offer nothing but afflicting pictures to his imagination; he already exists no longer; he is suspended in the void; he quits a rank which no longer suits him.

He knows that there are arguments against suicide that do not entirely rest on the wishes of God, and he mentions them.

> Some moralists, abstracting the height of religious ideas, have held that it is never permitted to man to break the conditions of the covenant that he has made with society. Others have looked upon suicide as cowardice; they have thought that it was weakness, that it displayed pusillanimity, to suffer, himself to be overwhelmed with the shafts of his destiny; and have held that there would be much more courage, more elevation of soul, in supporting his afflictions, in resisting the blows of fate.[24]

Yet in one little stroke he bats away the idea that one owes it to other people to stay alive, and the idea that it is against nature to kill oneself: "That society who has not the ability, or who is not willing to procure man any one benefit, loses all its rights over him; nature, when it has rendered his existence completely miserable, has in fact ordered him to quit it: in dying he does no more than fulfill one of her decrees, as he did when he first drew his breath."[25] He says no more about these life-affirming arguments—that individuals owe it to our communities to stay alive and that nature is opposed to it. He dismisses the first by saying that a man owes nothing to a community that has so let him down, and he denies the second by saying if you feel like killing yourself that must be what nature wants you to do. They are quite unfeeling comments and it is a strange kind of solace he offers next: "To him who is fearless of death, there is no evil without a remedy."

It is at this point that he arrives at the most heated part of his argument: "As to the superstitious, there is no end to his sufferings, for he is not allowed to abridge them. His religion bids him to continue to groan"; he is forbidden to escape into death, for if he did "he would be eternally punished for daring to anticipate the tardy orders of a cruel God, who takes pleasure in seeing him reduced to despair, and who wills that man should not have the audacity to quit, without his consent, the post assigned to him." This is d'Holbach's fury against the church and God, and he is certain that if people could see that the church is regularly wrong and that God is a bad invention of humanity, they would be more virtuous, more happy, less superstitious, and, in this particular case, they could die.

He sees how problematic this is, ending his tirade with a comment that many of his readers may fear that his maxims might encourage unhappy people "to cut the thread of life," but he believes that maxims can never actually lead to suicide. The real cause of suicide, he writes, is "a temperament soured by chagrin, a bilious constitution, a melancholy habit, a defect in the organization, a derangement in the whole machine," so no matter how much a philosopher might write about the rea-sonableness of suicide, such discussions will not lead readers to do it. Surely what he says has a little truth in it—pithy words encouraging suicide would not be enough to cause suicides on their own. However, just as surely, ideas do influence people. Thus d'Holbach feels safe in arguing with the church over suicide, having convinced himself that his writing can do no harm. In a distressingly uncharitable assessment he writes:

> Besides, what assistance or what advantage can society promise to itself from a miserable wretch reduced to despair, from a misanthrope overwhelmed with grief, from a wretch tormented with remorse, who has no longer any motive to render himself useful to others, who has abandoned himself, and who finds no more interest in preserving his life? Those who destroy themselves are such, that had they lived, the offended laws must have ultimately been obliged to remove them from a society which they disgraced.[26]

This claim recognizes that society will balk at throwing away one of its members, but the baron is certain that anyone who would actually kill himself must have been useless at best to society.

D'Holbach saves his most outrageous attack on religion for his footnotes. Here he reviews the history of suicide, noting that even religion has never been clear on the question. He invites his readers to consider "the fabulous Samson," who avenged himself upon the Philistines though it cost him his own life. Religious penitents who deny themselves to the point of death, he says, should also be considered suicides. Even Jesus, "the son of the Christians' God, if it be true that he died of his own accord, was evidently a suicide."[27]

In the footnotes he also cites the ancients, including "Seneca, the moralist," who is said to have allowed suicide. D'Holbach points out that those who died by storming into impossible battles have been held as models of heroic virtue. But what he gets wonderfully wrong is Cato's reputation. Because John Henley's work was so well known, d'Holbach writes not that Cato was celebrated for his virtuous last stand but that "Cato has always been condemned" for doing what seemed to d'Holbach the very height of honor, for "refusing to outlive the cause of liberty."

The philosophers of the Enlightenment advanced many of the ideas that are now the cornerstones of modern life. Their work broke down long-standing rules about who was fit to govern, and they loosened the rules about what professions various people were allowed to enter. They questioned social and sexual mores and advocated more freedom of choice. These agitations influenced contemporaries and the generations that followed. Much of this is commonly understood as change for the better. But along with many positive freedoms, some Enlightenment philosophers argued for the freedom to kill oneself. Given the perceived rise in suicide in this period, it is not surprising that some people made the connection between these deaths and the arguments of Enlightenment philosophers in defense of suicide. This question has not received much attention from historians, but it seems reasonable that if we can talk about the philosophers' influence in so many other domains of human behavior, we can also suppose that their writing in favor of the right to suicide also had an impact.

It is a rare observation, but not entirely unheard of: historian of suicide Jeffrey R. Watt relates the epidemic of suicides described by people of the time and asks, "Could it be that through their writings, the philosophs were, wittingly or unwittingly, helping unleash suicidal tendencies that Christian moralists had effectively restrained for over a millennium? Some contemporaries certainly thought so."[28] It is an important point. French critics noted a dramatic increase in suicides beginning in the 1760s and blamed it on "Anglomania" and on the irreligious arguments in favor of suicide.

Another way Enlightenment figures attacked the church's stance on suicide was to reject the punishments that were still being inflicted on the corpse and on the familial survivors of a suicide victim. The best example of this comes from Voltaire, one of the supreme Enlightenment figures. Voltaire is today remembered for his comic and philosophical short novel *Candide* of 1759, but in his own time he was most famous as a political agitator. He was one of the first to have used the press and public opinion to force action from governing bodies. In particular, he was a great crusader against the oppression and abuses of ordinary citizens at the hands of the Catholic Church. Voltaire's most extensive writing on suicide was in the entry "On Cato: Of Suicide" in the *Dictionnaire philosophique.* There, he tells of one suicide he was very close to: in October of 1769 a man whom he knew to be serious, professional, mature, and without vices had left a "written apology for his voluntary death," which Voltaire tells us was not made public out of fear of setting off a wave of other suicides. It is an astute early observation regarding suicidal influence. In this case the issue of suicidal influence was acute, as the victim's father and brother had killed themselves, and at the same age. Following this sad tale, Voltaire tells story after story and mentions the common belief that the English had lately been killing themselves more than the French but suggests that this perception merely reflects the publication of suicide statistics in England, a practice censored in France.

Voltaire writes approvingly of the lauded suicides of the

ancient world, praising Cato and calling Arria sublime, but he concludes with a critique of what the church of his time was still doing to the bodies of suicides:

> We still drag on a sledge and drive a stake through the body of a man who has died a voluntary death; we do all we can to make his memory infamous; we dishonor his family as far as we are able; we punish the son for having lost his father, and the widow for being deprived of her husband. We even confiscate the property of the deceased which is robbing the living of the patrimony which of right belongs to them. This custom derives from our canon law, which deprives of Christian burial such as die a voluntary death. Hence it is concluded that we cannot inherit from a man who is judged to have no inheritance in heaven. The canon law, under the head "De Poenitentia," assures us that Judas committed a greater crime in strangling himself than in selling our lord Jesus Christ.[29]

Voltaire's anger at the church is at the heart of the secular defense of suicide. Here the anger is directed at the cruelty inflicted on the families of suicide victims. As with Hume and d'Holbach, the defense of suicide issued by secular philosophy is pervaded by the conflict with religion. If the Catholic Church and other religious groups had never taken a fierce position against suicide, it seems unlikely that the philosophers of the Enlightenment would have taken up the subject, and if they had, it seems possible they would have followed the logic of their other opinions and given serious thought to the happiness and preservation of the individual.

Voltaire's fellow French Enlightenment philosopher the Baron Montesquieu (1689–1755) also wrote about suicide. Montesquieu is today remembered as the author of the idea of separation of powers, but in his own time was known as having described the character of various nations on the basis of environment, including such factors as whether the country was an island or mainland, the characters of its neighboring states, and its climate. For him, the ancient kind of suicide was very different from the contemporary; the ancient was a moral and political behavior, he explained, while suicides of his own time, especially the English, killed themselves without good reason. For Montesquieu the environment determined such tendencies.[30] He saw the English climate as having tremendous ill effect on its people, bringing on a "disrelish of everything." His analysis of the behaviors of various countries excited contemporary imagination, as it provided a whole new way of categorizing the acts of individuals. His claims sound today like grand generalizations, but in his own time what struck people was the scientific air that he gave such deliberations. Montesquieu contributed to the image of the Enlightenment philosopher as accepting of suicide, writing that if someone is miserable he ought to be able to take his own life, and without threat of posthumous punishment.[31]

We have seen that contemporaries believed that suicide was on the rise in this period and that this rise was the result of the new philosophical arguments in favor of it. The philosophers we have looked at so far either ignored this possibility or, in the case of d'Holbach, denied that such influence could really occur. Some philosophers, however, acknowledged a connection. Two important examples in particular felt responsible for increasing suicides in their own countries and in Europe at large because of things they had written. The first is Ma-

dame de Staël, a French-Swiss author who lived and worked in
the period following the Enlightenment and was noted for her
brilliance and modernity. She was famed for the influence of
her salon and her writings on culture and history. De Staël's
first work to touch on the subject of suicide, written in 1796,
was on the influence of various passions on people and nations. Here she opined, "There is something sensitive or philosophical in the act of killing oneself that is completely foreign
to a depraved being." Over the next several years de Staël was
often chided that such statements had encouraged suicides.
Partly because of the notoriety of that work, she took up the
subject again. Her *Reflections on Suicide* of 1813 was an attempt
to look at the question in objective, scientific terms. She is kind
in her consideration of victims of suicide, but now, instead of
praising them, she writes that they must not be celebrated:
"Inordinate misery makes people think about suicide. . . .
We must not hate people who are unhappy enough to detest
life, but neither should we praise the ones who give way under
an overload: If they could keep going, their moral strength
would be all the greater."[32] This switch in her approach to the
subject shows us how heavily the onus of having been blamed
for suicides weighed on some of the writers who defended it.

The same was true of Wolfgang von Goethe. His most
famous novel, *The Sufferings of Young Werther*, published in
1774, tells of a young man who falls in love with a married
woman, and whose lovesick sensitivity leads him to end his
life. The novel brought the subject before the public eye in a
brash, romantic way. *The Sufferings of Young Werther* was a
rejection of traditional religion, not in favor of rationalism but
in favor of the religion of the heart and the passions. In the
wake of its publication there followed a rash of suicides of people who indicated that they had been influenced by the book

by having it with them, often opened to the page of Werther's suicide. Some of the victims also dressed like Werther for the event, with a blue frock coat and yellow waistcoat. There were no statistics to confirm an increase in suicides, but that was certainly the widespread conclusion. But the book also gives voice to antisuicide sentiments, like the following uttered by Werther's rival, Albert: "You are certainly wrong when you compare suicide . . . to great actions, since no one can consider it as anything but a weakness. For it is certainly easier to die than bravely to bear a life of misery."[33] Albert's argument did not go unnoticed in discussions of the book, but Werther's reply was more passionate and commanded more attention. He claimed that it was absurd to call a person a coward for killing himself, as people could only take so much suffering. His most elaborate example was of a young woman abandoned by her lover and he describes her self-murder as beyond her control, such that in "the terrible agony of her heart, she throws herself into the depths to drown all her anguish in the embrace of death."[34] This was compelling in part because it described death as a consoling experience rather than the utter absence of experience. People were influenced by Werther's views on suicide in general, by his romantic language in writing about it, and by his own suicide at the book's conclusion.

Across Europe people spoke of Goethe's book as having inspired many to kill themselves, especially young men thwarted in love. Echoing this, Madame de Staël wrote, "Goethe has caused more suicides than the most beautiful woman in the world." Goethe came to sharply regret the work because of this. In later editions he included a note at the start of the book that said: "Do not follow my example." Because of the suicides it seemed to be causing, *The Sufferings of Young Werther* was banned by authorities across Europe, including in

Denmark, Saxony, and Milan. Clearly, d'Holbach was wrong to think that ideas had nothing to do with people's decision to kill themselves. Surely internal pain was the driving reason most people carried out the act, but words and ideas could also be a deciding influence. Goethe's *The Sufferings of Young Werther* is notable for giving new impetus to the tradition of suicide based on romantic love. Spurred on by Goethe's book and by rising cultural expectations of romantic love, this kind of suicide now became a common part of the culture.

Increasingly, even for this new phenomenon of love-sick suicide, doctors saw the problem as part of their purview and sought to implement a variety of cures, including bedrest as well as intense confinement and harsh water treatments. Medical science used rationalist language as it slowly led the culture away from speaking of demons and toward effective therapies. The medical world expressed its rationality in part by adopting a stance of moral impartiality. Throughout history, many diseases have been associated with character flaws, from the volatile heart patient to the reckless victim of venereal disease. As medicine emerged as a discipline, its practitioners and theorists tried to remain objective and scientific, sticking to the facts and offering no moral judgment. Suicide, once largely a moral question or the result of the devil's temptation, was now increasingly treated by medical science as the result of a mental or nervous disease.

Meanwhile, as these debates raged, authorities grew less interested in enforcing criminal law against suicide. In the sixteenth and early seventeenth centuries in Scotland and England, nearly all suicides were found guilty of murdering themselves, condemning themselves to profane burial and their heirs to property forfeiture. But by around 1750 nearly all suicides were found to be of unsound mind and suffered no official penalties. Much of what changed was the medicalization of madness. This happened in different patterns in different countries, and everywhere and at all times the conversation about suicide could be expected to retain elements of religious mixed with modern medical thought. But the trend was clear. As Michel Foucault has written: "the sacrilege of suicide was annexed to the neutral domain of insanity."[35]

Thus in the eighteenth and nineteenth centuries, suicide became medicalized, secularized, and decriminalized in mutually influential ways. In England medical opinion was at the forefront of that change, with doctors taking over the management of a variety of human behaviors that once had been handled by law.[36] In the rest of Europe, philosophical and romantic defenses of suicide sometimes led the way, undercutting the old criminal response to suicide and opening a space for medical theorists to step in. The result was essentially the same. Doctors were slowly taking over the territory of explaining suicide, legal powers were increasingly willing to exempt self-killing from criminal law, and ordinary people were more likely to think of suicide in morally neutral terms rather than as the very worst of sins.

All of this assuaged the previous age's brutality, but in its acceptance or tolerance of suicide, may also have led to an increase in the act. Certainly Goethe's *The Sufferings of Young Werther*, in which suicide is portrayed as an element of Romanticism, seems to have spawned suicides across Europe. It seems paradoxical that in the same era that brought the rise of medical science in dealing with suicide, more people began to take their own lives, but as we have seen, the old world had a host of ways of curbing suicide that the new world no longer had at hand.

5

The Argument of Community

I t is paradoxical that Plato gave us Socrates' famous death scene, history's most praised image of a suicide, and yet within that very dialogue, the *Phaedo,* Socrates categorically states that suicide is not right.[1] We have been proceeding chronologically so far, looking at the history of suicide from beginning of recorded history on—discovering the relatively tolerant attitude toward suicide in the ancient world and how that changed in the Middle Ages and in the eras that followed. In this chapter we double back to the start of our story in order to tease out a particular kind of thinking about suicide. It begins with the paradox of Socrates willingly drinking the hemlock but first telling his students that they themselves must eschew suicide. His reason, and the theme I will bring to light in this chapter, is that we owe it to the world and to our community to stay alive.

In the scene of Socrates' death, one of his followers, Cebes, asks him about suicide. Socrates says, "There is a doctrine uttered in secret that man is a prisoner who has no right to open the door of his prison and run away; this is a great mystery which I do not quite understand. Yet I, too, believe that the gods are our guardians, and that we are a possession of theirs. Do you not agree?" Cebes agrees, and Socrates then asks whether he would be angry if one of the animals he owned killed itself, having received no indication from him that he wanted it to die. Cebes acknowledges that he would, and Socrates concludes, "Then there may be reason in saying that a man should wait, and not take his own life until he is summoned, as I am summoned now." Socrates has been given a sentence of death. Shy of that, in his opinion, we have to stay alive. "A fool" may think that he should run away from his master and his duty, he says, but a wise person will see that the good choice is to stay with one's duty until the end. Socrates says it is better to let the larger forces make these decisions, and he says that life is where the good is, unless one is being taken out of life, in which case, one should go along with that too.

The Socrates whom Plato describes in the *Crito* also calls for people to stay alive because of what they owe their country and their countrymen. If our duty leads us to be wounded or to die in battle, so be it, but just as this may be our duty, so it is generally incumbent upon us to stay alive. A man must not take it upon himself to "yield or retreat or leave his rank" whether in battle or in a court of law, or in any other place.[2] To do so would be to do violence to the community. Socrates adds that it is clear that we must not do harm to our father or mother, and it follows that neither must we do harm to our country. Through history it will be remembered that in Plato's work the advice from Socrates and from Plato himself is that we owe it to each other to stay alive. Life is difficult, but we need each other and we must not leave our posts.

In *The Republic,* Plato further affirms that it is better to bear your sorrows than to try to escape them by ending your life. When someone is sad, Plato says, feelings of misfortune weigh upon him and seem to force him to indulge his sorrow, but at the same time there is something inside him that offers a strong guide to resist these feelings. Plato writes of this for-bearing strength as an inner principle of law and reason. We all experience trouble and pain. For some of us it is excruciat-ing, at least at times. The right thing to do, Plato counsels, is to wait. "To be patient under suffering is best. . . . We should not give way to impatience, as there is no knowing whether such things are good or evil; and nothing is gained by impatience; also, because no human thing is of serious importance, and grief stands in the way of that which at the moment is most required." What is most required is "taking counsel upon what has happened" and "raising up that which is sickly and fallen, banishing the cry of sorrow by the healing art."[3]

As with Socrates and Plato, it is worth returning to Aristo-tle with the specific question of what we owe one another. As we have seen, the narrative of suicide that arose in the Middle Ages held that suicide is a sin and a crime, and that the ancient world had praised suicide. Yet when we go back and study the great thinkers of the ancient world specifically for their thoughts on suicide and community, we find them offering strong words against suicide. Aristotle was direct about the strange nature of suicide as a crime and how hard it is to conceive of prosecut-ing people for doing harm to themselves. In an amusing turn of phrase he writes that "no one commits adultery with his own wife, burgles his own house, or steals his own property." So can suicide be thought of as wrong? Aristotle says yes:

> A person who cuts his throat in a fit of anger is
> doing this voluntarily, contrary to correct reason,
> and the law does not allow this; so he is acting un-

> justly. But towards whom? Surely towards the city,
> not himself, since he suffers voluntarily, and a kind
> of dishonor attaches to the person who has done
> away with himself, on the ground that he has per-
> petrated an injustice against the city.[4]

Aristotle's assessment reads as a cold depiction of the relationship between the individual and the community. Though Aristotle is clear in his rejection of suicide, he neither expresses
sympathy for the victim nor clearly says what the city is missing when it loses a man or a woman in this way. Still, it is an
eminent start to the development of the idea that we all need
one another and that suicide is wrong because we each matter
to all of us. Aristotle says suicide is contrary to the rule of life
and is unjust to the community.

This idea—that the world needs us to stay alive—was
beautifully reconfigured in the medieval Jewish world. The
scholar Moses Maimonides (1135–1204) stands out as one of
the greatest Jewish sages. Born in present-day Spain, he in-
herited a Judaism full of complex injunctions and contradictory rules; in reinterpreting these ideas over the course of his
life, he shaped much of what is recognizable centuries later as
Judaism, in practice and ideas. He was a profoundly rational
figure, claiming that when science and scripture clashed it was
best to follow science, because holy texts could be misleading
or misinterpreted.

So many wise sayings have come down to us from Maimonides that we do not have solid source attributions for them
all, but many of them bear his unmistakable tone and reflect
his signature themes. His emphasis was often on the problem
of how insignificant we can feel as individuals. Consider this
one: "One should see the world, and see himself as a scale with

an equal balance of good and evil. When he does one good deed the scale is tipped to the good—he and the world are saved. When he does one evil deed the scale is tipped to the bad—he and the world are destroyed." What is so poignant about this is its insistence on our individual importance. It is easy to see that if we all behaved badly, committing crimes and violence, the world would be a horrible place, but Maimonides declares that our actions matter on this grand scale even when considered individually. Regarding suicide Maimonides' key idea was this: "He who destroys himself destroys the world." It is a profound proclamation, dependent on a profound vision of our interdependence. The human world is held together by our optimistic trust that life matters to others and that the things we do in concert with others, even just living, are invested with that meaning. With a suicide, what is taken away is not only the person's presence but also her faith in life mattering, her hope in life, and her attachment to the future.

Religious writers over the centuries had the option of opposing suicide by calling it a sin and saying that God had legislated against it, but it is important to note that some concentrated their attention on the nature of humanity and argued that suicide was wrong because we each matter, because what each of us says and does creates our world. Within Christianity we see an efflorescence of this approach in the first part of the seventeenth century, in the ideas of a movement that has been called "devout humanism." Humanism was a manner of thinking that arose in the Renaissance and entailed turning away from religion and focusing attention on human culture and experience. As time went on some religious thinkers joined this conversation, though they made it clear that they saw faith in God as central to their thinking, and this was devout humanism. Here a writer might easily comment that God had ordained against suicide, but it was more characteristic for such thinkers to keep the matter in the human realm and to speak of our interdependence. John Donne has been understood as a devout humanist and despite his own writing in favor of tolerance for suicide, the poetry and prose that he published during his lifetime influenced the cultural conversation of the Western world toward understanding humanity as profoundly interconnected. Most famously, in his Meditation XVII of 1623, he wrote that when we hear that someone has died—announced in his time by the ringing of a church bell— this death must remind us of our own.

> No man is an island, entire of itself; every man is a piece of the continent, a part of the main. If a clod be washed away by the sea, Europe is the less, as well as if a promontory were, as well as if a manor of thy friend's or of thine own were: any man's death diminishes me, because I am involved in mankind, and therefore never send to know for whom the bell tolls; it tolls for thee.[5]

These stirring words have moved generations of people to consider the meaning of their lives as innately enmeshed in their communities. Other devout humanists drew on the idea of interconnection to make a direct argument against suicide. In this context they addressed the ancient suicides, writing that taking oneself away from the rest of humanity was an act of weakness, not strength. One of the devout humanists, the Jesuit Louis Richeome, writes that Cato

> killed himself, driven to an extreme by that very sin of pride. For having always fed his soul on the flies

of vanity and popular favors, which gave him no
substance nor solid reputation foreseeing that if he
were to fall into the hands of Caesar, his enemy, his
reputation would decline; beside himself with frus-
tration and despair and unable to endure that rival,
he ripped life from his body, taking the remedy of
a cowardly soul despite his seeming valiance, when
he disemboweled himself.[6]

Reverence for the heroes of the ancient world had been
an important element of secular humanism, so this critique of
Cato was a remarkable condemnation of suicide. There were
others. Another believing humanist, François de Sales (1567–
1622), the bishop of Geneva, also wrote about these issues and
his example shows us how strongly such thinkers felt they had
to attend to the specific stories of ancient suicide and to reject
the act in each particular case. Sales wrote about sadness and
melancholy with touching sympathy, but he warned against
ending that sadness through suicide. His argument shows us
that he expected his contemporaries to know of a great many
of the suicides of the ancient world, and he clearly thought
that on this question the ancients were a bad influence on people of his own time. How, Sales asked, could we think of the
Stoics as virtuous when they recommend killing oneself when
life became unbearable? Sales wrote that Seneca acted out of
pride and vanity and that Lucretius was wrong to kill himself.
Cato, he said, was no sage but a desperate man. Yes, Sales allowed, Cato had "a certain firm courage" that was praiseworthy, "but anyone wishing to follow his example must do so in
a just and good cause, not by killing himself."[7] The courage
was there in Cato, but for the rest of us the lesson should be to

apply that kind of ferocious courage to something worth dying for. Sales thought the Christian martyrs were to be praised in this way, but not the ancient world's suicides. Again his details show us that in his world these figures were well known. "Such was the case with our martyrs who with invincible hearts performed so many miracles of constancy and valor that the Catos, the Horatii, the Senecas, the Lucretias, and the Arrias deserve no consideration in comparison with them." The former had died for the community of Christians whereas the latter had taken their lives for their own reasons. Sales also cited Ecclesiastes, writing, "Sadness hath killed many, and there is no profit in it."[8]

As we can see, thinking about suicide in this era entailed a subtle and complex balancing of responses to several traditions. Amid this conversation we hear a variety of ways of arguing that we should stay alive for each other, for the community of which we are a part. The French philosopher Nicolas Malebranche (1638–1715) writes of many men and women joining monasteries or similar associations whose members believe that mystical communion with God can come through sometimes extremely harsh treatment of the body, which often ended in early death. He cannot help but see these as suicides and as wrong. Writing of the deprivations of abandoning oneself to God, he writes: "This is not to say that it would be permissible for us to take our own life, nor even to ruin our health. For our body is not ours—it is God's, it is the state's, our family's, our friends'. We ought to conserve it in its strength and vigor, according to the use we are obliged to make of it."[9] Malebranche was living in an era marked by increasing respect for the rights of the individual, and while this was much celebrated, it could also produce anxiety and isolation. His claim that our individual bodies are not our own but are in some sense owned by our loved ones could be a powerful antidote to feelings of alienation. To his mind we must not kill ourselves or ruin our health even through devotion—because we are part of something larger than ourselves, and we are needed.

The concern with the individual increased with time. John Milton, the great seventeenth-century poet and scholar, left us with meditations on staying alive that are among the most subtle yet robustly useful we will find. Milton had a life full of difficult reversals. He was terribly unlucky in marriage and in politics; his first wife left him and went back to her family from 1643 to 1645, helping to inspire his pamphlet advocating that divorce be permitted. She died in 1646. His second wife died, too, leaving him with three daughters. He later married again. As for politics, he backed Oliver Cromwell under the Commonwealth (the republic) of England, and after Cromwell died, Milton wrote tracts calling for the retention of government without a king. He was on the wrong side of history here, and with the Restoration he went into hiding to avoid execution. He was eventually pardoned but spent some time under arrest. He also went blind at age forty-four. His sonnet "On His Blindness" is crucial to our study, and I offer it in its entirety:

> When I consider how my light is spent,
>   Ere half my days in this dark world and wide,
>   And that one Talent which is death to hide,[10]
>   Lodged with me useless, though my Soul more
>   bent
> To serve therewith my Maker, and present
>   My true account, lest he returning chide,
>   "Doth God exact day-labour, light denied?"
>   I fondly ask. But Patience, to prevent

> That murmur, soon replies, "God doth not need
>   Either man's work or his own gifts. Who best
>   Bear his mild yoke, they serve him best. His
>   State
> Is kingly: thousands at his bidding speed
>   And post o'er land and ocean without rest;
> They also serve who only stand and wait.[11]

When he thinks about how his eyesight is gone (and how his days are spent) with half his life still to go, and when he thinks of his talent for writing buried in him because of his blindness, he wants to ask how he is supposed to do his work like this—it is day labor in the dark. But patience tells him that God doesn't need people's work. It is worth noting that when Milton wrote this, he had yet to write *Paradise Lost,* a poem based on the Hebrew and Christian Bibles yet marvelous in part because in it, Satan is drawn as a much more interesting and compelling character than God. Milton was nominally a Christian, if a rebellious one. By the end of his life, he called himself a monist, rejecting the content of any religion but believing that the world "is one" and that this "oneness" of the world is divine. In the sonnet, he writes of what God wants from people, but it is applicable to what people want from other people and from themselves. Often people demand a great deal from themselves and their lives and are despondent when reality does not measure up. Milton has long been understood as having offered consolation for this affliction, reminding us that we do not always have a say in the role that we play in the world and that sometimes we must learn to see the service we are giving when we are doing nothing but waiting.

In the final three lines, Milton's assertions feel surprising. While there are many ways to interpret these lines, they clearly speak to the virtue of patience. The work of waiting through suicidal dark periods is heroic. In the context of this book, Milton's insight is multilayered and particularly profound. It offers us the possibility that our quiet endurance will be rewarded as generously as any achievement. From this perspective, the failures or troubles that haunt a possible suicide may come to be more bearable.

It is also worth mentioning that among the few poems that we have of this stellar poet, one is *Samson Agonistes*— Samson the warrior. Samson had been a great warrior in his time, but after his capture by the Philistines, he becomes one of the Bible's few suicides, pulling down the ceiling and killing droves of his enemies, after declaring that he would die with them by doing it. Milton introduces the poem carefully because it is an antisuicide poem but a strange one. His preface reminds us that going through misery with a character in a book or on stage can make someone miserable feel better. He tells us that tragedy has always been considered the most consequential and useful of literary forms because, as Aristotle wrote, when we are made to feel pity, fear, or terror, it purges the mind of those and similar feelings. We give ourselves painful experiences in art so that we can handle them in real life. *Samson Agonistes* is a disturbing story of depression and suicide, and Milton informs us that he is telling us this story of melancholy to fight his own melancholy, and to help us fight our own.

It is a long poem, the length of a short book, yet it begins quite late, *in medias res*—Samson has already been captured and blinded, and is toiling away his days for the Philistines' amusement. His desolation is affecting, especially knowing that Milton himself lost his sight. Samson laments his situation, saying that he has become his own dungeon, and that this is the worst form of imprisonment. He is now permanently "shut up from outward light/to incorporate with gloomy night." Milton's Samson story is about the terrible depression Samson expresses as he is visited by Delilah, who wants forgiveness and love, and from his father, who wants to cheer him up. The culmination of the tale is a great bloody, loud, catharsis of an ending. Samson's father says he heard a noise and the chorus, in shocked phrases, responds:

> Noise call you it, or universal groan,
> As if the whole inhabitation perished?
> Blood, death, and dreadful deeds are in that noise,
> Ruin, destruction at the utmost point.

Samson's father exclaims that he hears a great noise and concludes that they have killed his son. The response that comes is, "Thy son is rather slaying them." Though of course, he too dies. It works as a harrowing end for the poem, but the catharsis is not for Samson, who is dead, but for his father, now "all calm of mind, all passion spent." It seems in this poem that Milton is not praising suicide, but that he is feeling so much darkness that he needs the contemplation of this murdering suicide in order to expiate his own agony and therefore live on, "all calm of mind, all passion spent." The father, the author, and the reader move on and put the suicide behind them.

Before we leave Milton, consider again his idea that "they also serve who only stand and wait." It is reflected in all the arguments against suicide that encourage people to stay alive, for to do so is a way of serving: serving the community, family, and friends—and themselves.

A hundred years later, in the eighteenth century, the French Enlightenment philosopher Denis Diderot framed a more specific argument against suicide. Diderot (1713–84) and his friend the mathematician Jean d'Alembert (1717–83) created one of the Enlightenment's quintessential projects, the *Encyclopedia*, a compendium of knowledge and know-how containing the old secrets of the guilds, the latest science and technology, and the most scandalous new ideas. It was considered very antireligious. Diderot himself is generally remembered as an atheist, though there were times when he seems to have believed the world had some kind of intelligent spirit to it.

Diderot was adamantly opposed to suicide. In his "The Marquise de Claye and the Count of Saint-Alban," the Count is weary of life and wants to end it, but the Marquise endeavors to convince him to stay alive. She tells him that his feelings are misleading him and that his desire to die will go away if he waits. She also tells him to remember the feelings of his family and his beloved and to try to live for them. Diderot also writes against suicide in his "Essay on the Reigns of Claudius and Nero," writing, "It is rare that one harms only oneself." For Diderot, Cato and Seneca gave no help to the cause of philosophy.[12]

In an article attributed to him in the *Encyclopedia*, Diderot rehearses the traditional arguments, including that God gives life and only he should take it, but he also declares that no one is useless to the community, even if he thinks he is. For Diderot, suicide was a rejection of one's role and responsibilities in society. He held that it was an egocentric act without regard to the harm inflicted on others. "As for the morality of this act," he writes, "it must be said that it is absolutely contrary to the law of nature."[13] The two most important reasons he offers are about our relationship with others and our duty to ourselves. First, writes Diderot. "We are not in the world only for ourselves. We are in close connection with other men, with our country, with our relatives, with our family. Everyone requires of us certain duties from which we may not exempt ourselves on our own." He explains that as he sees it, to willingly abandon our life and with it our fellows is a violation of the duties of society. Proclaiming that we owe it to society to stay alive, Diderot writes, "It cannot be said that a man could find himself in a situation in which he was assured that he is of no use to society. This situation is not at all possible." Even a person who thinks he has nothing left to offer, Diderot asserts, can, in fact, offer the example of courage and patience.

Diderot explains his second crucial reason for rejecting suicide with equal verve. He holds that human beings are obligated to attempt to make themselves happy and to always be improving themselves and their lot in life. "In depriving himself of life," the suicide "therefore ignores what he owes to himself." For Diderot this obligation to ourselves trumps all misfortune. We must not interrupt the possibility of our future happiness, and we must not make it impossible for us to go on improving ourselves in the future. He concedes that people who kill themselves think death might be a happier state than life but insists that "in this they reason badly." He cautions that even people who feel certain that there is an afterlife do not really know for sure.

Diderot still wants to fight with the church, so he turns his attention to the only argument for suicide written by a priest, the poet John Donne, and he attacks.

> Although it is not at all uncertain that the Christian church condemns suicide there have been Christians who wished to justify it. Among this number is doctor Donne, a learned English theologian, who, undoubtedly to comfort his compatriots, whom

melancholy often leads to cause their own deaths, undertakes to prove that suicide is not prohibited in Holy Scripture and was not regarded as a crime during the first centuries of the Church.

Diderot writes that Donne, in *Biathanatos,* declared that self-homicide is not always a sin and may in fact never be one. Diderot notes that this position did not get Donne rejected by the church. Diderot the rationalist is against suicide so he finds a way to show religion as pro-suicide. Still referring to Donne, he writes further of the theologian's tolerance for suicide:

> In his book he claims to prove that suicide is not against the law of nature, reason, or the revealed law of God. He shows that in the Old Testament, men acceptable to God caused their own deaths themselves, which he proves by the example of Samson, who died crushed under the ruins of a temple that he made fall on the Philistines and himself. . . . Everyone knows, among the pagans, the examples of Codrus, Curtius, Decius, Lucretius, Cato, etc. In the New Testament, he wants to strengthen his system by the example of Jesus Christ, whose death was voluntary. He regards a great number of martyrs as genuine suicides, as well as a host of hermits and penitents who caused their deaths little by little.[14]

Diderot also cites Donne as writing that during a persecution against the Christians by the Romans, the "fervor for martyrdom" was so great that the proconsul, tired of executions himself, had the public crier ask whether there were still Christians who wished to die for their faith. When a collective voice replied in the affirmative, the proconsul told them to go hang and drown themselves on their own in order to spare the judges the trouble of it. Donne made the point that these were suicides yet were approved of by the church authorities of their time. Diderot makes much of this:

> This proves that, in the early Church, Christians were hungry for martyrdom and offered themselves voluntarily for death. This zeal was subsequently checked by the council of Laodicea, and by the council of Carthage, in which the Church distinguished true from false martyrs and it was prohibited to risk death voluntarily.

Diderot managed, by skipping most of history, to highlight the aspects of the Christian narrative that seem to condone suicide, thus positioning himself as opposed both to suicide and to the church.

The common idea that Enlightenment philosophers were pro-suicide was clearly not based on all Enlightenment philosophers. The fact that this association was so strong, despite so many exceptions, is probably mostly the result of how much the pro-suicide arguments of Hume and d'Holbach shocked people and staked a claim on their memory. The philosophers who offered exceptions to the idea did so for a variety of reasons, but chief among them was sympathy for the individual and his or her family and friends. Julien Offray de La Mettrie (1709–51), a French Enlightenment philosopher, wrote with particular feeling about the harm done to others by suicide. He was a thoroughgoing materialist, his most influential book being *Man the Machine,* in which he denied the idea of a soul separate from the body. His works were burned and banned for their blasphemy. Despite his rejection of religion, like Diderot, he did not approach the suicide question according to that opposition, but instead judged suicide on its own terms and rejected it. In his "Epicurean System" he writes,

> No, I will not be the corrupter of the innate pleasure one takes in life. . . . I will make humble people see the great good that religion promises to anyone who has the patience to bear what one great man has called *le mal de vivre.* . . . The others, those for whom religion is only what it is—a fable—and whom one cannot retain by broken ties, I will try to seduce with generous sentiments. I will show them a wife, a mistress in tears, desolate children. . . . What sort of monster is someone who, afflicted with a momentary pain, tears himself away from his family, his friends, and his homeland, and has no other aim but to deliver himself from his most sacred duties.[15]

He sees a positive view of suicide as something that can corrupt life's pleasures. He hopes that anyone who can get help from religion on this question will do so, but for him religion is a fable. Instead, for people like him, the harm done to other people is a tremendously compelling reason to spare oneself. He reminds his reader that the worst of our pain is not constant, calling the pain that we suffer momentary. Finally, he reminds us of the range of people who need us, from family to friends to homeland, and he calls our continued presence among them a "sacred" duty. Except for calling the person who does fall into such behavior a monster, La Mettrie offers a beautiful example of a sensitive secular philosophy against suicide.

While Diderot and La Mettrie were certainly Enlightenment thinkers, the Genevan philosopher Jean-Jacques Rousseau (1712–88) has been seen as both an important Enlightenment figure and a central figure in what is often seen as the reaction against the scientism of the Enlightenment, Romanticism. He has also been remembered both as a proponent of tolerance for suicide and a strenuous opponent of suicide. The reason for this is a famous pair of letters in Rousseau's novel *Julie*. The first is from Saint-Preux, a young man in despair because he is in love with a virtuous married young woman. It begins, "Yes, Milord, it is true; my soul is oppressed with the weight of life." For a long time, he confesses, life has been a burden to him; he has lost everything that made life sweet, and only sorrows remain. "But they say I have no right to dispose of it without an order from the one who gave it me." Saint-Preux objects to this, addressing his position to Socrates. "Good Socrates, what are you telling us? Does one no longer belong to God after death?"[16]

The young man mentions Arria and Lucretia, Brutus, Cassius, and the "great and divine Cato." He claims that in the whole Bible one finds not one prohibition against suicide, and notes that when someone in the Bible takes his or her own life, "Not a word of blame is found against any of these examples." Samson, he notes, is even celebrated. He says the world is bad, and the good in it is mixed with evil. Somewhat shockingly, not only does he want to die, he advises the friend to whom he is writing, the Baron, whom he says he knows to be as miserable as he is, to put an end to his sorrows by taking his life too.

The Baron's response is magnificently furious. "Young

man," he begins, "you are being carried away by a blind transport; restrain yourself; do not give counsel while you are seeking it." He wisely says, "So you are entitled to cease to live? What I would like to know is whether you have even begun." He is sympathetic to the difficulty and pain of life, but insists that there is good in the world that is not mixed with evil. The Baron says it is one thing to help the end come sooner if you are in excruciating physical pain with no hope of survival. But "pains of the soul" are a different matter because, however acute, they eventually run their course and are over. When the sufferer endures the pain, the suffering ameliorates.

The Baron is particularly persuasive on the subject of usefulness to friends and the community. "But when you add, that your death does no one harm, are you forgetting that it is to your friend you dare to say this? Your death does no one harm? I see! To die at our expense hardly matters to you, you count our mourning for nothing." He reminds the young man that there are other people who would also suffer terribly from his suicide, people he claims to love desperately, especially the girl he is so broken up over. Indeed, he says, there may be someone who "loved you enough not to wish to survive you," and he asks whether the young man really thinks he owes such a person nothing. The Baron encourages his friend to think not only of what the world would miss from his own absence if he should carry out his "lethal designs," but also what the world would miss if, because of his own suicide, someone else died.

Rousseau has the Baron rebuke his friend for believing that just because he is not directly responsible for others, because he is neither a magistrate nor a father of a family, "you think yourself absolutely free." He asks whether his friend is not under some obligation to society, "to whom you are in-

debted for your preservation, your talents, your understanding?" He asks whether his friend owes nothing to his native
country, "and to those unhappy people who may need your
existence!" The Baron chides him that among the obligations
he has enumerated, he has omitted only those of a man and of
a citizen. His friend would never fight under a foreign prince,
just for the money, "because his blood ought not to be spilt
but in the service of his country" but he now, "in a fit of despair, is ready to shed it against the express prohibition of the
laws?" This is where the Baron makes his stand. "The laws, the
laws, young man! Does the wise man scorn them? Guiltless
Socrates, out of respect for them was unwilling to leave prison.
You do not hesitate to violate them in order to leave life un-
justly; and you ask, what harm am I doing?"

"You try to justify yourself with examples. You dare to
cite me Romans!" The Baron rightly points out that the lauded
Roman suicides were not about despair or love. "Did Cato rip
out his entrails for his mistress?" Furthermore, "What low es-
teem you hold Romans in, if you think they believed they were
entitled to take their lives as soon as they seemed onerous."
That is in fact what the Stoics said, but some of the examples
of Stoics who are said to have committed suicide, like Seneca,
were forced to do it. Rousseau's character is right to say that
the Romans did not really approve of ending their lives just
because their lives had become burdensome.

> Know that a death such as you contemplate is dis-
> honorable and devious. It is a larceny committed
> against mankind. Before you take your leave of it,
> give it back what it has done for you. But I have no
> attachments? I am of no use to the world? Philoso-
> pher for a day! Have you not learned that you could

not take a step on earth without finding some duty
to fulfill, and that every man is useful to humanity,
by the very fact that he exists?

He also says that every time the young man is tempted to
exit life, he should ask himself to do one more good deed before he dies. That act can be to help someone needy, to console
someone unfortunate, or to defend someone oppressed. With
this strategy, the time to kill oneself never arrives. Because the
first letter was more provocative, many people took Rousseau's
book as a defense of suicide. Read from this distance, however,
the second letter seems to be the one that locks up all the arguments and establishes itself as the more compelling truth. It is
worth noting that Rousseau himself was tormented by suicidal
thoughts, especially in the 1760s, but he did not do himself in.

Though he praised some ancient suicides, the great Enlightenment philosopher Voltaire also seems to have weighed
in on the side of living. According to Frederick II, Voltaire
once tried to kill himself, which the monarch guessed might
have been caused by cowardice, or philosophy, but there is
nothing to suggest he ever tried again.[17] What Voltaire wrote
was generally encouraging. He wanted "to make men return
to themselves, and make them feel that they are in effect only
victims of death, who should at least console one another."[18]
Even when writing in the voice of a fictional character Voltaire
reminds his reader that it is possible to be suicidal at times and
yet still find life worth living. In *Candide* a character known as
the Old Woman says, "I have been a hundred times upon the
point of killing myself, but still I was fond of life." In a letter
to a friend, a Madame du Deffand, Voltaire writes, "Amiable
people ought not to kill themselves; that is only for unsociable

spirits like Cato and Brutus. . . . Companionable people ought to live."[19]

In writing about the letter from Saint-Preux in Rousseau's *Julie,* in which the young man contemplates suicide, Voltaire comments, "His instructions are admirable. First he proposes to us that we kill ourselves, and he claims that St. Augustine was the first person who ever imagined it was not nice to kill oneself. The minute we are bored, according to him we should die. But Master Jean-Jacques, it's even worse when we bore others! What should we do then? Answer me. To believe you all the common people of Paris should run to bid adieu to this world."[20]

We come now to an interesting piece in the history of arguments against suicide. As we saw in the previous chapter, Hume's "On Suicide" was one of the best-known and influential texts in favor of the right to self-murder. When it was published, however, it was accompanied by an anonymous essay entitled "Anti Suicide."[21] The author of this lovely meditation on the subject first proposes that religion offers a sufficient answer to each of Hume's points, then turns to secular arguments. He repeats an anecdote from Montaigne about Cleomenes, king of Sparta, who rejected his friend's suggestion that they kill themselves: "Thinkest thou, wicked man, (said he) to show thy fortitude by rushing upon death, an expedient always at hand, the dastardly resource of the basest minds?" Better men than we, he continued, have given their lives in battle, "but he who, to avoid pain, or calamity, or censures of men, gives up the contest," should at least try to do something. "It is base to live or die only for ourselves. . . . In hopes, then, we may yet be of some use to others, both methinks are bound to preserve life as long as we can."

Having borrowed from the ancients, the anonymous author now turns to his own logical devices. He first insists that Hume's conclusion is contrary to sense: "No deduction, however plausible, can produce conviction in any rational mind, which originates in a supposition grossly absurd." He says the animals do not kill themselves so "in spite of all the sophistry [Hume] is master of, the question here will eternally recur, whether the wisdom of nature, or the philosophy of our author, deserves the preference." Nature must be right. He practically shouts that we just have to feel this one.

Moreover, he writes, "That a man who retires from life *ad libitum,* does no harm to society, is a proposition peculiarly absurd and erroneous." A society cannot live if it includes a principle the universal following of which would bring it to extinction. "It seems to be a maxim in human existence, that no creature has a right to decide peremptorily on the importance, utility, or necessity of his own being." The authority of this is cast in its simplicity. In the author's words, "There are an infinite variety of secret connections and associations in the vast system of things," and no one can know what he or she might be able to do sometime in the unforeseeable future.

Other Enlightenment writers also argued against what they perceived as the ancients' support of suicide. An author known only as Denesle wrote that those who defend suicide "are indistinguishable from assassins," and that the deaths of Cato, Brutus, and Porcia were crimes.[22] These ancient figures were important in the conversation because beyond being lauded suicides, they were also understood as people of great refinement. People of the Enlightenment saw themselves as highly refined as well, wiser and freer than the generations that had come before them. But was this entirely good for them? The Enlightenment author Henri de Feucher d'Artaize called suicide "the cowardly side of courage," and he connected it to the rise of reason: "It is a dreadful benefit of our high development; a refinement of liberty." He understood the suicides of Arria and Cato to have also been the result of the downside of sophistication and freedom, a refinement that had a kind of weakness as its corollary.[23] People who are depressed despite lives of comfort often feel guilty that they fail to appreciate their advantages, so it is important to note that throughout history "high development" and "refinement of liberty" have been cited as making a person's inner life tumultuous. Even many who value Enlightenment ideals of liberty and independence have worried that these principles, taken to extremes, might lead to anxiety and isolation. The sophistication of such famous ancient suicides as Arria and Cato made their cases particularly meaningful for antisuicide writers. Criticizing the suicides of Arria and Cato meant, by extension, also critiquing aspects of their refined, independent-minded culture and the Enlightenment version of these which had lately reappeared in Europe.

The German late-Enlightenment philosopher Immanuel Kant wrote movingly about suicide and the important relationship between the individual and society. His work stands out as strikingly original in these matters. Kant's *Critique of Pure Reason* is generally regarded as one of the great works of philosophy of all time. In it he argues that there are two aspects of reality: the one that we know with our senses and with our human conceptions of time and space, the phenomenal world; and the real but unknowable universe, which he calls the noumenal world. He believes that morality in human beings is a hint of the noumenal world. For Kant morality is a special quality of human life, and examining morality gives us insight into larger questions of meaning and our place among others. One of his key approaches to this question is the categorical imperative—the maxim to act only in such ways as you would want to be endorsed by a universal law; that is, to act in ways that would be fine if everyone behaved the same.

Kant claimed that suicide is wrong because it debases humanity and takes from the universe the goodness that is you. In his 1785 *Groundwork of the Metaphysics of Morals,* Kant begins his discussion of suicide by saying, in the first place, that most of us owe it to someone to stick around. Killing oneself is the crime of murder, he says. "It can also be regarded as a violation of one's duty to other people (the duty of spouses to each other, of parents to their children, of a subject to his superior or to his fellow citizen)."[24] But for Kant the crucial question is what one owes oneself and whether, "if I set aside all those relations, a human being is still bound to preserve his life simply by virtue of his quality as a person and whether he must acknowledge in this a duty (and indeed a strict duty) to himself." His answer, clear in the way he shapes the question, is emphatically yes.

Kant acknowledges the Stoics' belief that a sage should quit life "at his discretion (as from a smoke-filled room)" only to dispute it. Kant says that the very courage that makes it possible for someone to confront death proves the value of such a person and makes it imperative that that same strength of character should be devoted to staying alive. For Kant "a being with such a powerful authority of the strongest sensible incentives" should not take himself from life. Suicide is a violation of nature that, for Kant, is inherently immoral to other people and especially to oneself. Anyone strong enough to kill himself is more than strong enough to live, ought to let himself live, and is very much needed among us.

We are humanity, Kant says. Humanity needs us because

we are it. Kant believes in duty and considers remaining alive a primary human duty. For him one is not permitted to "renounce his personality," and while he states living as a duty, it also conveys a kind of freedom: we are not burdened with the obligation of judging whether our personality is worth maintaining, whether our life is worth living. Because living it is a duty, we are performing a good moral act just by persevering. In one of the most crucial statements in the history of suicide, Kant writes: "To annihilate the subject of morality in one's person is to root out the existence of morality itself from the world as far as one can, even though morality is an end in itself. Consequently, disposing of oneself as a mere means to some discretionary end is debasing humanity in one's person."[25] Human beings must understand themselves as a force of good, a force of morality. As human beings, it is our job to preserve these ideals. This goes a step beyond Aristotle's community or Rousseau's reminder of survivor's pain, and speaks instead of something larger. To be human is a powerful, profound thing that deserves a lot of patience.

Kant also famously offers his categorical imperative about our subject. His very first example of his maxim on morality is about suicide. Kant asks us to imagine someone who is sick of life and whose troubles have driven him to despair, but who is sufficiently in possession of his reason that he can think clearly about whether it would be right for him to kill himself. In order to come to such a decision the person asks himself whether "the maxim of his action could indeed become a universal law of nature." Kant understands the urge to kill oneself as coming out of one's "self-love." The man would be saying with his act that he subscribes to this maxim: "I make it my principle to shorten my life when its longer duration threatens more troubles than it promises agreeableness." The man's thinking would thus revolve around his own self-interest. For Kant, to know whether something is right we have to look beyond ourselves and ask "whether this principle of self-love could become a universal law of nature." He concludes that it "is seen at once" that a natural law that impelled beings toward death would be a contradiction and could not be sustained. For Kant, the categorical imperative shows suicide to violate human beings' duty toward one another.[26] In some ways this is the perfect example of the categorical imperative, because the crux of the categorical imperative is that true morality is to be judged on the basis of whether an action writ large would enhance or undermine society, and nothing can provide a more unambiguous answer than the actual survival or death of society's members.

Similarly, other philosophers and writers have argued that individuals should not take their own lives because of their innate value to the people around them and humanity at large. This idea is common in the fiction of the late nineteenth and early twentieth centuries, in which characters are often tempted to suicide. Herman Melville (1819–91), in *Moby-Dick,* famously considers the mystery of the ocean and the emotions it brings forth, so it is fitting that when he wanted an ancient suicide to illustrate his theme, it was to Narcissus that he turned. Melville writes that Narcissus "could not grasp the tormenting, mild image he saw in the fountain"—an image Melville says we all see reflected in all bodies of water—and for that reason he plunged into it and was drowned.[27] Scholars of *Moby-Dick* have seen the mention of Narcissus's suicide in the beginning of the book as a foreshadowing of the vain suicidal mission into which Ahab would lead the society of the *Pequod.*[28] Melville had intimate experience of the disruption of suicide: his son Malcolm died at eighteen of a self-inflicted gunshot wound.

Melville's interest was in the torments of the individual, but some fiction writers, like some philosophers, wrote about the influence the suicide has on other people. The great French novelist Victor Hugo, in *Les Misérables,* writes a few striking sentences about profound inner pain and our duty to bear it and live through it: "You want to die, I want that too, I who am speaking to you, but I don't want to feel the ghosts of women wringing their hands around me. Die, so be it, but don't make others die. . . . Suicide is restricted. . . . As soon as it touches those next to you the name of suicide is murder."[29] It is striking to hear a character answer a desire for suicide by confessing that he too harbors that wish and then go on to say that suicide is prohibited precisely because of what it does to other people, even to the point of influencing them toward death.

The early-twentieth-century author G. K. Chesterton made the same kind of emotional plea based on what we owe the world, but in terms that resonate with some of the philosophical arguments we have already seen. Chesterton's most enduring works are novels, such as *The Man Who Was Thursday,* a wonderfully cryptic tale which inspired Jorge Luis Borges and other unconventional writers. He also wrote rather straightforward nonfiction, such as *Orthodoxy* (1908), in which he offers his philosophy of life and his opinion on many aspects of his culture. Here he explains that he is sharply against suicide and that he resents the rationalist's defense of it. Chesterton writes: "Grave moderns told us that we must not even say 'poor fellow' of a man who had blown his brains out, since he was an enviable person, and had only blown them out because of their exceptional excellence. Mr. William Archer even suggested that in the golden age there would be penny-in-the-slot machines, by which a man could kill himself for a penny." Chesterton rejects this idea that social progress entails ever more acceptance of suicide: "In all this I found myself utterly hostile to many who called themselves liberal and humane. Not only is suicide a sin, it is the sin. It is the ultimate and absolute evil, the refusal to take an interest in existence; the refusal to take the oath of loyalty to life." His notion of an oath of loyalty to life is an important variation on the theme of what we owe humanity. He also explores this in a way that reminds us of Maimonides and Kant, writing, "The man who kills himself, kills all men; as far as he is concerned he wipes out the world." For Chesterton it is the rejection of what life has to offer that does the calamitous harm. "The thief is satisfied with diamonds," he writes, "but the suicide is not: that is his crime. He cannot be bribed, even by the blazing stones of the Celestial City. The thief compliments the things he steals, if not the owner of them. But the suicide insults everything on earth by not stealing it. He defiles every flower by refusing to live for its sake." Chesterton well understands the agony that life can bring in its terrible confusions and endless losses. Still, he hotly rejects answering life's pain by rushing toward death. The suicide, for Chesterton, is most awful for the rejection it delivers to everyone living.

> There is not a tiny creature in the cosmos at whom his death is not a sneer. . . . Of course there may be pathetic emotional excuses for the act. . . . But if it comes to clear ideas and the intelligent meaning of things, then there is much more rational and philosophic truth in the burial at the cross-roads and the stake driven through the body, than in

> Mr. Archer's suicidal automatic machines. There is
> a meaning in burying the suicide apart. The man's
> crime is different from other crimes—for it makes
> even crimes impossible.[30]

Chesterton here even supports the old religious idea of burying the suicide apart because he wants it clear that this is a profoundly damaging injury to humanity. We might advise that the suicidal person consider that whatever burden she thinks she presents by staying alive, it is a worse burden to kill oneself. As Chesterton eloquently puts it, "When a man hangs himself on a tree, the leaves might fall off in anger and the birds fly away in fury: for each has received a personal affront."

We may balk at the accusatory tone of Hugo and Chesterton, but their positive message is more important. The writings of Hugo and Chesterton can both be thought of as tools for those who are tortured by thoughts of suicide but searching for a way to embrace living. If suicidal thoughts always inexorably led to suicide, there would be little point in arguing against the act. But in fact, many people have testified that parts of their lives were lost to an excruciatingly painful vacillation between the choices of life and death. Herman Hesse's *Steppenwolf*, first published in 1927, contains a poignant commentary on the situation of the suicidal person. The book is a novel but it has been understood as substantially autobiographical, and Hesse reported that in the period prior to writing the book he experienced despair and suicidal thoughts. Hesse's narrator tells us that the suicidal person must struggle toward life, and that the struggle can be pervasive and exacting:

> All suicides have the responsibility of fighting against
> the temptation of suicide. Every one of them knows

very well in some corner of his soul that suicide, though a way out, is rather a mean and shabby one, and that it is nobler and finer to be conquered by life than to fall by one's own hand. Knowing this, with a morbid conscience whose source is much the same as that of the militant conscience of so-called self-contented persons, the majority of suicides are left to a protracted struggle against their temptation. They struggle as the kleptomaniac against his own vice.[31]

The narrator of *Steppenwolf* also contends that many more people than kill themselves are still essentially suicides, in that they think about killing themselves and have to work against doing so. Hesse's testimony to the struggle is touching. One of the main ends of my argument is to erect an adamant prohibition against suicide and thereby mitigate the struggle over it. No one should be left alone to fight for her life without the benefit of all the great minds who have offered resolute advice to keep living.

Surely there are people who commit suicide with the intention of hurting others. Such a person would be unmoved by damage his own death would inflict on the world. In Arthur Miller's *After the Fall,* the tormented Quentin says, "A suicide kills two people, Maggie. That's what it's for." Attestations abound that suicide can devastate those close to the victim. In *Dream Songs,* the luminous twentieth-century poet John Berryman pitied Ernest Hemingway at the end of his life and asked his own long-dead father not to kill himself so that he, the poet son, would not have to suffer over it his whole life.[32] Hemingway's father took his life, and in 1961 Ernest followed suit. Then on July 1, 1996, one day before the anniversary of her grandfather's suicide, Margaux Hemingway killed herself. In a poem called "On Suicide," Berryman wrote that he was possessed by reflections on his own father and on suicide.[33] His aunt had also taken her life. Eventually the poet committed suicide as well. The dramatic monologist Spalding Gray, author of *Swimming to Cambodia,* was likewise haunted by suicide. In an interview in *Io* magazine Gray said, "I was darkly convinced that at age fifty-two I would kill myself because my mother committed suicide at that age."[34] Gray lived a decade longer than his mother, but jumped to his death from the Staten Island Ferry in 2004.

These reprises of a suicidal theme suggest, conversely, that by simply staying alive one gives heart to others, even to the point of keeping them alive. Surely within families biological tendencies may also be a factor, but for Berryman and others like him, the fact of the suicide was hauntingly influential. They report being ravaged by a choice someone had made. The good we do by staying can be equally compelling. We tend to think of our contribution to another person's life as a balance sheet: on one side things done well, on the other, things done poorly; we tend to forget the immense good accomplished by agreeing, in the face of pain, to life.

Suicide can seem like a quintessentially solitary act, but as the authors I have cited make clear, its meanings for the community are monumental. Today when we discuss the harm suicide does to others, we think in terms of the psychological. We talk about how survivors feel responsible and are ashamed that they were not able to help the victim. We speak about how survivors feel rejected. It is important to see that this question of the harm the suicide inflicts on others has been discussed as a central issue in philosophy and literature.

Philosophers in this chapter have invoked courage. Kant

allowed that there was courage in the suicidal person, but claimed that this courage should be "a still stronger motive for him not to destroy himself." Some of the writers discussed in this chapter argued that the death contemplated by the would-be suicide is morally wrong. As Rousseau put it, suicide "is a larceny committed against mankind." Every person is useful to humanity, by the very fact that he or she exists. Just stay alive and you serve us mightily because you are an integral part of our hearts and minds and because of the influence your death would have on ourselves, our children, our friends, and our society. As Rousseau and Hugo both stated, it may even influence others to likewise die.

As Rousseau and others suggested, if you have any energy at all for participating in this world, perhaps live now only for those small kindnesses and consolations you can render. Perhaps seek to help those equally burdened by sadness. Confess your own sadness to those in sorrow. Your ability to console may be profound. The texts urge human beings to try to know that they are needed and loved. We all deserve each other's gratitude for whatever optimism and joy we can hustle into this strange life by sheer force of personality, even by that most basic contribution, staying alive.

6

Modern Social Science on Community and Influence

I t has long been suggested that one person's suicide is destructive for other people and that suicides sometimes come in clusters. Recall, for instance, that the young women of Miletus suddenly started killing themselves at an alarming rate several hundred years before Plutarch wrote about the story in the first century B.C.E. These suicides have commonly been understood as a chain of influence.

A few early attempts to examine suicidal influence in scientific terms came in the nineteenth century. In 1845 Amariah Brigham, the first editor of the *American Journal of Insanity*, approvingly cited the medical statistician William Farr's finding that imitation is often a source of suicide. Farr put it in the dramatic terms that "a single paragraph may suggest suicide to twenty persons."[1] As he explained it, the act, as well as its particular details, seizes the imaginations of those who learn of them, and who, in a moment of distress, are powerfully drawn to repeat it. A later editor of the same journal also wrote of suicidal influence and explained that some of this imitation occurs because one victim uses the fact of an earlier suicide to justify his own.[2]

Some observers even tried to warn their communities against publicizing a suicide. In 1837 the physician Isaac Parrish wrote of a suicide cluster. He told of an adolescent woman who killed herself a few months after the young woman had witnessed the male head of her household, called J.S., attempt suicide. Closer to her own death she had read a newspaper report of a man's death by the intentional swallowing of arsenic. This was the method of suicide by which she herself died. Nine months later, J.S. killed himself as well. Jacob Heckstor, who lived five blocks from J.S., killed himself soon after. In the same year Albert Davis, who also lived five blocks from J.S., took his own life as well. Parrish concluded that these deaths were connected and that the newspaper reports of them were a powerful force behind the cluster. He presented his findings to the American medical profession, along with cautions against newspaper reports of suicide, but his suggestions were not heeded.[3]

Also in the nineteenth century, we find evidence of coroners refusing to return an object used in a suicide to the victim's family, fearing that the gun, cup, or razor might take on a pernicious fascination and be used for the same purpose again. Likewise, coroners counseled against broadcasting any unusual method or place of suicide lest it enact a dangerous attraction upon others. Some even wrote of "emotional contagion," while others simply spoke of imitation.[4]

Today's sophisticated statistical research bears out these intuitions. Sociological studies have found evidence that a person taking his or her own life increases the likelihood of another person doing so. Parent suicides are easily the most dramatic and damaging influence, but there are examples in other communities, such as workplace, school, and neighborhood, as well as suicide clusters centered on popular culture. Media reporting on suicide can also result in suicides. One insight from this research is that "like affects like." Suicide influence is strongest on those who are *close* to the victim in some way, or *like* them, in all meanings of that word. It has been repeatedly demonstrated that the report of suicide results in a rise in suicides of those similar to the victim in age and gender. Beyond the sociological and epidemiological studies, the notion of suicide influence is a common truth of clinical psychology. Counselors consider it a risk factor for suicide when a person reports having known someone who died this way. The sociological fact that suicide influences suicide leads to a philosophical idea: that it is morally wrong to kill oneself. A key predictor of suicide is knowing a suicide, and that means that in killing yourself you are likely to be killing someone else too, by influence. This claim can be shown to be valid in poetic as well as scientific terms, but here we are concerned with what we can measure.

The first step in demonstrating suicidal influence is to look at the fatal harm a parent's suicide often causes. A 2010 study from Johns Hopkins University in the May 2010 issue of the *Journal of the American Academy of Child and Adolescent Psychiatry* showed that children (eighteen years old or younger) of suicide victims are three times as likely to commit suicide at some future point, compared with people who reach eighteen with neither parent having committed suicide.[5] The study looked at the whole Swedish population over thirty years. Investigators in Sweden and the United States examined suicides, psychiatric hospitalizations, and violent crime convictions in more than 500,000 Swedish children, teens, and adults under the age of twenty-five who had lost a parent to suicide, accident, or disease compared with nearly four million children, teens, and young adults with living parents. A suicide by a parent while a child was under the age of eighteen tripled the likelihood that that child would commit suicide. Children under thirteen who lost a parent to illness had no increased risk for suicide when compared with children with living parents. The study also found that children who lost parents to suicide were almost twice as likely to be hospitalized for depression as those with living parents; those who lost parents to accidents had a 30 percent higher risk for hospitalization for depression, and for those who lost parents by illness the risk was 40 percent higher.

To be sure, the case of parents is complicated. Being left voluntarily by a parent causes anguish no matter how the parent goes; mental illness can have a genetic component; and parents displaying tortured behavior can traumatize a young person such that the child becomes suicidal. Any of these factors might suggest that what happens to the child is not necessarily due to knowing that the parent took his or her own life. Yet the numbers overpower these objections. When a parent leaves, or dies unintentionally, or displays emotional torment, it may cause a lot of sadness, but it doesn't *triple* the children's suicide rate. From this numerical relationship alone we can see that suicide's influence to cause suicide is enormous. We have seen that children of a suicide have reported feeling haunted by thoughts of that parent and his or her fatal final act. Friends of someone who has committed suicide have reported experiencing a similar obsession. This study of parents and children, however, shows that the experience of suicide in this relationship is the most cataclysmic. As further evidence that the biological inheritance factor was not dominant, the researchers did not include children with psychiatric or developmental disorders who were treated before the parent's death; thus the influence of parental suicide may be even more marked than the study suggests.

It is hard not to think of Sylvia Plath killing herself in her kitchen in England, while her children slept, and some forty-six years later and half a world away, her son Nicholas Hughes taking his own life, too.

Researchers have found that women with dependent children often feel inhibited from committing suicide, except for those who have been victims of incest.[6] More generally, women who have been raped are thirteen times as likely to attempt suicide as those who have not.[7] But the aspect of being an incest survivor seems to be particularly life-threatening, and it is striking to see that even having young children offers little protection against a suicidal impulse. This contrast, though, is important to note. It means that both the past and present circumstances of people's lives—their psychic scars as well as the obligations of the parent of young children—contribute to their assessment of the permissibility of suicide. It also reconfirms that the concept that we need one another is already in place, though perhaps too localized, restricted to children needing mothers, when in fact it is all of us needing one another.

Another measure of suicide influence is the phenomenon of suicide clusters. These spikes in the suicide rate of a local population are well documented. The consensus of many studies is that, through often quite remote influence, the early suicides in a cluster partially cause the later ones. We will consider the phenomenon of adult clusters before moving on to the much more heavily documented cases of suicide clusters influencing young adults.

In sociological or epidemiological literature it is often

said that suicide clusters are largely exclusive to teens and young adults. They certainly appear to be, as we mostly notice them in high schools and colleges. However, suicide clusters of a sort may also happen with adults, just less visibly. The meaningful relationships of people past the age of thirty may be too geographically spread out to allow us to notice that a feeling of connection to a person who has committed suicide has influenced other people to commit suicide.

Among adults, geography camouflages our spheres of influence. Finding out that your old friend killed himself can be painful. Even if you had not seen one another for a long time; even if the last time you spoke, you were annoyed with each other. Different work-related communities have different levels of personal interaction, but all groups that have blogs, websites, and listserves, as well as actual hangouts and annual conferences, are social fields that can be sensitive indeed to what happens to one of their own. We cannot know how many people feel an acute loss when someone commits suicide. There is also the factor of a sense of permission, that if suicide was a route out of problems for one person, it might be considered by the second person as an acceptable route out of her own problems. By full adulthood, we have met so many people, studied with so many, worked with so many, and lived in so many communities, that each of us may belong to a multitude of distinct groups touched by suicide. We can measure the impact only by asking people whether they have been emotionally distressed by having known, or known of, someone who killed himself. In my canvassing of the literature and of survivors, the answer is that suicide strikes most people with crushing force. Close friends report grievous suffering over many years. Casual friends report an increase in suicidal thoughts, also for years. It must be recognized that staying alive though suicidal is an act of radiant generosity, a way in which we can save each other.

In his book *Suicide Clusters,* Loren Coleman points out the suicide clusters in adult professions.[8] One of his examples is what Coleman called "town fathers." In the period of 1973 and 1974 the town of Dueren experienced a wave of suicides among prominent town members. One of the best-known doctors was the first, shooting himself in the head. Next was a notary who used a noose. Then a chief doctor in the local hospital took poison, and in the next month a local official hanged himself. The victims all knew each other. Another cluster Coleman cites occurred among policemen. In one week in 1986 three Boston policemen died at their own hands by gunshot. In the next month, a private detective working in the same area also shot himself. Another police suicide cluster occurred in New York City, with seven police suicides in the same year, and yet another early the next year in nearby Suffolk County.

Coleman notes that generally such phenomena are interpreted as related to the stress of the job, but that behavior contagion seems to be an important factor that should not be overlooked. He also notes suicide clusters in the 1970s and 1980s involving gay men, particularly those diagnosed with AIDS. The phenomenon was severe enough to register with some researchers as a suicide epidemic. Finally, Coleman speaks of a cluster of suicides by farmers. In 1985 an indebted farmer shot himself, and in the aftermath the country experienced an increase in farmer suicides. The chief of statistics at the Minnesota Department of Health reported that between thirty and fifty of the state's four hundred suicides each year were from farm families. As with the other clusters there were intense pressures acting on the group as a whole, in this case the crisis in agriculture, but there is also an implication of cultural scripting or contagion. One person in a given situation deals with his problems by committing suicide and others are both struck by the loss and influenced to see suicide as a way out of their own difficulties.

A quarter of a century after Coleman's book was published, the staggering losses to suicide in the military constitute one of the worst suicide clusters in history. The number of suicides in the U.S. Army set records in 2007, 2008, and 2009 (hitting 162 in 2009). In June 2010 alone, the branch had 32 suspected suicides. There may have been even more, as is explained in an article in *Harvard* magazine: "If accidental death through risky behavior—such as drinking and driving, or drug overdose—is included, more soldiers now die by their own hands than die in combat."[9]

Shocking new Pentagon data showed U.S. troops were killing themselves at the rate of nearly one a day in 2012; the final count for the year was 349—more than died in combat. The army lost 182 soldiers to suicide, as compared with the 176 members lost to Operation Enduring Freedom. Overall, since the war in Afghanistan began more members of the U.S. military have taken their own lives than have died in the fighting there. Across the United States military suicides were up 16 percent from 2011.[10] This is all the more striking since historically the civilian population always had a significantly higher suicide rate than the military. The reason for the shift is not well established, but repeated tours of duty have given rise to a higher rate of posttraumatic stress disorder, which in turn generates an increase in suicide attempts. But there are limits to this explanation. An article in *Time* magazine's July 2012 issue entitled "One a Day" makes the important point that nearly a third of the suicides in the five years from 2005

to 2010 were among troops who had never deployed, 43 percent among those who had deployed only once, and only 8.5
percent among those who had deployed three or four times.[11]
This *Time* article does not mention suicide influence on other
suicide but an online *Time* article on the subject (by one of the
same authors) mentions that issue: "There is a sense, some service members say, that suicide—or at least suicide attempts—
can be contagious." A study released in June of 2013 showed
that in the years from 2008 through 2011 a full 52 percent of
military suicides were people who had never been deployed.
These numbers suggest that the military suicides are a result
not of individuals being exposed to horror but of a community that has now experienced so many suicides that voluntary
death has become part of the culture.[12]

Looking specifically at soldiers, a study by Russell B.
Carr showed the profound and devastating impact on both
comrades and caregivers. In his commentary on Carr's paper,
suicide expert Matthew K. Nock writes that recent research offers better prediction of who is in danger, through genetic and
behavioral inquiry.[13] There is some evidence for the benefit of
prevention programs employing physician educators, training
"gate-keepers," and restricting suicidal opportunities.[14]

In another look at adult cases suicidal influence has been
understood as "cultural scripting." A study of suicide in the
U.S. Mountain West found that older American and European
men were apt to kill themselves after being diagnosed with a
serious illness, and concluded that these men had a cultural
script of defending one's masculinity by responding to illness
with suicide.[15] The authors held that suicide is culturally pat-
terned and that each man who enacts this script keeps it potent for the other men around him.

In the past suicide has been most prevalent among the

young and in elderly men, but lately there has been a rise in the rates of suicide among middle-aged Caucasians, especially middle-aged white women. The category is broad, but it is worth asking whether some aspect of suicide clusters or cultural scripting is contributing to the phenomenon. According to a study from Johns Hopkins University, from 1999 to 2005 the overall suicide rate rose 0.7 percent, while the rate for white men aged forty to sixty-four rose 2.7 percent and the rate for middle-aged white women rose a full 3.9 percent.[16] Another way of looking at this is that baby boomers killed themselves at a relatively high rate as adolescents, and they continue to do so in middle age. Sociologist Ellen Idler of Emory University has posited that the earlier suicides contribute to the current rise. She cites clinical studies that have shown that knowing a suicide makes one more prone to suicide and concludes that the higher rate of teen suicides a few decades ago may be having a reverberating effect now.[17]

The example of celebrities can give us further insights into the likelihood of suicide influence among adults. When celebrities die by their own hand, there is a rise in suicide nationally. The sociologist David Phillips first began writing about this phenomenon in 1974. In the month following Marilyn Monroe's overdose, there was a 12 percent increase in suicides in America, with 197 more cases than usual. Phillips called it the "Werther Effect," alluding to Goethe's novel. Phillips's "Werther Effect" was met with some skepticism at first, but gradually became the sociological consensus on the subject.

Phillips's research showed a strong relationship between the age and gender of the particular famous person who died by his or her own hand and the age and gender of the population whose suicide rate then spikes. This relationship, too, has held up under scrutiny. A famous young female suicide yields a rise in young female suicides. It works for older women and for older men too. When Phillips couldn't find a significant rise in suicides in young males after a suicide by a famous young male, he found, instead, that one-person fatal car accidents involving young males did increase—enough to close the gap.[18]

We do not always know whether suicides in a certain demographic were well known to others in that demographic, but we do have studies of close communities in which a suicide was known to all. The authors of one study report an epidemic of six inpatient suicides in a psychiatric hospital in Finland.[19] They found that the timing and the methods of the suicides were influenced by suggestion and identification. The authors report that an increase in inpatient suicide rates has been reported from many countries, and the Werther effect is thus likely to be of considerable importance in psychiatric hospitals. People who are already severely depressed and/or anxious are particularly susceptible to suicidal influence, so psychiatric hospitals are likely to be particularly vulnerable to suicide clusters. Furthermore, members of small communities may have unusually strong influence on one another, and for this reason too, psychiatric hospitals may find it important to offer a robust response to patients in the wake of a suicide. That might take different forms in different circumstances, but in general, directly discussing the problem seems to be beneficial, as does giving patients additional contact with their psychiatric caregivers.

Some researchers have been able to isolate particular aspects of suicidal influence. The authors of a 1998 article reported that within the population studied in Manitoba it is common after a suicide for people to experience dreams of the suicide victim beckoning them to follow the victim into death.[20] This phenomenon of dreaming that a suicide victim is waiting for the dreamer in the afterlife and encouraging the dreamer to join him or her has been noted by other researchers. In the Manitoba First Nations community discussed in this article, there were six suicides in a population of fewer than fifteen hundred in three months, and several other suicide attempts occurred in the same time frame. The community was notably isolated. First Nations communities are particularly hard hit by suicide clusters, and studies of the phenomenon reach back several decades. One such article, from 1977, reveals that suicides were brought on by various specific stressors, including a loss of extended family and lack of a sustaining social life, but the authors conclude that the influence of knowing a previous suicide acted as a kind of "last straw" factor.[21]

Exceedingly careful theorists still caution against assuming that every suicide cluster is due to contagion; after all, in some cases similar stressors acted on each victim independently. Furthermore, some studies have found no rise in suicide due to media reporting, for instance. (Still, there are many more articles supporting suicide contagion than arguing against it.) The theory still has some skeptics, but even challengers often find the evidence troubling.[22]

It is also true that sometimes when scientists report that a cluster is not specifically due to contagion from the first victim to the next ones, they are merely acknowledging that rather than strict imitation, the first person's suicide saddened the next person, whose depression then led its own course toward suicide.[23] Both these definitions fit under other researchers' definition of contagion, and both are included in what we are trying to establish here: that a suicide can contribute fatal harm to others. On this point there is a great deal of agreement.

We have touched on a number of themes already, but

the main point up to now has been to highlight suicide imitation in adults or groups containing adults. We now turn to the more plentiful literature arguing that suicidal influence is real and powerful among younger people.

Some studies concerning suicide in and around the teenage years highlight personal contagion, while other studies look at media contagion. Both often also discuss "postvention," the term researchers and psychologists use for action taken to prevent a suicidal cluster from occurring after an initial case. Though research often combines personal contagion and media contagion, we will largely examine personal contagion first. In looking at media contagion, adult suicide clusters are also often discussed alongside those of young people, so there will be some overlap here as well.

On the subject of personal contagion in young people, consider, for instance, the findings of a 2001 study of high school suicide contagion.[24] Focusing on several secondary schools that had each experienced at least one student death in this manner, the researchers examined whether a suicide at a school predicted more suicides. They were able to show that after the first event, indeed, the number of additional suicides at the school increased markedly beyond chance. However, schools that provided "talk-throughs and psychological debriefing" by a mental health professional saw no new suicides. The study examined crisis intervention in three secondary schools following the suicides of five students, focusing on the relation between suicide contagion and crisis intervention. The contagion hypothesis was supported. There is agreement among experts that intervention in a community can be very effective. Influence is real and it works in both directions, toward death or toward life.

A group of researchers from Sweden studied two suicide clusters.[25] In the first cluster, three teenagers who knew one another committed suicide by hanging within an eleven-month period. Two lived in the same industrial community adjacent to a city where the third victim lived. The first case was a seventeen-year-old boy who regularly attended a church to which the parents of the third suicide victim belonged. His parents perceived him as being "depressed" the last few months before the suicide. He never received psychiatric treatment. Eight months later, a seventeen-year-old girl committed suicide. She lived and worked close to where the first young man lived. She did not exhibit problems at school and had many friends. Eleven months after the first victim, the third teenager, a fourteen-year-old girl, committed suicide. She had known the young man as a friend. Almost from the day he committed suicide she expressed suicidal thoughts. The parents contacted a child and adolescent psychiatric clinic and attended several sessions with a psychologist.

In the second cluster, three teenagers committed suicide by jumping from a tower and by hanging within a seventeen-month period. They lived on the same block in the same city and they knew each other. The first case was an eighteen-year-old boy who had a history of problems with schoolmates. He spent more time at home than usual before the suicide and was described by his parents as reserved. Some time before the suicide he disappeared from home, and his concerned parents found him near the tower from which he later leaped. A seventeen-year-old boy was the second victim fourteen months later. He was uneasy at school, and his parents had noticed that he had been quieter the last few days before the suicide. He told them that he was going to visit a friend, but instead he went to the same tower from which the first boy had jumped, left a suicide note there, and leaped to his death.

Three months later the third case, a sixteen-year-old girl, committed suicide. She identified the second victim by name in her suicide note, saying that she was now going to talk to him. During her last year, she had an intense interest in suicide-related information, such as newspaper articles about suicide and music by artists who had committed suicide.

Frank J. Zenere, the author of another article that considers personal suicidal contagion, was called in as a consultant on several suicides. He was asked to determine whether the events were, indeed, a cluster.[26] What he found was that over a thirteen-month period, six violent deaths of teenagers were reported, five clearly suicides and the other suspected to be so. All the victims were male; four went to the same school, the two others to a school nearby. The rate of suicide exceeded that which would be normally expected. One victim survived for a brief period before dying, and a large number of young people kept a bedside vigil, including some of the teens who eventually killed themselves as well. One victim was a pallbearer at the previous victim's funeral. The day before the fourth victim's suicide, the third victim's mother gave him some of the clothing of her deceased son; the fourth victim used that clothing to hang himself. The fifth victim lived four houses away from the fourth. Victim six was a friend or classmate of victims one and three and attended their funerals. All six had been diagnosed with forms of depression or showed signs of mood disorders. Based on these facts Zenere concluded that these tragic events were, with a high probability, eventuated by a strong imitative contagion. He also noted that school psychologists can do much in identifying the factors that promote contagion, and that suicide is a public health problem that should be addressed with a public health solution.

This thesis is reiterated in David Miller's *Child and Ado-*

lescent Suicidal Behavior: "A primary purpose of postvention procedures is to prevent any further instances of suicidal behavior, a phenomenon known as suicidal contagion."[27] Knowing someone who commits suicide is here identified as a more potent factor than media influence, but both were shown to be significant.

School bullying of gay and lesbian students today is considered a clear danger for suicide. The author of a recent article shows that as a result of bullying and suicidal influence, a school district's young people experienced an increase in suicides, attempted suicides, and calls to crisis centers regarding suicide.[28]

The authors of another study point out that the evidence suggests that it is not the closest friends of the suicide who are most at risk but rather peers who have psychiatric vulnerabilities.[29] It is important to recognize that subsequent victims do not need to have been close to the previous victims. There are times when suicide contagion is brought on when a person desperately misses a person who has committed suicide, but other times it is more about the example set by the previous victim.

There also has been extensive study on the effect of media on suicide. Media depictions of suicide are dangerous to susceptible people in all age groups but seem to be particularly so to young people. We might begin by quoting the surgeon general of the United States, writing in 1999 that "evidence has accumulated that supports the observation that suicide can be facilitated in vulnerable teens by exposure to real or fictional accounts of suicide." That was based on a great many studies, and these studies have continued to appear.

An article by A. Schmidtke and H. Hafner reviewed the evidence from several studies.[30] In a West German study researchers looked at the suicide rates after a twice-broadcast television program featuring a suicide. In this study, it was possible to prove the Werther effect in suicides that occurred after the victims had watched fictional models. The program was a fictional miniseries called *Death of a Student* showing the railway suicide of a nineteen-year-old male student; it was broadcast once in 1981, and once in 1982. The researchers found such striking confirmation of suicide influence that their analysis has affected broadcast standards. What the researchers called "imitation effects" were most clearly observable in the groups whose age and sex were closest to those of the model. The effect lasted a couple of months. In the seventy days after the first time the show was broadcast, the number of railway suicides among fifteen-to-nineteen-year-old males went from an average of 33.25 for a period that length to 62, up 175 percent. For girls of the same age there was a rise of six suicides, and for other age groups there was smaller increase, and for this population the effect faded much faster.

Researchers found that increases observed after the first and second broadcast for men younger than thirty closely corresponded with the respective audience figures for the two showings. After the second showing the result was smaller but still significant on males, up seventeen, or 54 percent, and for young women, the increase was nine. During this time suicide by other methods did not decline, and the rate for all suicides stayed higher than average throughout the year. This strongly suggests that the suicides were not simply happening sooner rather than later or by different means because of the broadcast, but rather the broadcast was influencing people who would not otherwise have killed themselves.

Schmidtke and Hafner also report the results of another study concerning the airing of an episode of the British soap opera *The Eastenders* in which a woman takes an overdose of pills.[31] In the following weeks, twenty-two overdosed patients came into the emergency room where the authors worked, compared with a weekly average of 6.9 for the previous ten months and 6.7 the previous ten years.

In a letter published in 1992 in the *New England Journal of Medicine,* researchers Elmar Etzersdorfer, Gernot Sonneck, and Sibylle Nagel-Kuess reported on the possible effect of the print media's coverage of Vienna's subway suicides.[32] Since opening in 1978, the Viennese subway repeatedly has been used as a method of attempted and completed suicide. Though the number of suicides was low in the early years, suicides and suicide attempts began to increase in 1984. Dramatic reports on these suicides in the major Austrian newspapers raised concern about the effects of imitation in suicidal behavior. The Austrian Association for Suicide Prevention created media guidelines and requested the press to follow them beginning in June 1987. After these guidelines were released, the character of reporting on suicides changed considerably. Sensational articles ceased and the papers either printed only short reports, frequently on inside pages, or refrained from reporting the suicides at all. The number of suicides in the subway decreased abruptly from the first to the second half of 1987, and the rates remained low in the years examined. The overall suicide rate in Vienna decreased steadily (by 13 percent) from 1987 to 1990. The authors found that the striking relation between the change in reporting by the media and the number of subway suicides in Vienna supports the hypothesis that press reports of suicides may trigger further suicides.

In the United States studies of suicide contagion have increased awareness of the phenomenon and influenced the way the media tell us about suicide.[33] One study shows what the researchers call a "dose-response" correlation between the amount of media attention a particular suicide drew and the increase of suicide in the general population.[34] The U.S. government has for decades issued recommendations for reporting suicide, based on the findings of such studies, in the hope of minimizing the contagion.[35] Many news outlets adopt the government guidelines or establish standards of their own to minimize any negative effects of their reporting. Typical print guidelines include omitting from the headline the fact of suicide, or at least its method, announcing instead merely that the person has died. The text of the article often informs readers that the death was a suicide, but journalists are frequently requested not to mention the method of suicide. Reporters are cautioned against sensationalizing any account of suicide, and often are advised, to that effect, to refer to suicide as a public health issue, not a crime. For the same reason many editors decline to print photographs of the victim in death, or pictures of grieving survivors, or of the funeral, instead showing an image of the person in life. If there is a suicide note, an account might mention that fact without quoting from the document. And instead of using such common phrases as "unsuccessful suicide attempt" and "successful suicide attempt," articles often describe suicide attempts as either "completed" or not. Many editors believe that articles should not suggest that a suicide was brought on by a particular event or disappointment, in order to avoid the implication that suicide is an appropriate response to a setback. Instead of quoting from first responders to this particular suicide, journalists are often encouraged to consult with and quote suicide experts. Finally, some media outlets make it a policy to include in any such article information to help the reader find guidance if she or someone she knows seems to be at risk for suicide.

Adoption of guidelines like these appears to be benefi-cial. A study by Madelyn Gould, a psychology professor at Co-lumbia University, and Patrick Jamieson and Daniel Romer, researchers at the University of Pennsylvania, suggests that suicidal influence from media is real and can be mitigated.[36] The authors find abundant evidence from the literature on suicide clusters and the impact of the media to support the hypothesis that suicide is contagious. This contagion can be understood within the larger context of behavioral contagion: the rapid spread of any distinct behavior through a group. Another way of understanding contagion is through social learning theory.[37] Citing a wide variety of research sources, the authors state that young people, in particular, are suscep-tible to the influence of reports and portrayals of suicide in the media. They found the evidence strong for the influence of news reports on suicide, citing several studies that have found dramatic correlation between televised portrayals and increased rates of suicide and suicide attempts using the same methods displayed in the shows. While acknowledging dis-senting voices, the authors conclude that suicidal contagion should no longer be in doubt.

Fictional portrayals of suicide can have powerful nega-tive effects, too. Studies in the 1980s found after the showing of a TV movie that included a suicide, there was an increase in hospitalization of adolescents who had attempted suicide.[38] All of those interviewed reported having seen the program. Still, because there is less evidence that exposure to fictional suicides leads to more actual suicide, fewer guidelines exist for these portrayals. Gould, Jamieson, and Romer have ar-gued that the influence of fictional suicides in popular media is considerable and that we ought to have better guidelines for it. They suggest reducing the harmful effects of both factual reporting and fictional portrayals by educating journalists and media programmers about ways to present suicide so that imitation will be minimized, and by encouraging media outlets to urge troubled viewers or readers to seek help.[39]

It is worth noting that television programmers focus more on murder than suicide. Considering that in America and across the world, more people die every year by suicide than by homicide, it is particularly surprising to note how many more murders than suicides are shown on television. According to Gould, Jamieson, and Romer, however, the number of suicides in movies has been increasing exponentially in recent years.

A recent study by Frank J. Zenere sums up the prevailing literature in an interesting way.[40] He writes that there are three contagion vectors that influence people in the wake of a suicide. The first is "geographical proximity," which extends from those who are eyewitnesses to the event or those exposed to the immediate aftermath of the suicide, all the way to those who are simply in the same community.[41] The second is "psychological proximity," which has to do with how closely the person in question identified with the suicide victim, taking into account such cultural commonalities as both being "victims of bullying, team members, classmates," as well as other common characteristics.[42] Finally there is "social proximity," the closeness of the relationship that the person had with the deceased. Those at risk along this vector are family, friends, romantic partners, and others of the same social circle. As Madelyn Gould and others have shown, a victim of a suicide cluster generally is acquainted with the first suicide but not a close friend.[43] A person who is implicated in more than one of these vectors is at the highest risk, especially if he also has a history of mental illness or traumatic experience. A further factor that increases contagion is a sense of responsibility and helplessness for having failed the first victim by missing signs of his or her intentions.

Alex Mesoudi, a London researcher, designed computer programs that highlighted similar sets of factors and found that the mass media play an important role in either encouraging or discouraging copycat suicides: "The computer simulations strongly support the proposed link between the mass reporting of a prestigious celebrity's suicide and an increase in national suicide figures."[44] Mesoudi distinguishes "point clusters," defined as people actually around the suicide victim, from "mass clusters," which have more to do with those hearing about the event through mass media. The simulations suggested that social learning did generate point clusters: some people who knew the victim of a suicide imitated the behavior. On the other hand, in some cases of suicides among a group of people, the reason might not strictly be imitation but an affinity among friends initially drawn together because of their common depression or other mental health issues. In mass clusters Mesouidi demonstrates that prestige and identification are also factors in the influence that occurs after a celebrity suicide. Essentially the more famous and respected the first victim was, the more copying of the behavior occurs, and the closer the resemblance—especially in age and gender—between the celebrity victim and potential copycats, the more that population would be at risk.

Researchers have assessed the aftermath of the Seattle musician Kurt Cobain's suicide in 1994.[45] Cobain's death raised immediate concerns among suicidologists about the need to pre-empt suicide influence and copycat suicides. Data collected from the Seattle Medical Examiner's Office and from the Seattle Crisis Center suggested that there was no significant rise in completed suicides but that there was a significant increase in suicide crisis calls following his death. The authors hypothesized that the lack of an apparent copycat effect in Seattle might be due to various aspects of the media coverage, and to the impact of the crisis center and community outreach interventions.[46] The marked increase in phone calls to the suicide crisis center suggests that influence is very real, that one person's suicide can inspire or increase suicidal feelings in many other people. The apparent success of local intervention is encouraging.

Just as caring and realistic discussion of suicide can help curtail suicide influence, sensitive, informed depictions of suicide in media can do the population good rather than harm. In one study of three television movies including a suicide, suicide increased after two, both of which concentrated their attention on the suicide victim. The one that was not associated with a rise in the suicide rate concentrated on the grieving parents.[47]

All the caveats about suicidal influence are points to be considered. My argument that suicide harms the community as it fatally harms its immediate victims seems clearly confirmed by the research. Imitation or contagion may be insignificant among those who are psychologically healthy, but those with a history of depression seem to be highly influenced. If nothing else, the example of primary suicide may increase the sense in those with some risk factors that suicide is a reasonable way to deal with their problems.

People in the counseling professions are very much aware of suicidal influence. Psychologists assessing people's suicide risk ask whether the troubled person has lost someone to suicide. It is one of the most important risk factors that mental health professionals consider. The common suicidal risk factors, here quoted from the physician and medical writer Matthew Hoffman on the respected health website WebMD, are as follows:

> One or more prior suicide attempts
> Family history of mental disorder or substance
>   abuse
> Family history of suicide
> Family violence
> Physical or sexual abuse
> Keeping firearms in the home
> Incarceration
> Exposure to the suicidal behavior of others.[48]

I especially want to stress the third and the final items, but we should note the high-risk company they keep, such as family violence, past sexual abuse, and nearby guns.

It is worth thinking about the effects of using the term "contagion." Obviously it is a metaphor, since the term refers to a phenomenon that involves pathogens passing from one host to another, and there is, technically considered, no pathogen here. What *is* contagious is an idea. Suicide begins as an idea. Remaining alive after one has contemplated suicide also begins as an idea. It may be possible to encourage antisuicide contagion.

For each suicide, there are many who are profoundly affected. Suicide researcher Edwin Shneidman argued in 1973 that each suicide affects six people. The website USA Suicide: 2009 Official Final Data estimates, "If there is a suicide every 14.2 minutes, then there are 6 new survivors every 14.2 minutes as well."[49] According to suicide expert Alan L. Berman, empirical study of the question suggests that the number of survivors for each suicide is between six and thirty-two.[50]

Beyond those people considered survivors, many more also feel connected to the loss. Researchers randomly called people and asked each whether he or she knew someone who had committed suicide in the past year, thereby discovering that about 425 people are connected to each suicide. This broader category of people touched by suicide makes up 7 percent of the population of the United States.[51]

Some poignant recent suicides have been people who had lost a friend to suicide. In 2010 the fashion designer Alexander McQueen killed himself after his close friend and supporter Isabella Blow had killed herself a few years earlier. In July of 2011 the Olympic skier Jeret "Speedy" Peterson took his own life, and among several tragedies in his history, he too had a friend who had died this way. Indeed, the friend shot himself in front of Peterson, and years later Peterson used the same method. It is heartbreaking but important to note that he got his nickname because he wore an oversized helmet that made him look like the cartoon character Speed Racer, but the helmet was considered more protective than others. He stood out for trying to take care of himself until such a time as he became his own worst enemy. The biggest threat was what was in his head, not assaults from without. It is a keen parallel with what happened with the ancient hero Ajax and his longed-for armor: he ended up dying because of his inner distress, not because of his body's weakness.

I ask for soldiers and veterans in despair to think of other soldiers and veterans and the influence they have on them, and to try to stay alive for their sake as well as their own. Young people might be convinced to have the same concerns. A middle-aged woman must think of other middle-aged women struggling with mental and emotional anguish, especially women she has known. She might consider it a pact of a sort to stay alive to spare the other. Some pacts fail, but some succeed. An older man must consider his place and influence among older men. College students in despair need to consider the influence they have on one another and commit to the rather heroic act of keeping one another alive. High school students must meditate on the other high school students who feel agonized and think nothing will get better. They have to encourage one another, if only by refusing suicide for themselves. Rejecting suicide is a huge act within a community. I also think it changes the universe. Either the universe is a cold dead place with a little growth of sentient but atomized beings each all by him- or herself trying to generate meaning, or we are in a universe that is alive with a growth of sentient beings whose members have made a pact with each other to persevere.

7

Hope for Our Future Selves

I n July 67 C.E. the man who would become the great
Jewish and Roman historian Titus Flavius Josephus was
trapped in a cave with forty fellow soldiers. Josephus was
a Jewish commander in the first Jewish-Roman war
when the Romans burst into his garrison and slaughtered
thousands. In hiding, Josephus and his companions discussed
the situation and agreed that all was lost; they decided that instead of allowing the Romans to kill them, they would commit
suicide. Their method was similar to the one used at Masada:
they drew lots to establish the order in which each man would
kill another. When they carried this out, Josephus was one of
the final two, and these last two men together decided not to go
through with it. They surrendered to the Romans and Josephus
went on to write his books, become an adviser to the Roman
emperor, marry several times, and father many children. This
story has long served as a reminder that surviving a near-sui-
cide can lead to a life full and rich beyond all expectation.

In his *Essays,* Montaigne writes that Josephus was caught
in danger "so clear and so imminent . . . that logically there

could be no way out." He might have accepted death, but as Montaigne expresses it, "he did well to hang on stubbornly to his hopes; for fortune, beyond all human reason, so reversed this situation that he saw himself delivered from it without any mishap."[1] One never knows what life might bring. Montaigne had a pervading sense of the world as unknowable to human beings. For him there is so much reality beyond what our senses can report that we always must remain humble in our attempt to understand the universe and our place in it. This uncertainty carried through to Montaigne's ideas about melancholia: our despair, he observes, generally hinges on troubles that are specific only to a particular moment in our lives. Montaigne was against suicide because people can never know enough about their situation and their future to make anything but a premature judgment on the question. Montaigne scholar Hugo Friedrich wrote that for Montaigne, "Actuality, which is always laden with what is different, and which cannot be hauled in or anticipated by any judgment, takes away life's right to throw itself away."[2] Montaigne wrote of his own struggles with the anguish of life, from kidney stones and other painful ailments to keen loneliness and sadness, but he opposed suicide because of his belief in life and in its surprises. Indeed, he tells us that some of his best friendships came late in life, as did richer happiness.

Just as Montaigne reminds his reader that, sometimes, in short order, bad fortune can turn to good, some have emphasized that sorrowful moods also change—sometimes in short periods of time. Voltaire wrote, "The man who, in a fit of melancholy, kills himself to-day, would have wished to live had he waited a week."[3] To put the matter in another way, we are complex beings who feel very differently at different times, such that the "you" in any given moment should not have the authority to end life for the many yous of many other moments.

Utilitarianism, the doctrine of the greatest happiness for the greatest number, holds that government should not be set up to protect people from their own decisions. If a person wants to walk over an unsound bridge, a utilitarian would say, no authority should step in and stop him. In John Stuart Mill's words, "The only purpose for which power can be rightfully exercised over any member of a civilized community, against his will, is to prevent harm to others. His own good, either physical or moral, is not a sufficient warrant. . . . Over himself, over his body and mind, the individual is sovereign."[4] One might think that as a principal philosopher of utilitarianism, Mill would believe in a person's right to end his own life, but it is not the case. Mill argued in *On Liberty* that since the essence of liberty is the power of the individual to choose, any choices that deprive a person of all further choices must be rejected.

Mill writes that in his and most other civilized countries, a contract made in which a person sells him- or herself as a slave would be null and void, "neither enforced by law nor by opinion."

> The ground for thus limiting his power of voluntarily disposing of his own lot in life, is apparent, and is very clearly seen in this extreme case. The reason for not interfering, unless for the sake of others, with a person's voluntary acts, is consideration for his liberty. His voluntary choice is evidence that what he so chooses is desirable, or at the least endurable, to him, and his good is on the whole best provided for by allowing him to take his

own means of pursuing it. But by selling himself
for a slave, he abdicates his liberty; he forgoes any
future use of it, beyond that single act. He therefore
defeats, in his own case, the very purpose which is
the justification of allowing him to dispose of himself. He is no longer free; but is thenceforth in a
position which has no longer the presumption in
its favor, that would be afforded by his voluntarily
remaining in it. The principle of freedom cannot
require that he should be free not to be free. It is
not freedom, to be allowed to alienate his freedom.[5]

Thus despite all one might have assumed about utilitarianism,
"It is not freedom to be allowed to alienate [one's] freedom." It
is a powerful idea. It could also be argued from the perspective of utilitarianism that suicide does not serve the greatest
happiness for the greatest number, because while ending the
pain, and existence, of one person, it creates profound grief in
those left behind. It has a negative influence, furthermore, not
only on those who actually grieve, such as family and friends
and closer acquaintances, but also on complete strangers who
know about the suicide, especially if they have qualities in
common with the victim.

Along very different lines the invaluable German philosopher Arthur Schopenhauer (1788–1860) also expressed the
idea that the suicidal owe it to themselves to stay alive. In his
masterful work *The World as Will and Representation,* he describes all the action in this life as will, hunger, and desire, over
which human beings have little control. He sees suicide as a result of suffering after one's will is thwarted.[6] Schopenhauer was
not a cheerful fellow, and though his writing is lively, his conclusions tend to be downbeat. For him, because of the hard-

ships and horrors of human existence, "Optimism . . . seems to me to be not merely an absurd, but also a really wicked way of thinking." Still he believed suicide to be above all else a mistake. For Schopenhauer, the overarching point of human existence, the only element that has real truth behind it, is the achievement of insight, and the suicide gives up all possibility for future insight. This loss is especially acute, Schopenhauer believed, because the pains that we suffer afford us additional possibilities for real understanding. As awful as they can be, the tribulations of life provide a mortification of the will which allows for unusual levels of knowing truth. As such, suicide is an evasion of a precious challenge.

The other reason Schopenhauer saw suicide as a mistake is that the attempt to eradicate oneself doesn't actually work. You stay who you are. Even though you demolished your physical being, your nature is essentially indestructible. Schopenhauer illustrated the problem with a metaphor of trying to remove a rainbow from a waterfall by scooping the water with a bucket. You cannot remove yourself from the world. As Schopenhauer scholar Bryan Magee has put it, for Schopenhauer, the suicide "neither gains what he hopes to gain nor loses what he wants to lose."[7] He does not lose what he wants to lose because, Schopenhauer points out, the act of ending life freezes life in the situation that inspired the suicide. He does not gain the escape he sought to gain because escape means getting to someplace better. You have to feel this suffering to get to something better; death is no place and no escape. Schopenhauer, who was influenced in part by Eastern religions, advises the person in distress that this enormously challenging experience will eventually bring exceptional wisdom and peace of mind.

Real insight into ourselves and our world comes with time, and that insight is our salvation. In his *Parerga and Para-*

lipomena, Schopenhauer takes pains, though, to distance himself from religious antisuicide, offering a contrarian position from the perspective of atheistic rationalism: "The only valid moral reason against suicide . . . lies in the fact that suicide is opposed to the attainment of the highest moral goal, since it substitutes for the real salvation from this world of woe and misery one that is merely apparent. But it is still a very long way from this mistake to a crime, such as the Christian clergy would like to stamp it." Along these same lines, some of his remarks make him seem almost prosuicide: "They tell us that suicide is the greatest piece of cowardice . . . that suicide is wrong; when it is quite obvious that there is nothing in the world to which every man has a more unassailable title than to his own life and person."[8] His defense of suicide is all about how wrong the church is in its condemnation of it. Schopenhauer points out that the Bible does not call suicide a sin or a crime, so when the clergy fulminate against the act they are doing so for their own reasons. In his estimation the secret reason for religious rejection of suicide is that a suicide puts the lie to the religious claim that God and his world are good. They denounce suicide, he explains, to escape being denounced by it. As with other philosophical defenders of suicide, Schopenhauer is arguing mostly against religion. But as we have seen, elsewhere Schopenhauer makes clear that having title to one's own life and person does not mean you should do whatever you want with yourself. There is your own future to think about. Schopenhauer writes to identify and work out the mistake of suicide, the way it seems to offer a release but does not, as all possibility for release and safe haven are only available by living. He discusses this idea in *The World as Will and Representation:* "Whoever is oppressed by the burdens of life, whoever loves life and affirms it, but abhors its torments, and in particular can no longer endure the hard lot that has fallen to just him, cannot hope for deliverance from death, and cannot save himself through suicide. Only by a false illusion does the cool shade of Orcus allure him as a haven of rest."[9] Then he segues into a Zen-like reminder that it matters little what individuals do:

> The earth rolls on from day into night; the individual dies; but the sun itself burns without intermission, an eternal noon. Life is certain to the will-to-live; the form of life is the endless present; it matters not how individuals, the phenomena of the Idea, arise and pass away in time, like fleeting dreams. Therefore suicide already appears to us to be a vain and therefore foolish action; when we have gone farther in our discussion, it will appear to us in an even less favorable light.[10]

That less favorable light is that for Schopenhauer, suicide is an act of will that is trying to destroy a person's acts of will, so it cannot be successful. The only success life can have, he believes, is the slow, difficult, even excruciating process of learning to conquer one's will, to see an end to it and thus be wiser, for only when you quiet the distortions and noise of the will can you begin to see the world around you. By conquering one's will one is not only wiser but also happier, because that is what happens once you accept that you are not going to get a lot of what you want. What the suicidal person who rejects suicide has chosen to say, Schopenhauer tells us, is this: "I do not want to avoid suffering, because it can help to put an end to the will-to-live, whose phenomenon is so full of misery, by so strengthening the knowledge of the real nature of the world now already dawning on me, that such knowledge may become the final quieter of the will, and release me forever."[11] What Schopenhauer calls the will-to-live is full of desire that makes us miserable, but suffering can give a person a much clearer vision of the world as it actually is, so that the noisy will is at last quieted and the person is free. All this can take place only while one is alive and among the living.

Schopenhauer also makes the compelling argument that the ancient Stoics had it wrong on the suicide question because their whole agenda was to live with a kind of indifference to life. The struggle to survive pain is the only real escape from pain. The very meaning of the term "escape" includes the notion that you leave for another place, not just that you disappear from a set of circumstances. (It might be worth noting here that the etymology of the English word *escape* is French, from a word meaning to "get out of one's cape, leave a pursuer with just one's cape"—so escaping is really getting out with your life intact, quite the opposite of suicide.)

From yet another perspective, Schopenhauer writes, "It was just the suffering it thus shunned which, as mortification of the will, could have led it to the denial of itself and to salvation, so in this respect the suicide is like a sick man who, after the beginning of a painful operation that could completely cure him, will not allow it to be completed, but prefers to retain his illness.[12] The pain, Schopenhauer insists, is what you need to gain the wisdom that will lead you out of pain.

Another poignant work about the problem of suicide was penned by the poet and novelist D. H. Lawrence (1885–1930). In his poem "The Ship of Death" Lawrence, using Hamlet's best-known soliloquy as a starting point, suggests that a calm interior existence is to be found only in life, difficult though that journey may be:

> And can a man his own quietus make
> With a bare bodkin?
>
> With daggers, bodkins, bullets, man can make
> a bruise or break of exit for his life
> but is that a quietus, O tell me, is it quietus?
>
> Surely not so! For how could murder, even
>   self-murder
> Ever a quietus make?
>
> O let us talk of quiet that we know
> That we can know, the deep and lovely quiet
> Of a strong heart at peace!
>
> How can we this, our own quietus, make?[13]

Lawrence's use of "bodkin" suggests not only *Hamlet* but also the story of the daughters of Orion, who killed themselves with their bodkins and looms in order to protect their city from plague. Lawrence asks whether the kind of break with life that people make themselves can ever deliver calm and peacefulness. "Surely not so!" he exclaims. As many before him had done, he likens suicide to murder and dismisses it as a false path to "quietus." Uncertain though we may be how to make our own peace other than by preparing for the death we cannot avoid, Lawrence declares that there is a goal: the true "deep and lovely quiet / of a strong heart at peace."

In another poem, Lawrence gives us a better idea of what he means by seeking a strong heart at peace. Here is "Healing" in its entirety.

> I am not a mechanism, an assembly of various
>   sections.

> And it is not because the mechanism is working
>   wrongly, that I am ill.
> I am ill because of wounds to the soul, to the deep
>   emotional self
> and the wounds to the soul take a long, long time,
>   only time can help
> and patience, and a certain difficult repentance
> long, difficult repentance, realization of life's
>   mistake, and the freeing oneself
> from the endless repetition of the mistake
> which mankind at large has chosen to sanctify.[14]

What could be a more astute reading of the effort of healing oneself? Again, as difficult as it is, it is possible, and it is possible only here among the living.

In 1910 Rudyard Kipling wrote his famous poem "If," which contains a rallying cry for staying long after everything in you has given up.

> If you can force your heart and nerve and sinew
>   To serve your turn long after they are gone,
> And so hold on when there is nothing in you
>   Except the Will which says to them: "Hold on!"[15]

The conclusion of the poem advises that if you can do this, if you can just hold on, "Yours is the earth and everything in it, / And—which is more—you'll be a Man, my son." Pain and exhaustion are to be suffered because if you can press through them, you have the chance of obtaining the highest goals. To be at peace with yourself makes you master of the earth and everything in it, and the paragon of a full human being.

These poems, like Schopenhauer's observation, remind

us of the future selves we can be if we can only endure the present. To return from poetry to philosophy, the twentieth-century Austrian-British philosopher Ludwig Wittgenstein (1889–1951) famously struggled with depression and with thoughts of suicide. Horribly, three of his four brothers killed themselves. Despite that, he wrote about suicide only twice, both times quite briefly. But his ruminations are deeply meaningful. When Wittgenstein speaks to the puzzle of human morality in his *Notebooks,* he contends with the immorality of suicide:

> If suicide is allowed then everything is allowed. If anything is not allowed then suicide is not allowed. This throws a light on the nature of ethics, for suicide is, so to speak, the elementary sin. And when one investigates it, it is like investigating mercury vapor in order to comprehend the nature of vapors.[16]

This is so important that it deserves much more attention than Wittgenstein gave it. In fact, he turned his back on it a bit: the little philosophical observation ends with a doleful, "Or is even suicide in itself neither good nor evil?" He stops there but we need to give his comment its due and learn from its perception. Wittgenstein says here that suicide is the elemental wrong and that what is wrong about it can tell you about all other wrongs.

What could he have meant by this? Maybe that what is wrong about lying and stealing is not just that it hurts the other person but that it breaks faith with the human project. To invest ourselves in our own lives and to engage positively in the lives of others is thus "right" in a way that turning our back on our sense of life mattering is "wrong." This is perhaps what

Wittgenstein meant when he said that if suicide is allowed, everything is allowed. Our loyalty to feelings of life mattering is the basis for our morality. We feel our lives as full of wants, needs, fears, anxieties, love, and grief, all of which feel real, all of which matter and *mean*. We feel a kind of communion with other human beings, and what we do to enhance that feeling is right, and what we do to erode or break with that feeling of significance is wrong. In that sense nothing, as Wittgenstein says, could be more wrong than suicide.

As with so many other philosophers who discuss suicide, Wittgenstein puts the weight on the negative—suicide is the primary wrong—but it is worth considering that the primary good gesture is to stay alive. Our chief moral duty is not to keep from infringing on the property and rights of the next person; rather, our chief moral duty is to maintain the significance of life whether or not we believe in a higher power. When people are sorely taxed by life and they break some of the rules that reinforce communal and individual meaning, they weaken it for themselves and for others, whether the breach is lying, stealing, cheating, or being cruel. For Wittgenstein, if there are any moral rules at all, if we can say that we owe one another anything, than the first thing we are responsible for is rejecting suicide.

The other comment that Wittgenstein left us regarding suicide seems to have been influenced by Schopenhauer's theory. In a letter written in 1920, Wittgenstein confesses that he is "in a state of mind that is terrible to me." He will not resort to suicide though, and he explains, "I know that to kill oneself is always a dirty thing to do. Surely one cannot will one's own destruction and anybody who has visualized what is in practice involved knows that suicide is always a rushing of one's own defenses. But nothing is worse than to be forced to take oneself by surprise."[17] Here Wittgenstein follows Schopenhauer's idea that we cannot will the destruction of the will. What then, he asks, occurs with a suicide, if the act is not one which the person in question fully wants. The answer is that the aspect of the person who wants to end his or her life is only one part, and it has to plot against the rest of the person and circumvent objections of the rest by a sneak attack, by taking the person by surprise. What may look like an integrated person making an impulsive move might also be seen as a person in a particular mood acting quickly so as not to allow input from him- or herself in different moods.

Sometimes the feeling that life matters and has meaning resides "in our other selves," and we do not always have access to it. Sometimes it is necessary to wait and to refuse to be taken by surprise by one's own inner saboteur.

Sigmund Freud's understanding of suicide also involved doing something rather different from what you want to do and sparing your future self. As Freud put it, "Probably no one finds the mental energy required to kill himself unless, in the first place, in doing so he is at the same time killing an object with whom he has identified himself, and, in the second place, is turning against himself a death-wish which had been directed against someone else."[18] Symbolically harming the parent or other victimizer is too painful, so the victim turns his or her anger inward. Another way of seeing it is that the parent has been so profoundly internalized that the victim is in fact attacking the other when he or she commits suicide. In both these interpretations, suicide is a mistake, an error in judgment. The answer to what is, for some of us, at times, the seemingly unbearable anguish of life, is to talk about the inner life until it becomes clear that the self is not the true target of

our feelings of rage and despair. Freud and most of his followers acknowledged that this can be a very long process, but it is
also something constructive that one can do with one's pain.
One can use it to find the trail out of a longing for death and
instead learn to feel as an independent individual; the result
will be a much more pleasurable existence, where suicide is
no longer a consideration. The person in the future deserves
to exist, deserves to live through the dark time associated with
this error in judgment about the real source of his or her pain
and anger.

Freud also spoke of a "death instinct" and saw this in our
attempts to lose ourselves in entertainment, or in drugs, or
even just in sleep. Sometimes it goes all the way to thoughts
of suicide and suicidal wishes. Freud theorized that at times
some people direct the impulse outward in the form of aggres-
sion, cruelty, murder, and destructiveness. This too, of course,
is far from the response of a healthy ego and personality.

Thus one of the most astute interpreters of the mind was
convinced that the suicidal person is not harming the person
she thinks she is harming. Through talking about feelings in
a psychotherapeutic setting, the would-be suicide might be
able to become aware that her anger is not strictly localized on
the self and may be released and managed without actual violence to herself or to others. If a cure is possible through talk
therapy, then the future self ought to have a chance to live to
that point where the person no longer wants to die.

How can we ask ourselves to stay for someone else, and
for our own futures, or even for a person in the abstract—that
is, some unknown person whom we might influence? Here
it is helpful to consider the work of the twentieth-century
French Talmudic scholar and philosopher Emanuel Levinas.
Levinas considered philosophy to be the "wisdom of love" in-

stead of the "love of wisdom," such that our acts of friendship are the most real and knowable aspect of the entire universe. His philosophy insists that ethics comes first, that "ethics precedes ontology": the first thing we know is our own being, and the way that we know everything else is through the other person. For Levinas even one's own self is possible only with its recognition of "the Other," and this recognition carries responsibility to what is irreducibly different. The emphasis is on a relationship of respect and responsibility for the other person. The Other is a real person whom you really know, as well as a concept pointing toward all the others whose existence matters even in the abstract. Put another way, subjectivity is primordially ethical, not theoretical. Our responsibility for the other is not secondary to our subjectivity but rather founds our subjective being by giving it a meaningful direction and orientation, without which we are lost. Levinas's thesis of "ethics as first philosophy" claims that the traditional philosophical pursuit of knowledge is secondary to a basic ethical duty to the Other. To meet the Other is to have an idea of infinity. Levinas further encourages us to stay by invoking the hope of greater understanding. He does not deny that life can be terrible but emphasizes that the pain is inextricably connected to love of being, and joy:

> In its opposition to being (that is, suffering pain), the I seeks refuge in being itself (that is, in the gift of life and the "goodness" that accompanies it). Suicide is tragic, for death does not bring a resolution to all problems to which birth gave rise, and it is powerless to humiliate the values of the earth—whence Macbeth's final cry in confronting death, defeat because the universe is not destroyed at the same

time as his life. Suffering at the same time despairs
for being riveted to being—and loves the being to
which it is riveted. It knows the impossibility of
quitting life: what tragedy! What comedy. . . . The
taedium vitae is steeped in the love of the life it rejects; despair does not break with the ideal of joy.[19]

Macbeth complains, "I 'gin to be aweary of the sun / And wish
th' estate o' th' world were now undone."[20] But the world cannot be undone. Escape and even suffering can happen only
here, alive on earth. In one poignant passage Levinas writes,
"Prior to death there is always a last chance; this is what heroes
seize, not death."[21]

Levinas declares himself unambiguously against suicide.[22] According to him there is no ethical case for taking
one's own life. Death cannot be chosen. This is in part because
suicide is a logically and metaphysically contradictory concept, but also because in the choice of death, ethical responsibility turns into irresponsibility. Meanwhile, many people are
desperately in need of escape, not from life but rather from
themselves. In this, too, the only course from Levinas's perspective is through new and different attention to the Other:
the persons around one, their practical needs in daily life, and
their more abstract needs as representatives of humanity. We
have to keep looking forward to further human connection:

> In the innocence of our daily lives, the face of the
> other (or the neck or the back) signifies above all a
> demand. The face requires you, calls you outside.
> And already there resounds the word from Sinai,
> "though shalt not kill" which signifies "you shall
> defend the life of the other." . . . It is the very ar-

ticulation of love of the other. You are indebted to someone from whom you have not borrowed a thing. . . . And you are responsible, the only one who could answer, the noninterchangable, and the unique one. . . . In this relation of the unique to the unique there appears, before the purely formal community of the genus, the original sociality.[23]

It may be true that no one wants to die; the suicidal, rather, simply do not want to keep living the way they are feeling. If Levinas is right that our very being is constituted through confrontation with the Other, then the crisis of suicidal misery is an opportunity. The misery requires us to ask for help or at least to express our distress to another person. In doing this we begin the long and difficult trip out from our loneliness into a real engagement with humanity and thus with ourselves. "The possibility of deliverance (and the temptation of suicide) arises in the anxiety of death." Death is nothingness, but bearing anxiety can be everything and essential. "Such is a responsibility stronger than death, affirmed by Plato in his own fashion in the *Phaedo* when condemning suicide."[24] In Levinas's work suicide seems like a real temptation against which he has to struggle, and he copes with it by recounting the ways in which we have a responsibility to stay around and learn more about the real nature of things and the persons we can come to be.

Of the nearly thirty-eight thousand people in the United States who took their lives in 2010, how many of them, two years or even two months earlier, might have been sorry to know that this was the end that they were to come to? A case can be made that they were obliged to give their future selves the same chance to look back and be glad still to be with us.

The person who wants to take his own life is not necessarily "out of his mind"—people often seem almost cheerful, "back to normal," in the days before they have planned to take their own lives. But being sane does not necessarily mean knowing, at that critical moment, what is best for one's life. Everyone changes, but at a given moment, we tend to feel that this is the way we always have been. With depression, that despair of the possibility of change is even more intense; the depressed person is convinced that she will never come out of it. But even that person has had periods of happiness. It is the nature of existence that this happiness will return—if we stay around to enjoy it.

One of the best-known sayings about suicide alludes to the impermanence of the pain. As the talk-show host Phil Donahue put it, "Suicide is a permanent solution to a temporary problem." It is a pithy reminder that if you live you will have to continue to face this difficult life, but that the particular element that you despise in your life today may be utterly gone tomorrow, or soon after. Of course, depression is more durable than any given setback, but even depression is not permanent. One characteristic of major depression is that it feels as if it will never end, but in fact, even untreated it waxes and wanes, and with treatment most people will experience considerable improvement. There is always hope for a better life in the future, a life that may be sufficiently rich and strange, creative and beautiful, peaceful and vibrant to have made the wait worthwhile.

8

The Twentieth Century's Two
Major Voices on Suicide

Emile Durkheim and Albert Camus were the two towering figures in thinking about suicide in the twentieth century. Both are remembered as having deeply considered suicide in light of modern ideas about our place in the universe, but it is less well known that each took a decided stance against it. How they came to this conclusion is the subject of this chapter.

In the social sciences, Durkheim was easily the most significant interpreter of suicide of the twentieth century. His book *Suicide* was published in 1897, and because it relied on statistics, it is generally considered to be the original modern sociological monograph. The book has since been subjected to a good deal of criticism on a variety of counts—for instance, Durkheim did not believe that suicide has a significant imitation factor, an opinion which is now widely rejected—but it is remarkable how much the book's statistical revelations and its descriptive language of suicide have held up. Durkheim established that suicide rates are generally higher in men than in women (though childless women begin to catch up as the years go by); that rates are higher for single people than for the married, higher for childless people than for parents, higher for soldiers than for civilians, higher among Protestants than among Catholics and Jews, higher in times of peace than in times of war, higher in Scandinavian countries than elsewhere, and higher among the educated than among the uneducated.

Durkheim identified four kinds of suicide, and his language is still in use today. He divided suicides into egoistic, altruistic, anomic, and fatalistic. Egoistic suicide occurs in a person who lacks a sense of belonging to the community and who becomes overcome by feelings of meaninglessness, apathy, and depression. Altruistic suicide is the opposite: the victim is so profoundly enmeshed in the ideals of the group that upholding these ideals becomes more important than life itself. Anomic suicide is characterized by an individual's moral confusion, uncertainty, and lack of direction, usually related to dramatic social and economic upheaval. Fatalist suicide is the opposite of anomic: it is a response to being chronically oppressed so that one's own desires are endlessly thwarted. All these could be combined to produce various results.

These terms gave sociologists a classification framework that has lasted more than a century. They are of use to clinicians but also to people who are suffering and experiencing isolation and can recognize themselves in Durkheim's descriptions. This is especially true today, when our understanding of depression tends to be divided between biological explanations and familial explanations; it is useful to be made aware of broader sociological explanations as well. Durkheim's key message was that in most of the modern Western world, people feel cut off from their communities and uncertain about how they fit into the world. Suicide in the West was, for Durkheim, a crisis caused by insufficient social integration. He wrote that suicide was the most obvious symptom of a widespread need for more feelings of human connection. Too much individualism was not a character flaw, it was a social problem. Durkheim was doubtful that religion or science could provide a cure. Instead, he hoped that some new form of community connection would arise. He proposed that it might be some kind of "corporation," using the word in a noneconomic sense. He hoped his imagined corporations or something like them would replace the collective force that functioned in society before modern life. For Durkheim, the lack of this collective force was precisely what was causing modern suicide. "First of all," he wrote, "it can be said that, as collective force is one of the obstacles best calculated to restrain suicide, its weakening involves the development of suicide."[1] With a strongly integrated society, individuals feel deeply connected to something larger than themselves, something that "forbids them to dispose willfully of themselves." People feel they have to stay alive and fill their roles.

Even depression, for Durkheim, was best described in terms of its sociology and the alienation of the individual from society: of "melancholy suicide," he wrote, "This is connected with a general state of extreme depression and exaggerated sadness, causing the patient no longer to realize sanely the bonds which connect him with people and things about him."[2] Present-day investigations of suicide also focus both on the state of extreme depression and the disconnection of the victim from the rest of society, but they do not ascribe the former so strictly to the latter. (Today, depression is usually discussed less as a function of society than as biological and/or based in a difficult childhood or a traumatic experience.) It is important to remember that Durkheim, contrary to most of today's researchers, doubted that what we call suicidal contagion is real. He believed that those who killed themselves after a publicized suicide would have done so anyway, though perhaps a little later. We may attribute Durkheim's certainty on this matter to his commitment to the idea that European suicide was to be explained through his concept of the egoistic results of the disruption of tightly knit communities.

Durkheim attached incalcuble importance to the disappearance of the small town and of the closer relations people had before city industry, trains, and changing mores separated the average person from his community. People feel integrated through family, community, and the state, and modernity supplied less community than earlier periods. Individuals were now conscious of society and their dependence upon it only in relation to the state. The state, however, is relatively remote and can have only a distant, periodic influence over them. Individuals' feelings of being subsumed in a society thus become weak and inconstant.[3] For most of people's lives, Durkheim continues, nothing draws them out of themselves and instills restraint on them. Inevitably, they lapse into egoism or anarchy. People cannot become attached to higher aims if they do not feel they belong to anything. Thus, for Durkheim, freeing people from all social pressure abandons them to themselves, and to sorrow. So it seems that for people sensitive to melancholia some kind of deeper sense of belonging is necessary, though difficult.

Though Durkheim's work was primarily a sociological study—based in statistics and using an objective, scientific tone—toward the end he makes some philosophical statements about the meaning of life and comes to the resolute conclusion that suicide is immoral. Durkheim describes the aspect of humanity that he calls "the cult of man"—something not unlike culture and mutual feeling—and discusses how it brings us together. "This cult of man is something, accordingly, very different from the egoistic individualism, . . . which leads to suicide." Instead of alienating people from society and driving them to think only of themselves, the cult of man "unites them in one thought, makes them servants of one work."[4] Human beings are not just what each of us is on our own, Durkheim says, we are also humanity in some ideal form as created by a given people at its moment in time. To be well, we need to be drawn out of our individual personalities, to feel the overarching culture within and beyond us. The state is bound by these ideas as well. "Our dignity as moral beings is therefore no longer the property of the city-state; but it has not for that reason become our property, and we have not acquired the right to do what we wish with it."[5] With this, Durkheim concludes that suicide is wrong:

> Under these conditions suicide must be classed among immoral acts; for in its main principle it denies this religion of humanity. A man who kills himself, the saying goes, does wrong only to himself and there is no occasion for the intervention of society; for so goes the ancient maxim *Volenti non fit injuria.* This is an error. Society is injured because the sentiment is offended on which its most respected moral maxims today rest, a sentiment almost the only bond between its members, and which would be weakened if this offense could be committed with impunity. How could this sentiment maintain the least authority if the moral conscience did not protest its violation? . . . No matter that the guilty person and the victim are one and

the same; the social evil springing from the act is
not affected merely by the author being the one
who suffers.

In this proclamation Durkheim reverses his usual focus on
what society ought to be doing for the individual, and what
it fails to do for the suicidal, and asserts the obligation of the
individual to not kill him- or herself for the sake of the common society of the community of humanity. This is not too far
from Kant's claim that suicide does deep damage to humanity,
or from Maimonides' notion that he who destroys himself destroys the world.

Durkheim makes it clear that he does not intend to blame
suicide victims or sympathize with abuses of earlier times. Having said that suicide is wrong he adds, "Of course, this does not
mean that we must revert to the ferocious penalties imposed
on suicide during the past centuries." These, he says, were created when the entire system of public repression was enforced
with undue ruthlessness. "But the principle that homicide of
one's self should be reproved must be maintained."

Durkheim did not feel he had to tell his reader about the
ferocious penalties that were inflicted on suicides in past centuries, but his may have been the last generation that could
take such knowledge for granted. Twentieth-century discussions of suicide rarely mentioned the torturing of corpses, or
if they did, it was with a good deal of explanation. Yet meditations on suicide continued to be animated by a rejection of
interference with the individual's control over his or her own
life. In defiance of God and the state, some claimed that suicide was a fundamental choice that belonged to every human
being. This was particularly true in conversations about the
philosophical movement of existentialism.

Though existentialism has roots in nineteenth-century philosophy, it became an influential philosophical movement only after World War II. Different values have been associated with this rubric, but one theme common to them all is that human beings come to existence and then make up a purpose for themselves. In Jean-Paul Sartre's words, "man first of all exists, encounters himself, surges up in the world—and defines himself afterwards." Of all of the thinkers involved with this movement, French existentialist Albert Camus stands out for having written specifically on suicide in a way that reached average people rather than just philosophers.

Camus opens "An Absurd Reasoning," the first essay in his collection *The Myth of Sisyphus,* with these words:

> There is but one truly serious philosophical problem, and that is suicide. Judging whether life is or is not worth living amounts to answering the fundamental question of philosophy. All the rest—whether or not the world has three dimensions, whether the mind has nine or twelve categories—comes afterwards. These are games; one must first answer.[6]

He makes the seriousness of the question clear by essentially threatening to think through the problem, come to an answer, and then carry out that answer, even if it means to die. With a fierce wit he judges that his subject is urgent compared with other questions of philosophy, writing, "I have never seen anyone die for the ontological argument."

Nodding toward Durkheim, Camus tells us that suicide has been dealt with only as a social phenomenon and that he is instead concerned with the connection between individual thought and suicide. The problem he lays out is the overall meaninglessness of existence and how absurd that makes our lives of sound and fury. But the absurd is tolerable. Camus writes that it is no more than wordplay to conclude that because life has no ultimate meaning it is not worth living.[7] The lack of overall purpose or goal does not imply that there is no value to living. For Camus, killing oneself is an unwarranted "insult to existence," even though life is painful.[8] He acknowledges that he is keenly aware of the sorrow and struggles of human life; he knows that it can be exhausting, repetitive, anxious, and depressing, but he concludes that once we fully recognize the absurdity of it all, a kind of love and joy arise. His philosophy sympathizes with anguish but cajoles the fellow sufferer to embrace life, all the more so because it makes no sense. We should, Camus writes, accept that our desires do not match up with the world as we know it, and yet love the unanswerable strangeness of it all.

Toward the end of the essay, Camus makes some compelling remarks about staying alive. He says that the absurd teaches us not to make the mistake of valuing certain kinds of lives and their experiences over other kinds of lives. "For the mistake is thinking that the quantity of experiences depends on the circumstances of our life when it depends solely on us. Here we have to be over-simple. To two men living the same number of years, the world always provides the same sum of experiences. It is up to us to be conscious of them." There is nothing more than being aware of one's life, whatever form it might take. For Camus, "one's revolt, one's freedom," is this awareness, and it is the essence of living "to the maximum."[9] There is no life that is higher.

This is an unusual stance in philosophy. Philosophers are much more often found encouraging people not to worry

about an early death, saying that we all die in the end and that
it is of no importance how long our span of life is. Camus specifically argues with the ancient philosophers for teaching that
a short, brilliant life is as good or better than a long, ordinary
one. To his mind, the experience of being alive and feeling life
is more important than anything in particular that life may
offer. Such advice is aimed at those who have a painful fear of
death and who cling so tightly to life that they forget to enjoy
it as it passes. Camus, however, is aiming his advice at those
who are, to some degree, disappointed by life and entranced
by the idea of death. That is why Camus gives more weight
to the quantity of life than to the quality. He believes that the
great gift that life offers is the same for all of us and builds up
over the years, so no matter how difficult one's life seems, it
would be a terrible mistake to cut it short. That leaves premature death as a real problem to be feared, and Camus acknowledges this. It is often a matter of luck whether we have a long
or short life, and Camus says that this is the one real trouble
we must face.

These ideas turn philosophy on its head. Instead of wisdom consoling the mass of common people who are frightened of death, Camus sees a somewhat more hidden distress
of humanity, which is being fed up with life. Instead of saying
that death does not matter, Camus addresses the part of us that
already believes that death might be preferable to life, and he
says that once we have understood the absurdity of life and accepted it, we will see that more life is always better: "One just
has to be able to consent to this. There will never be any sub-
stitute for twenty years of life and experience."[10] People feeling
depressed and disheartened by life might feel that they are just
marking time, getting through one day after another without

much reason. Camus insists that there is a reason for getting through the days even when one does not feel joyous. He is certain that when we see the absurdity of the human condition, just living adds up to a rich experience that is, in its own way, joyful. In this sense Camus adds his voice to those who have said that we must not kill ourselves because of what we owe to our future selves.

Camus's ideas are sorrowful but cheerful. No matter how much he believes in the fact of depression, he embraces life. In his words, "the point is to live."[11] He understands despair—"polar night, vigil of the mind"—but says, "I draw from the absurd three consequences. Which are my revolt, my freedom, and my passion. By the mere activity of consciousness I transform into a rule of life what was an invitation to death—and I refuse suicide. I know, to be sure, the dull resonance that vibrates throughout these days. Yet I have but a word to say that it is necessary."[12]

Camus counsels a kind of revolt, which means for him that we must have knowledge of the certainty of our ultimate fate—death—but refuse to be resigned to it. It is a paradoxical revolt in the face of acceptance—a very tricky idea but one which Camus feels sure we can manage. This is why suicide is anathema to his philosophy of the absurd experience. He says that people consider suicide the ultimate revolt, but the contrary is true. Life in the face of its pain, he writes, is the ultimate revolt. Suicide "is acceptance in the extreme."[13] Our challenge is to be aware of death and at the same time reject it. The tension between being keenly aware of death yet not being resigned to it is what creates the absurd, and keeping the absurd alive keeps the person alive.

Camus writes that it is essential that we do not die of our own free will because our embracing the absurd leads us to take all of life and give what we have. "Suicide," he writes, "is a repudiation. The absurd man can only drain everything to the bitter end, and deplete himself. The absurd is his extreme tension, which he maintains constantly by solitary effort, for he knows that in that consciousness and in that day-to-day revolt he gives proof of his only truth, which is defiance."[14]

In the title essay of *The Myth of Sisyphus,* Camus famously describes our human lives as similar to the torture of Sisyphus, who was condemned to roll the same stone up the same hill, just to have it roll down again, over and over until the end of time. Sisyphus was being punished in part because he had escaped the underworld once and lived some years enjoying life on earth. Now he is back in the underworld at his quintessentially meaningless task. Camus finds this absurd and he finds coping with the absurd heroic. Sisyphus perseveres and resists the lure of suicide. Camus holds that suicide tempts us with the illusory promise of freedom, but the only real freedom is to embrace the absurdity:

> You have already grasped that Sisyphus is the absurd hero. He *is,* as much through his passions as through his torture. His scorn of the gods, his hatred of death, and his passion for life won him that unspeakable penalty in which the whole being is exerted toward accomplishing nothing. This is the price that must be paid for the passions of this earth.[15]

Camus asks us to fully imagine the huge effort Sisyphus must make, straining his body to push the huge stone, a hundred times over. We must see his face screwed up with the effort of it, his cheek pressed hard against the stone, his shoulder fully braced against its dirty surface, his foot wedging it to keep it from falling backward. At the end of his tremendous effort, "measured by skyless space and time without depth," he is successful. Then he watches the boulder fall back down the hill in a matter of moments. Down he goes again to restart his toil. It is during that return, that pause in concerted effort, that Sisyphus most interests Camus. That time is when Sisyphus is most conscious. He is not distracted by the work but is fully facing the absurdity of his situation. At those moments, Camus writes, Sisyphus "is superior to his fate. He is stronger than his rock.[16]

We are stronger than our rock. Sisyphus and the rock can be a man and his tedious, repetitive work, but the rock is also life itself, even if there is no task to perform that is as onerous as the labor of Sisyphus. Every day must be borne, and the reward for bearing it is another day. Still, Camus sees reason to rejoice as well as weep. He says that it is in the descent of our rolled-up rock that we are most aware of our predicament. "If the descent is thus sometimes performed in sorrow, it can also take place in joy. This word is not too much." The chief sorrow, he tells us, was in the beginning. Now when images of better times, like Sisyphus's recollection of earth, become dominant in one's mind, and when the desire for happiness becomes too much to resist, "melancholy rises in a person's heart and grief is too heavy to bear." Even this grief has an antidote: "Crushing truths perish from being acknowledged."[17]

Even Oedipus, Camus tells us, was in the end resigned to what fate had unfolded for him and concluded that all was well. Sisyphus is exhausted but continues. He even continues well. "His fate belongs to him. His rock is his thing." The person who understands the absurdity of the human condition is strengthened by it. He or she still has to work unceasingly to bear up under the weight of being, but it is worth it.

There is no higher destiny, Camus declares. The absurd man is the master of his days. When he gazes backward over his life, he contemplates that series of unrelated actions which becomes his fate, created by him, and like Sisyphus and his rock, the whole seemingly unreasonable effort turns out to have meaning, just because it constituted his life. Thus, even while we are convinced that all human meaning comes from human beings, and not from outside them, we are still able to be impressed by its meaning if we allow ourselves to be. Camus says that each of us, like Sisyphus, is like a blind man who wants to see and yet knows the night has no end, but who is still "on the go." Meaning and joy are inherent in our simple, yet heroically effortful, persistence. "The rock is still rolling."[18] We endure.

He ends the essay with a famous passage that combines all his strange pessimism and optimism.

> I leave Sisyphus at the foot of the mountain! One always finds one's burden again. But Sisyphus teaches the higher fidelity that negates the gods and raises rocks. He too concludes that all is well. This universe henceforth without a master seems to him neither sterile nor futile. . . . The struggle itself toward the heights is enough to fill a man's heart. One must imagine Sisyphus happy.[19]

It is not a simple kind of happiness, but Camus asks us to perceive that it is happiness all the same. For those who find life hard to bear—or perhaps for all of us when we find life hard to bear—Camus is an odd but wonderful companion, entirely empathizing with our despair, yet cheering us on to live and even see a happiness in our struggle.

Jean-Paul Sartre, like Camus associated with existential-ism, wrote an illuminating analysis of Camus's 1942 novel *The Stranger*. Sartre describes the novel's protagonist, Meursault, as beyond suicide: "The absurd man," Sartre writes, "will not commit suicide; he wants to live, without relinquishing any of his certainty, without a future, without hope, without illusions . . . and without resignation either. He stares at death with pas-sionate attention and this fascination liberates him. He expe-riences the 'divine irresponsibility' of the condemned man."[20] Sartre also wrote about the possibility of suicide as an asser-tion of authentic human will in the face of absurdity. Sartre was fascinated with suicide as both a practical and a symbo-lic way of reacting to a godless world. Still, the real act of sui-cide was for Sartre the abandonment of all liberty.

It is worth noting here that even though Camus and Sartre reject suicide, they do consider it each person's right, precisely because for them there is no God and no outside meaning, no framing significance that comes from outside the self. Neither has much faith in other people, and neither sug-gests that the community provides sufficient "outside mean-ing" to militate against suicide. Instead, for them the embrace of absurdity is a way of conceptualizing one's commitment to living. In this sense, Camus champions the importance of the future self, without focusing on what that future self deserves.

Despite Camus's stance against suicide, he is sometimes most remembered for the importance he gave the question. Be-cause of his insistence that the thinking person must make a de-cision about whether life is worth living, he is often considered a supporter of the option to take one's own life, and he is grouped with the secular thinkers who have actively accepted suicide.

As false as that association may be, secular philosophy has been an undeniable force in the trend toward neutral or even positive attitudes toward suicide. The nonreligious view of the world is often thought of as a brave look into the abyss. Here is how one of the happier secular philosophers, Diderot, described existence: "To be born in imbecility, in the midst of pain and crisis: to be the plaything of ignorance, error, need, sickness, wickedness, and passions . . . never to know where you come from, why you come and where you are going! That is what is called the most important gift of our parents and nature. Life."[21] But just as with the suicide question itself, the question of the abyss is keenly shaped by religion. Because religion addresses particular kinds of ideas, like an afterlife or the efficacy of prayer, the absence of those ideas is felt as a deficit. The world without them seems a world of despair. But as many can attest, especially people raised without religion, at some distance from these religious ideas, God and the afterlife are not always missed.

Without the worldviews of various religions, the universe has often been imagined as a dark, boundless place. Belief that life is meaningless has become widespread. In much secular literature, people worry that their actions don't matter in a world without significance. Characters express sadness over losing the specific comforts of modern Western religion. Atheist philosophers Arthur Schopenhauer and Friedrich Nietzsche elaborately embroidered this mood, as did such novelists as Fyodor Dostoyevsky and Virginia Woolf and other authors of the nineteenth and twentieth centuries. Here is Schopenhauer on life:

> Many millions, united into nations, strive for the common good, each individual on account of his own; but many thousands fall as a sacrifice for it. Now senseless delusion, now intriguing politics, excite them to wars with each other; then the sweat

and the blood of the great multitude must flow, to
carry out the ideas of individuals, or to expiate their
faults. In peace, industry and trade are active, in-
ventions work miracles, delicacies are called from
all ends of the world, the waves engulf thousands.
All strive, some planning, some acting; the tumult
is indescribable. But the ultimate aim of it all—
what is it? To sustain ephemeral and tormented individuals through a short span of life, in the most
fortunate case with endurable want and compara-
tive freedom from pain, which, however, is at once
attended with ennui; then the reproduction of this
race and its striving.[22]

It seems reasonable to reply that such dark visions under-
report love, trust, hope, and community. The good is worth
saving. The bearable can become sweet, and sometimes there
is joy in love, and art, and the absurd.

For an individual, when life seems too hard even to endure, the idea of saving the world may not be on the table.
Nevertheless, as Camus might say, the choice to get through
the day, made over and over, is the heroic action that the world
requires from you. The argument against suicide put forward
by Durkheim also points to how to live: be engaged. To be
connected to the rest of us, at least conceptually; to cultivate within ourselves an ability to feel the sustaining force of
the human culture in which we live. If we take Durkheim and
Camus together, it seems the job is to try to feel your connection to the world, and to try to stay curious about what is
happening and about what might happen—to experience life
despite its capacity to seem as brutal and pointless as the hard
labor of Sisyphus, for some people, some of the time.

9

Suffering and Happiness

S o what do we do with the pain of living? Many people who have questioned religion have rejected the religious advice that one should just accept and be reconciled with suffering. Secular thinkers have pointedly accused religion of being a cult of pain. Judaism became a new kind of religion during the Babylonian captivity when the Israelites in their sorrow began blaming themselves instead of their God for their misfortune. When the Jews met with adversity again throughout history, often they blamed themselves and tried to make amends with God. The Buddhist way of embracing suffering is very different, and yet arrives at a similar conclusion: a measure of self-denial will lead to more happiness. From the outside both these religions have seemed, to some observers, to be too resigned to suffering.

Early Christianity took the idea of embracing suffering to new extremes. Consider Jesus' acceptance of torture at the hands of the soldiers, then consider the flagellants—medieval monks who thrashed themselves bloody—and consider the hundreds of thousands on barefoot treks for religious pilgrimages. In May 2010 Pope Benedict told a crowd of followers in Portugal that the infirm must "overcome the feeling of the uselessness of suffering which consumes a person from within and makes him feel a burden to those around him when, in reality, suffering which is lived with Jesus assists in the salvation of your brethren." For the religious, suffering can have great value. Secularists in all times reject religion for its praise of suffering, which seems cruel in a world already so full of pain.

Still, secular culture desperately needs some way of valuing suffering. Life has suffering in it no matter what you do; no one escapes. As we have seen, there is a secular tradition that honors the hurt we have had in our lives, without suggesting that we invite more.

The poet John Keats wrote that the world is a "vale of soul-making," explaining that we become something greater than ourselves if we live through difficulties.

> I will put it in the most homely form possible—I will call the *world* a School instituted for the purpose of teaching little children to read—I will call the *human heart the horn Book* used in that School—and I will call the *Child able to read, the Soul* made from that *school* and its *hornbook*. Do you not see how necessary a World of Pains and troubles is to school an Intelligence and make it a soul! A Place where the heart must feel and suffer in a thousand diverse ways! Not merely is the Heart a Hornbook, It is the Mind's Bible, it is the Mind's experience, it is the teat from which the mind or intelligence sucks its identity.[1]

Keats saw the terrible pain of life as necessary to the development of a full human being. While the heart suffers acutely, the mind is nurtured and matured through the information garnered by the anguished heart. In his extended metaphor there is no other way for a human being to be tempered into personhood. In that sense the world, with all its difficulties, is a school. As we saw, Montaigne, too, believed that suffering brought one to a greater experience of life, and Schopenhauer taught that through the process of life and its anguish one attains a better vantage point from which to know the world.

In modern secular culture the phrase "no pain, no gain" is generally heard only in conjunction with physical exercise and sport, but the expression might be rehabilitated to describe the challenge of attaining not a gym body but rather emotional and intellectual maturity. We need to recapture some of the philosophical stance toward suffering, not only because pain can have value but because it is cruel to let people feel they are suffering needlessly when in fact they might be gaining wisdom. In psychotherapy especially, the pain of living can lead to solace and freedom. Childhood formed us all, and the more we suffered then, the harder it can be to accept ourselves as adults. True, the road to self-awareness is arduous. Some realizations bring us to low feelings much like grief, and much like grief the only solution is to live through it. We come out wiser on the other side. As Robert Frost wrote, "The only way around is through."

Nietzsche provides important insight into the profound importance of suffering. In *The Gay Science* he writes of how difficult it is to know one another's suffering and of the attempts we make, out of pity, to console one another:

> It is the very essence of the emotion of pity that it strips away from the suffering of others whatever is distinctively personal. . . . The whole economy of my soul and the balance effected by "distress,"

the way new springs and needs break open, the way
in which old wounds are healing, the way whole
periods of the past are shed—all such things that
may be involved in distress are of no concern to
our dear pitying friends; they wish to help and have
no thought of the personal necessity of distress, al-
though terrors, deprivations, impoverishments,
midnights, adventures, risks, and blunders are as
necessary for me and for you as are their opposites.
It never occurs to them that, to put it mystically,
the path to one's own heaven always leads through
the voluptuousness of one's own hell. No, the "religion of pity" . . . commands them to help, and they
believe that they have helped most when they have
helped most quickly.

Nietzsche compels his readers to examine their own attitudes
and see whether they too do everything in their power to ex-
punge suffering from their experience. He warns us that the
common refusal to tolerate suffering even an hour signals an
unproductive devotion to the "religion of comfortableness."

For Nietzsche, the common idea that displeasure is a defect of existence disguises the truth that pain is inherent in
existence and part of our path toward wisdom. Comfort, he
writes, is in opposition to real happiness. Happiness and unhappiness, he explains, "are sisters and even twins that either
grow up together or . . . remain small together."[2]

Nietzsche urges us to see that human suffering is necessary, but what is not necessary is painfully regretting that
suffering. Our condition hands us difficulty, and unless we are
careful to stop ourselves, we add more difficulty to our lot by
fearing and loathing that difficulty. We suffer and then hate

ourselves for suffering. We are much better off accepting the pain, seeing it as universal, noting that it can be borne, and, when possible, expressing it.[3]

Pain is rarely praised these days. Yet some still engage with the idea that crucial kinds of growth are achieved through suffering. Author Calvin Trillin writes that his late wife Alice responded to tragedy with rare insight. She wrote to a young woman who had been violently attacked, saying that no one would ever choose to be throttled by life: "But you don't get to choose, and it is possible at least to . . . begin to understand the line in 'King Lear'—'Ripeness is all.' You might have chosen to become ripe less dramatically or dangerously, but you can still savor ripeness."[4] Living through anguish can give a person uncommon depth. Today we often refuse to "listen to suffering"—we pretend it is noise with no content and try only to get rid of it. We might consider listening to it. Especially for those who are suicidal, whose suffering is so intense that they cannot hear clearly what it is saying, psychotherapy can help.

Another way of listening to pain is to listen to others' stories of pain and survival. Consider Erica Jong's "Dear Colette," an epistolary poem addressed to the French author of the title, thanking her for being a strong woman writer. Colette's books meant so much to Jong that for decades the poet has hung a picture of the French author above her desk. So many female writers, Jong observes, were either suicides or "spinsters," but Colette was neither. In the poem, Jong cites the unmarried Jane Austen, Sylvia Plath gassing herself in the oven, and Virginia Woolf drowning herself, among others. She thanks Colette for marrying, for having a complicated love life, for having a child, for singing and dancing and always still writing. She thanks Colette for enduring, for having "never willingly let go," and concludes by saying that Colette's example has held her to this life, which, we can fairly deduce, she hopes will be an example for her own readers.[5]

Such connections are exceedingly important. We feel our suffering in isolation. But suffering may also unite us if we make that communal suffering visible to ourselves. The social idea to take one's own life, within the context of a deeply enmeshed society, may have a direct mirror in a social idea to preserve yourself for the sake of others, within the context of a society like ours, marked by independence. In the Great Depression of the 1930s many individuals took their lives, either when they lost all their money in the stock market crash or during the period afterward, with its grinding unemployment. When we think of it now it seems surprising that people could take these widespread hardships so personally, but this seems to be how the mind works—all misfortune feels local. In any era, recognizing that many people are in pain may help individuals to live through their own worst times. Collective suffering is a powerful notion because it can help convince people that they are not to blame for their suffering and because it can add a sense of companionship to life. The idea of collective suffering can also bolster the idea of collectively rejecting suicide.

Throughout history, some traditions and prejudices of a given culture that have long been assumed to be good or neutral—foot binding, or dueling, slavery or repressing homosexuals—have been flipped in a generation or two, so that the good migrates to the other side. Kwame Anthony Appiah's *The Honor Code* shows that a culture's shifting sense of what is honorable is more efficacious than top-down legislation in changing behavior. The notion of what is honorable is resilient, but it can evolve.[6] Appiah points to so-called "honor killings" in the Muslim world as a tradition that might also respond to the same kind of social awareness and thus become increasingly rare. Perhaps if we pay attention to Kant, Schopenhauer, and other voices advocating that we live through the pain, surviving a suicidal impulse could be added to this list of the honorable.

Appiah cites Kant's declaration, in *Groundwork of the Metaphysics of Morals,* that the highest reason for doing good is not "inclination towards honor" but acting in order to do the right thing, which Kant calls acting from duty. "But Kant himself says we should 'praise and encourage' righteous acts motivated by honor. That seems only sensible. After all, if people find it hard (as they evidently do) to act from duty, we have cause to make sure they have other reasons for doing what is right."[7] Why not adapt the call of Kant and Appiah to include praise and encouragement for those who are tempted by suicide and yet reject it?

It is an intellectual and moral mistake to see the idea of suicide as an open choice that each of us is free to make. The arguments against suicide ask us to commit ourselves to the human project. They ask humanity to set down its daggers and cups of hemlock and walk away from them forever. Let us be done with bare bodkins.

If we take seriously the arguments against suicide that we have rehearsed in the course of these pages, it seems right to ask each other to survive, to stay on this side of the guardrail. The suicidal should be aware that they are doing something noble when they make a cup of tea and stare at the sky through the branches. If we take seriously the arguments against suicide, we have to ask the suicidal person to see herself as a Lucretia who survives.

Suffering and surviving are ways of serving humanity, and that, in and of itself, can bring some happiness. The twentieth-century humanitarian Albert Schweitzer spoke poignantly on the subject. Addressing a group of school boys, Schweitzer said that he sometimes got letters asking him how to live.

> And when I answer such letters I add . . . "Seek a humble sort of thing." Our hearts often look for something very big, something wanting a lot of sacrifice, and often our heart does not see the humble things. At first you must learn to do the humble things and often they are the most difficult to do. In those humble things, be busy about helping someone who has need of you. You see somebody alone—try and be with him, try to give him some of the hours which you might take for yourself and in that way learn to serve: and then only will you begin to find true happiness. I don't know what your destiny will be. Some of you will perhaps occupy remarkable positions. Perhaps some of you will become famous by your pens, or as artists. But I know one thing: the only ones among you who will be really happy are those who have sought and found how to serve.

As Eleanor Roosevelt put it, "In all our contacts it is probably the sense of being really needed and wanted which gives us the greatest satisfaction and creates the most lasting bond." At the end of his *Conquest of Happiness,* the philosopher Bertrand Russell wrote, "The whole antithesis between self and the rest of the world, which is implied in the doctrine of self-denial, disappears as soon as we have any genuine interest in persons or things outside ourselves. Through such interests a man comes to feel himself part of the stream of life." Maybe the service one does for others and for oneself in staying alive through suicidal times is sufficient to garner some of these positive feelings.[8]

A person in crisis may find it too hard to do anything for himself, let alone for someone else. In crisis it may be too hard to think. Yet it may be possible to think through these ideas ahead of time, so that useful responses are at the ready when one needs them. One needs to practice believing in the power of small actions to change the way one feels. In an acute state of misery, it may be impossible to initiate this kind of belief: one tries to imagine connecting with others and gets nowhere. Just as we cannot get drunk by thinking about vodka, we cannot feel the good feelings that come with being connected with people by thinking about connecting. We have to act, and then be aware of how acting changes our outlook, and vigilantly remember the experience. If we have done the work of thinking about these things in advance of our dark times, they may become accessible to us when we need them to help carry us through to better days. When we think of being of use, we should start small, thinking first of our past service and how we honor that by simply staying alive. We may also think of the service we can do for people by honestly bearing witness to our own pain, in writing or in conversation. There is also the small yet meaningful service of asking people in our lives about their feelings and listening with patience and understanding. There are small acts of service that we can do in response to need, without necessarily committing ourselves to long-term activities. Many people who do a great deal of service describe starting small and following the good feelings that these first small actions bring them, then slowly increasing the commitments, which bring them ever more peace of mind. We should not be unduly optimistic about this, but neither should we be unduly pessimistic. We can take seriously the fact that severe misery sometimes befalls us and that when severe misery strikes, very little is possible, yet we can practice being aware that if we can hold out for them, better days will come.

There are two people who committed suicide whom I want to quote on the pain of life. The first is David Foster Wallace, in a passage in which he brings to vivid attention the agony of tedium:

> Enduring tedium over real time in a confined space is what real courage is. Such endurance is, as it happens, the distillate of what is, today, in this world neither I nor you have made, heroism. Heroism.... The truth is that the heroism of your childhood entertainments was not true valor. It was theater. The grand gesture, the moment of choice, the mortal danger, the external foe, the climactic battle whose outcome resolves all—all designed to appear heroic, to excite and gratify an audience. . . . Gentlemen, welcome to the world of reality—there is no audience. No one to applaud, to admire. No one to see you. Do you understand? Here is the truth—actual heroism receives no ovation, entertains no one. No one queues up to see it. No one is interested.[9]

One of the beautiful things about this piece of writing is that it concentrates on the trials of ordinary life. We often associate pain in life with either horrendous misfortune or terrible mental health disorder, like hospitalized depression. Many times, however, people feel extreme despair while they continue to function in everyday life. Wallace here reminds his reader that it is legitimate to feel that despair, and likewise it is legitimate to recognize the heroism of continuing on. The notion goes well with Camus's idea of the absurd. We did not make this world, Wallace's speaker says, and our childhood inclinations about how to succeed in it turn out to be wrong: often our courage is needed not to dramatically change reality but to accept it and persist in it. Camus advises us to cope with this strange reality by concentrating our attention on the strangeness of it; not by making sense of it, but by aligning ourselves with the absence of sense. Camus's idea of the absurd is not a doctrine that counsels us to do service for others, but Camus's own act of writing his ideas and giving them to the world was itself an act of service. If we think about writing and publishing for the sake of self-aggrandizement, we will probably be disappointed—as we can see from the many stories of successful people who report misery or even kill themselves, success does not always feed the hunger as we think it will. If instead we think of the community of sufferers and understand our writing as a way of connecting to them, we may well feel better ourselves. We can write about loneliness without noticing that our readers make us part of a community, but if we do the work of noticing this and remembering it, it can save our lives.

The second person who committed suicide from whom I want to offer a quotation, on the pain of life, is the poet Anne Sexton:

> I don't want to live. . . . Now listen, life is lovely, but I Can't Live It. I can't even explain. I know how silly it sounds . . . but if you knew how it Felt. To be alive, yes, alive, but not be able to live it. Ay that's the rub. I am like a stone that lives . . . locked outside of all that's real. . . . I wish, or think I wish, that I were dying of something for then I could be brave, but

to be not dying, and yet . . . and yet to [be] behind a
wall, watching everyone fit in where I can't, to talk
behind a gray foggy wall, to live but to not reach or
to reach wrong . . . to do it all wrong . . . believe me,
(can you?) . . . what's wrong. I want to belong. . . .
I'm not a part. I'm not a member. I'm frozen.[10]

Sexton's expression of anguish is extraordinary. Yet such
feelings are not uncommon. To live through this painful feeling is hard work and requires prodigious courage. That courage comes first from recognizing that we are not alone. Sexton's confession here is of feeling cut off from community, yet
she expresses something that a huge number of people experience. If we can grasp that commonality, the pain can become
easier to bear. The courage to live may also come from having
shared with other people, through reading or conversation,
that despite pain it is worth finding the courage to live—for
the sake of other people and for the sake of our future selves.
None of us can save Sexton or Wallace, which is a brutal pity.
We might, however, be able save one another and ourselves,
in part by becoming more aware of the community and especially of the community of sufferers. It can feel like we are
alone, unseen, frozen out, but that is not the case. There is a lot
of company on the dark side of life.

In a memorable article in the New Yorker, Tad Friend
wrote about the "suicide magnet" quality of the Golden Gate
Bridge. Friend advocates that a barrier be erected to prevent
the suicides—a measure that has encountered an odd resistance on aesthetic grounds. Those opposing the barrier have
argued that people kept from killing themselves on the Golden
Gate would simply find someplace else to do it, perhaps in a
way dangerous to others. Friend cites a study from 1978 that

followed up on 515 people who were stopped from jumping off the bridge between 1937 and 1971. At that point the average time elapsed was more than twenty-six years, yet 94 percent of those who had tried to commit suicide on the bridge were still alive or had died of natural causes.[11] He also mentions that several people who have jumped off the bridge and survived reported regretting the decision only moments after having made the leap.

On high precipices where guard rails have been put up, it is possible that the guardrail fence not only physically prevents people from jumping but also reminds them that the community cares and is trying to watch after them. When the kind of English gas ovens that made it so easy for Sylvia Plath to kill herself were replaced, the suicide rate in England went down. When the United Kingdom banned the sale of acetaminophen in bulk, permitting only sales of packets of sixteen pills, there was a marked decrease in the rate of suicides and suicide attempts.[12] Surely, if barriers to physical, actual means of suicide can make a difference, then conceptual barriers to the whole idea can also make a difference. Arguments against suicide can provide such a conceptual barrier. We have only to spread the word, make suicide resistance part of our culture, attach a sense of honor to perseverance. The hope is that these ideas can take suicide off of one's list of options, preempt it as an emotional possibility the way a physical barrier can preempt the physical act of jumping. If we can take suicide off the docket for the moment, that moment may turn out to be enough.

Works that put forth an argument for living might be imagined as notably cheery, but they often come out of a tradition of seeing the harsh side of life. The dark vision of life is also present in heartwarming stories. The quintessential

American film about suicide is Frank Capra's *It's a Wonderful Life*. Part of what makes the film so compelling is that it argues that life is worth living despite its suffering and darkness. Jimmy Stewart's George Bailey is miserable and frustrated near the beginning of the film. He has sacrificed his big dreams for the sake of his small town and his family. Now his nemesis Henry Potter steals his money, and it seems as if all the sacrificing was in vain. In his desperation, wracked with anguish, George makes his way to a bridge with thoughts of jumping. This is a movie of magic, and an angel, Clarence, is dispatched to help George. Clarence finds him on a bridge on Christmas Eve, thinking about jumping. What Clarence does is to show him how important George has been by giving him a look at what his town would be like if he had never existed. Much that turned out wholesome and good with George's help turned out seedy and sad without him. When he realizes that he wants to have lived, his world is restored to him and he is grateful, especially as his friends throughout the town and beyond collect money for George to make up for his loss. Despite the movie's portrait of friendship and generosity, Potter never gives the money back; in fact, his act of thievery is never discovered. By a cruel twist of fate, the money just seems to have vanished. Life is not shown to be very wonderful at all, really. What it is, though, is important. George's friends and family need him and love him, and that turns out to be the crucial matter. The pain of loss is overpowered by the call back to life.

Many authors have celebrated the sweetness of life, and for those who are feeling good it can be wonderful to read of happiness. Here we have seen that some thinkers in history have written about how difficult life is, but have encouraged us to see that difficulty as a necessary part of the wisdom and joy we may get from life. Such ideas can be companions to us in our darkest times. We are all in this together. The twin insight is that, first, you have a responsibility not to kill yourself; and second, the rest of us—and you yourself—owe you our thanks and respect. We are indebted to one another and the debt is a kind of faith—a beautiful, difficult, strange faith. We believe each other into being.

10

Modern Philosophical Conversations

It is not uncommon today to hear someone express the idea that everyone has a right to suicide. Sometimes the speaker is thinking primarily of the terrible pain and decrepitude of fatal illnesses. As I noted in my introduction, for someone in agony because of a fatal disease, it may be inappropriate to think of self-administered death as suicide; rather we might think of it as the way that person has chosen to manage the death that cancer, for instance, had made inevitable. That is not what this book has been about. This is an important difference to keep in mind, because fierce antagonism exists between those who would allow suicide in extreme illness and those who hold a belief—generally based in religion—that no tampering with life is permissible. The extreme position of those who would prohibit all suicide sometimes has the effect of pushing those on the more tolerant side of the argument to a broader stance, perhaps inspiring them to defend suicide for people who are healthy but sad, or fed up with life. At the very least we need to notice that these are two different issues that deserve to be adjudicated separately, each on its own terms.

Some people argue for a right to suicide because having the option to end their lives gives them some solace. Nietzsche wrote that the thought of suicide got him through many a bad night. Sometimes when a person is feeling very bad and perhaps very scared, it can be a comfort to know that if she ever comes to a place where the pain is too much, she would have an out. I have no wish to deprive anyone of consolation, especially since most people whom the option would comfort are unlikely ever to follow through with the act. If a person is faced with a terrible fear—of losing a child, say, or of being brutalized in a particular way—that person might take solace from thinking, "I can dismiss worrying over this unlikely suffering because should it come to pass, I will end my life." Maybe such thoughts are harmless, but maybe they are not. Would it not be better, and more useful, for that fearful person to comfort herself by remembering that the intelligence and strength that got her through past trials are apt to get her through further trials as well? It is crucial to see that deciding against the principle of suicide creates its own practical strengths: it commits one to the human project and to one's own life in a way that gives rise to solidarity and resilience. And when one speaks of such commitment to living, others may be encouraged to live and to find the resources to survive pain.

Of course, there are times when a person suffers from despair so intensely and for so long that it can seem merciful to let him or her end life. Perhaps there is a level of constant emotional anguish that is more reasonably considered alongside painful fatal illness in regard to the appropriateness of suicide. There are many things that we say are wrong that yet have some exceptions. I think it is right to say, along with many incisive thinkers throughout history, that suicide is wrong. I believe the vast majority of people who think about suicide are tortured by their suicidal thoughts and wish to be rid of them. It can be a tremendous comfort to learn that great minds have concluded that no individual need wonder whether his or her life is worth living. It is worth living.

Three modern philosophers have some useful thoughts on this subject, and though each has been seen as having written in support of suicide, their approaches are more nuanced than is often suggested.

The first, Romanian-born French philosopher Emile M. Cioran (1911–95), is important because of his thoughts on vacillating between the desire to kill oneself and the desire to live. Cioran wrote, in *The New Gods*, "The obsession with suicide is characteristic of the man who can neither live nor die, and whose attention never swerves from this double impossibility."[1] Cioran's use of the word "obsession" helps provide a strong vision of the person whose "attention never swerves" both from imagining death and from rejecting it. Zilla Gabrielle Cahn has written of Cioran that "throughout his work one finds this refrain: I cannot live, I cannot die."[2] Cioran speaks of this vacillation as intensely painful in itself and sympathizes with others in his situation. Camus joked that most of us are in this situation, writing that "just as one does or does not kill oneself, it seems that there are but two philosophical solutions, either yes or no. That would be too easy. But allowance must be made for those who, without concluding, continue questioning. Here I am only slightly indulging in irony: this is the majority."[3] Like Camus, Cioran seems almost morbid in his willingness to speak about death and suicide so openly, but it is essential to note the philosophical distinction between accepting suicide and accepting thinking about it. Living can be too hard, and we can find ways to refuse to do it, at least in the ways that we were taught it had to be done. But though we may refuse a version of life, we must also refuse voluntary death. Cioran is much more interested in suicide than popular culture's purveyors of life-affirming sentiments, but he does not actually advocate suicide.

The modern philosopher who most clearly does countenance suicide is the French savant Michel Foucault. Foucault defends the right to suicide and even seems to celebrate it. To him it seems a grand act of self-determination. He considers modern suicide to be somewhat less grand than the "moral and political form of behavior" Montesquieu cited for the "Roman suicide," but he does not idealize the ancient suicides. Rather, he seemed to exalt in a kind of suicide precisely not in the service of the family or the state.[4] Foucault attempted suicide as a young man in 1948 and several times afterward. His school doctor attributed the early attempt to homosexual guilt, but it was probably a more complicated suffering.[5] Throughout his career Foucault shocked people with his sympathy for suicide. In a short essay of 1979, "The Simplest of Pleasures," Foucault wrote that he was not attempting to legalize suicide or make it moral, saying that "too many people have already belabored these lofty things."[6] His intention, he explained, was instead to contradict the humiliations and shady doings that the detractors of suicide have associated with it. He advocated a world that was amenable to the potential suicide and allowed him to take his time, openly choosing his method and moment. Foucault spent his life decrying the suppression of social deviancy that he felt characterized medicine, psychiatry, and law. He fought for the freedom of a host of behaviors that are policed in modern society, and within that context it makes sense to see his championing of suicide. I find much of Foucault's writing very persuasive, but I question his conclusion on this particular subject. It is one thing to try to free the human being from social constraints and to defend difference of all types; it is another thing to help usher people into the grave.

Finally we must consider the psychiatrist and philosopher Thomas Szasz (1920–2012). Szasz famously argued that there is no connection between mental illness and suicide, and that no mental health professional ought to consider it her natural duty to step in to prevent suicide. Szasz argued that people should be able to choose when to die at any time, with no intrusion by medicine or the state, just as with contraception they are able to choose when to conceive without medical or state interference. He cites suicide as one of the most fundamental rights. In 1963 Szasz coined the phrase "therapeutic state." The therapeutic state responds to unwelcome activities, opinions, and feelings by repressing them—or, as representatives of the viewpoint would put it, curing them—through an alliance between psychiatry and government. Thus suicide is considered to be a sickness that needs to be treated, along with unusual religious beliefs, unhappiness, anxiety, shyness, sexual promiscuity, overeating, gambling, smoking, and illegal drug use. Szasz disagrees sharply with this control and considers all these behaviors choices made by sane people who should not be interfered with. These are dramatic claims against the backdrop of our state laws and social rules, and these dramatic claims are what people think of when they consider the work of Szasz. It is crucial to note, however, that Szasz believed that anyone who did not want to die should by all means avail himself of whatever help he could find in keeping himself from committing suicide. Szasz wrote, "Let me state that I consider counseling, persuasion, psychotherapy, and other *voluntary measures,* especially for persons troubled by their own suicidal inclinations and seeking help, unobjectionable and indeed generally desirable interventions."[7]

Szasz's opposition is to coercive measures that would prohibit a person from committing suicide, even after the onset of a horrible disease. Szasz points out that no doctor would institutionalize a patient for not taking his medicine or otherwise not acting in his own best interest, even to the point of death, but suicide attempts routinely result in such action. His ideas got a considerable hearing, and he has influenced modern thinking on the subject. His theories have also inspired a robust counterargument. In defense of intervention, his opponents have argued that the urge to suicide is often relatively brief in duration, that it presents itself within the fluctuations of depression, and that it is often deeply ambivalent.[8]

Here we are not primarily concerned with the amount of control doctors legally have over people who say they intend to kill themselves. Rather, we are looking at those through history who have counseled people against suicide, and we are doing so with the particular aim of nudging secular philosophy toward a robust rejection of suicide, and of nudging individuals too. As we have seen, one can advocate all sorts of liberties for humanity and still try to convince people to draw the line at self-murder.

Some might argue that counseling others against suicide is not our business, as private citizens, that antisuicide advocacy might better be left to mental health professionals. But a recent study showed that worldwide relatively few suicidal respondents had received treatment, from 17 percent in low-income countries to 56 percent in high-income countries.[9] The researchers' conclusion was that "most people with suicide ideation, plans and attempts receive no treatment."[10] The dominant reason given by respondents was low perceived need. So one reason we need a more pervasive cultural argument against suicide is that many people do not have therapists or others in a professional capacity looking after them. Health care professionals are not the only ones whose responsibility it is to protect individuals from self-harm. A social and philosophical argument has the potential to take up different space in the culture and act, on its own, as a gatekeeper. Ideas have force and can dramatically reshape behavior and societal norms.

Consider the anguish and turmoil of the person considering suicide. Consider the terrible aftermath of a completed suicide. Consider the tremendous numbers of people that death affects. We as a society do very little to save the lives of people suffering and contemplating suicide. Isn't it time for us to try a little harder to save these lives? To save our own lives?

Conclusion

As we have seen, suicide has captured the attention of most of the finest thinkers in Western civilization. The story of suicide, as fact and as idea, runs through Socrates and Aristotle, Cleopatra and Cicero, Judas and Jesus, Augustine and Aquinas, Dante and Maimonides, Chaucer and Shakespeare, Voltaire and Wittgenstein. The history of Western philosophy and religion is, among many other things, one long dialogue on the propriety of taking your own life.

This history reveals that even in the intensely personal matter of choosing whether or not to go on living, the ideas and beliefs of others can be a deciding factor. Thus it is critical that people have at least heard the arguments against suicide. My chief goal in writing this book has been to place these arguments on the shelf of common ideas, so that people have access to them. I believe fiercely in the position I have here put forward, but rather than seeking to convince everyone that my position is the only correct one, I am seeking to make sure that alongside arguments in favor of the right to suicide, people are also aware of this argument that we must endeavor to live. One man or woman in extreme distress might be beyond reaching, but another might be reached. No argument will convince everyone, but no one should die for want of knowing the philosophical thinking on staying alive.

The arguments against suicide are precious because they may save lives and also because they may help make life happier. As we have seen, many thinkers have reported on the terrible experience of living with the temptation of suicide. People who have bouts of depression find life difficult enough without feeling as if it is up to them to justify their continued existence. I hope it will bring solace to know that there is a philosophical thread extending over twenty-five hundred years that urges us to use our courage to stay alive.

Religious people may be able to use these largely secular arguments against suicide, for belief in God is not always enough to stop a person from killing him- or herself. Still, the nonreligious reasons to stay alive chronicled in this book are especially important for those who do not believe in God, or at least not a God who is concerned with these matters. In particular, in our culture it is widely believed that secular philosophy is without exception open to suicide, and that the more decidedly nonreligious a philosophy is, the more decidedly affirming it is of suicide. We have seen where that idea came from, and we have seen that it is not true. A few secular thinkers have argued that we all have a right to suicide, but suicide was roundly rejected by Plato, by Aristotle, by Kant, by Schopenhauer, by Wittgenstein, and by Camus. We have seen that throughout history various authors and institutions have taken steps to influence people away from suicide. Our own era needs such influences as well. Many of the techniques used in the past do not make sense for us today—we certainly would not want to threaten people with postmortem exposure or torture. For us, knowing our history may be most valuable, as it shows us the broader context of our troubles.

Clear as it is that suicides can cause more suicides, it is clear that talking to people about rejecting suicide can help them reject suicide. Ideas matter. To stem the awful rise of suicide in our time, many things are surely needed, from easier access to mental health professionals to a general rise in economic security. Yet some of the problem can be addressed by talking about it. We need to actively reject suicide, and get this into our collective minds by reading it, speaking it, and hearing it, both one-on-one and in large communal settings. We sometimes need to be reminded that life is where everything happens, all forgiveness and all reunions. We can forget that we live in a web of significance and emotional interdependence with hundreds of other people. Sometimes the web is subtle, even imperceptible, but it is real. We forget to thank each other for staying. People can feel isolated in their dark thoughts, and learning that all of humanity suffers, at least some of the time, from such thoughts can help us to feel less alone.

Let us consider one last time the version of human existence depicted in Rembrandt's painting of Lucretia. She has been wronged, she is deeply troubled, she is contemplating suicide, but she is still alive. There is something magical about this moment: she is in a state of inestimable significance. If we follow the logic set out by Kant, or that proposed by Wittgenstein, a person choosing to die or to live exists in the very crucible of human morality and meaning. Certainly it is a frightening thing to think about, but it yields fascinating insights about what it means to be human. From a practical standpoint, too, it makes sense to give thought to these issues. If we try to suppress the whole subject, if we quarantine suicide from our consciousness and from public conversation, we run the risk of suddenly confronting it, alone and unarmed, when we are most vulnerable. It is much better to remember that this is part of the human experience and to avail ourselves of the conceptual barriers to suicide that have been provided through history. When we cannot see our own worth and are tempted to leave life, we are doing a shining service to our community and to our future selves when we choose to stay. If there is one factor universally recognized as a route to happiness, it is to be of use to others. When you are tempted by suicide and you make the decision to reject it in part for the sake of community, you may gain some of the happiness that derives from simply being of use.

None of us can truly know what we mean to other people, and none of us can know what our future self will experience. History and philosophy ask us to remember these mysteries, to look around at friends, family, humanity, at the surprises life brings—the endless possibilities that living offers—and to persevere. There is love and insight to live for, bright moments to cherish, and even the possibility of happiness, and the chance of helping someone else through his or her own troubles. Know that people, through history and today, understand how much courage it takes to stay. Bear witness to the night side of being human and the bravery it entails, and wait for the sun. If we meditate on the record of human wisdom we may find there reason enough to persist and find our way back to happiness. The first step is to consider the arguments and evidence and choose to stay. After that, anything may happen. First, choose to stay.

Notes

Introduction

1. Deaths and Mortality, 2009 data, http://www.cdc.gov/nchs/fastats /deaths.htm/.

2. Number of deaths from 113 selected causes by age: United States, 2005, http://www.disastercenter.com/cdc/Age%20of%20Deaths%20113%20 Causes%202005.html.

3. Greg Jaffe, "VA Study Finds More Veterans Committing Suicide," *Washington Post,* February 3, 2013, http://articles.washingtonpost.com/2013 -02-01/national/36669331_1_afghanistan-war-veterans-suicide-rate-suicide -risk.

4. On HIV/AIDS see R. N. Anderson, K. D. Kochanek, and S. L. Murphy, Report of Final Mortality Statistics 1995, *Monthly Vital Statistics Report* 45 (11 suppl. 2), Hyattsville, Md., National Center for Health Statistics, as cited in Kay Redfield Jamison, *Night Falls Fast: Understanding Suicide* (New York: Vintage, 1999), 23.

5. "Ten Leading Causes of Death and Injury," Centers for Disease Control and Prevention, http://www.cdc.gov/injury/wisqars/LeadingCauses .html.

6. "Mental Health," World Health Organization, http://www.who.int /mental_health/en/; "Suicide Statistics," Befrienders Worldwide, http://www .befrienders.org/info/index.asp?PageURL=statistics.php.

7. Shelby D. Burns, "Suicide Rates Climbing, CDC Urges Intervention," PsyWeb.com, http://www.psyweb.com/news/treatment/suicide-rates -climbing-cdc-urges-intervention.

8. David Hume, *Essays on Suicide and the Immortality of the Soul* (Basil, U.K.: Collection of English Classics, 1799), 2.

9. Pat Conroy, *My Reading Life* (New York: Nan A. Talese, 2010), 11.

10. Robert Burton, *The Anatomy of Melancholy,* ed. Thomas C. Faulkner, Nicholas K. Kiessling, and Rhonda L. Blair (Oxford: Clarendon, 1994), 1: 6.

1

The Ancient World

1. All biblical citations are from the King James Version.

2. Pseudo-Apollodorus, mythographer, first century B.C.E., in *Gods and Heroes of the Greeks: The Library of Apollodorus,* trans. Michael Simpson (Amherst: University of Massachusetts Press, 1976), 3.15.4.

3. Hyginus, *Poetic Astronomy* 2.4; Pseudo-Hyginus, mythographer, first century B.C.E., both quoted in *The Myths of Hyginus,* ed. Mary Grant (Lawrence: University of Kansas Press, 1960), 186.

4. Hyginus, *Fables* 141, 117.

5. Euripides, *Iphigeneia in Aulis: The Greeks,* ed. Od Hatzopoulos (Athens: Kaktos, 1992), 1375–78.

6. Anton Liberalis, *The Metamorphoses of Antoninus Liberalis: A Translation with a Commentary,* trans. Francis Celoria (New York: Routledge, 1992), 84.

7. Ovid, *Metamorphoses,* trans. Stanley Lombardo (Indianapolis: Hackett, 2010), 372.

8. Ibid., 96.

9. Euripides, *Iphigeneia in Aulis,* 1249–52.

10. Euripides, *The Madness of Hercules* (Cambridge: Loeb Classical Library, Harvard University, 1979), 3: 1347–52.

11. Plutarch, *Parallel Lives* (Cambridge: Loeb Classic Library, Harvard University, 1918), 120–23.

12. Plutarch, "The Bravery of Women," in *Moralia,* trans. Frank Cole Babbitt (Cambridge: Harvard University Press, 1931), 11: 249.

13. *Hippocrates,* trans. William Henry Samuel Jones (Cambridge: Harvard University Press, 1967), 2: 185–217.

14. Epicurus, "Letter to Menocéceus," in Diogenes Laertuis, *Lives of the Eminent Philosophers,* trans. Robert Drew Hicks (Cambridge: Harvard University Press, 1972), 649–50.

15. M. J. Cooper, "Greek Philosophers on Euthanasia and Suicide," in *Suicide and Euthanasia,* ed. A. B. Brody (Dordrecht, The Netherlands: Kluwer Academic Publishers, 1989), 9–38.

16. Lucretius, *On the Nature of Things,* trans. and ed. Anthony M. Esolen (Baltimore: Johns Hopkins University Press, 1995), 26–27.

17. Pliny the Younger attributes his information to a conversation he had with Arria's granddaughter, Fannia. Pliny the Younger, *The Complete Letters,* trans. P. G. Walsh (Oxford: Oxford University Press, 2006), 152–53.

18. Ibid.

19. Virgil, *The Aeneid,* translation mine, end of chapter 4. For a full modern translation, see: Virgil, *The Aeneid,* trans. Sarah Ruden (New Haven: Yale University Press, 2009), 89.

20. Cicero, *Tusculan Disputations,* trans. J. E. King (Cambridge: Harvard University Press, 1950), 1.48.116–17.

21. Plutarch, *Parallel Lives,* 247. Porcia's suicide is also discussed in Cassius Dio, *Roman History,* trans. Earnest Cary (Cambridge: Loeb Classical Library, Harvard University Press, 1927), 5: 217; Appian, *Roman History,* trans. Horace White (Cambridge: Loeb Classical Library, Harvard University Press, 1913), 4: 371; and Valerius Maximus, *Memorable Deeds and Sayings* (De factis dictisque memorabilibus), trans. Henry John Walker (Indianapolis: Hackett, 2004), 145.

22. Lucius Annaeus Seneca, *Letters to Lucilius,* trans. E. Phillips Barker (Oxford: Clarendon, 1932), 77: 15; George Minois, *History of Suicide: Voluntary Death in Western Culture,* trans. Lydia G. Cochrane (Baltimore: Johns Hopkins University Press, 1999), 51.

23. *The Works of Josephus,* trans. William Whiston (Peabody, MA: Hendrikson, 1987), 389–406.

2
Religion Rejects Suicide

1. Eusebius Pamphilius, *The History of the Church,* trans. Valesius (Cambridge: John Hayes, Printer to the University, 1683), 146–47.

2. Kalman Kaplan, "The Death of Jesus and Anti-Semitism," in *Jewish Approaches to Suicide, Martydom, and Euthanasia,* ed. Kalman J. Kaplan and Matthew B. Schwartz (Northvale, N.J.: Jason Aronson, 1998), 38.

3. Ibid., 39.

4. Ibid., 43.

5. Ignatius, *Epistles: Early Christian Writings,* ed. B. Radice (Baltimore: Penquin, 1968), 9.

6. Augustine, *City of God,* trans. Marcus Dods (Peabody, Mass.: Hendrickson, 2009), 29.

7. Ibid. On "Thou shall not kill," 24–25; on Lucretia, 22–23.

8. The Councils of Antisido, Braga, and others are mentioned in Nils Retterstol, *Suicide: A European Perspective* (Cambridge: Cambridge University Press, 1993), 17.

9. Koran, trans. Yusuf Ali, 4: 29–30.

10. Sahih al-Bukhari, vol. 8, book 73, no. 126.

11. Emile Durkheim, *Suicide,* ed. George Simpson, trans. John A. Spaulding and George Simpson (New York: Free Press, 1979), 327.

12. Maher Hathout, "The Suicide Culture," Muslim Public Affairs Council, http://www.mpac.org/programs/anti-terrorism-campaign/islamic-views-regarding-terrorism-and-suicidem/the-suicide-culture.php.

13. Muhammad S. al-Munajjid, "Ruling on Committing Suicide Because of Depression," Islam QA, http://islamqa.info/en/ref/111938.

14. George Minois, *History of Suicide: Voluntary Death in Western Culture,* trans. Lydia G. Cochrane (Baltimore: Johns Hopkins University Press, 1999), 55.

15. The Council of Hertford and the Canon attributed to King Edgar are mentioned in Michael MacDonald and Terence R. Murphy, *Sleepless Souls: Suicide in Early Modern England* (Oxford: Clarendon, 1990), 18–19. The Council of Toledo is noted in George Howe Colt, *The Enigma of Suicide* (New York: Summit, 1991), 158.

16. Thomas Aquinas, *Summa Theologica,* trans. Richard Murphy (New York: McGraw Hill, 1965), 55–73.

17. Michel Vovelle, *La mort et l'Occident: De 1200 a nos jours* (Paris: Gallimard, 1983); Pierre Chaunu, *La mort à Paris: XVIe, XVIIe, et XVIII siècles* (Paris: Fayard, 1977).

18. Minois, *History of Suicide,* 9.

19. Quoted in MacDonald and Murphy, *Sleepless Souls,* 50.

20. Flavius Josephus, *The Jewish War,* trans. H. St. J. Thackeray (Cambridge: Harvard University Press, 1997), book 2, 107.

21. *The Ethics of the Fathers,* 4: 22, http://www.chabad.org/library/article_cdo/aid/2032/jewish/Chapter-Four.htm.

22. Minois, *History of Suicide,* 75.

23. Martin Luther, *Memoirs,* ed. and trans. Jules Michelet (1854; Paris: Mercure de France, 1990), quoted in Minois, *History of Suicide,* 72.

24. Quoted in MacDonald and Murphy, *Sleepless Souls,* 60–61.

25. John Foxe, *Book of Martyrs; or, The Acts and Monuments of the Christian Church* (Philadelphia: Smith, 1856), 471.

26. See Lynn Hunt, *Inventing Human Rights: A History* (New York: Norton, 2007).

3
To Be or Not to Be

1. Francesco Petrarca, *Petrarch's View of Human Life,* trans. Mrs. Dobson (London, 1791), 310–12.

2. Ibid., 307–8.

3. Minois dates this as beginning around 1570. George Minois, *History of Suicide: Voluntary Death in Western Culture,* trans. Lydia G. Cochrane (Baltimore: Johns Hopkins University Press, 1999), 66.

4. John Harington, British Library manuscript, cited in Paul S. Seaver, "Suicide and the Vicar General in London," in *From Sin to Insanity: Suicide in Early Modern Europe,* ed. Jeffrey R. Watt (Ithaca, N.Y.: Cornell University Press, 2004): 25–47, quotation on 39.

5. Fedja Anzelewsky, *Durer: His Art and Life* (London: Alpine Fine Arts Collection, 1992), 191.

6. William Shakespeare, *The Arden Shakespeare: Complete Works* ed. Richard Proudfoot, Ann Thompson, and David Scott Kastan (London: Thomson Learning, 2001), 82.

7. Ibid., 309.

8. Ibid., 271.

9. Ibid., 158.

10. Ibid., 657.

11. Seaver, "Suicide and the Vicar General," 28–29.

12. Michel Montaigne, "A Custom of the Island of Cea," in *The Complete Essays of Montaigne,* trans. Donald M. Frame (Stanford: Stanford University Press, 1957), 253.

13. Ibid., 253.

14. Ibid., 254.

15. Ibid., 254–55.

16. Ibid., 255.

17. Hugo Friedrich, *Montaigne,* trans. Dawn Eng (Berkeley: University of California Press, 1991), 272.

18. Montaigne, "Of Cruelty," in *Essays,* 308–9.

19. Ibid., 309–10.

20. Pierre Charron, *Of Wisdom,* ed. George Stanhope (London: Tonson et al., n.d.), 230.

21. John Donne, *Biathanotos: A Declaration of that Paradox or Thesis, that Self-homicide is not so Naturally Sin, that it may never be otherwise* (London: Humphrey Moseley, 1648), 18.

22. Ibid., 191.

23. Robert Burton, *The Anatomy of Melancholy,* ed. Floyd Dell and Paul Jordan-Smith (Kila, Mont.: Kessinger, 1991), 2: 499–500.

24. Ibid., 1: 16.

25. Ibid., 2: 884, 964, 949, 970.

26. Ibid., 2: 942.

27. Vera Lind, "The Suicidal Mind and Body: Example for Northern Germany," in *From Sin to Insanity: Suicide in Early Modern Europe,* ed. Jeffrey R. Watt (Ithaca, N.Y.: Cornell University Press, 2004), 64–80, esp. 67–77.

28. Ibid., 77.

29. Arne Jansson, "Suicidal Murders in Stockholm," ibid., 81–99.

30. Ibid., 99.

4
Secular Philosophy Defends Suicide

1. Michael MacDonald and Terence R. Murphy, *Sleepless Souls: Suicide in Early Modern England* (Oxford: Clarendon, 1990), 5.

2. Quoted in George Minois, *History of Suicide: Voluntary Death in Western Culture,* trans. Lydia G. Cochrane (Baltimore: Johns Hopkins University Press, 1999), 180.

3. MacDonald and Murphy, *Sleepless Souls,* 69.

4. Joseph Addison, *Cato: A Tragedy* (London: J. Tonson, 1713), 53.

5. Minois, *History of Suicide,* 187.

6. Ibid., 181.

7. Ibid., 190.

8. Sir Thomas Browne, *Religio Medici,* ed. W. E. Greenhill (London: Macmillan, 1904), 69.

9. John Henley, *Cato Condemned; or, The Case and History of Self Murder, Argued and Displayed at Large, on the Principles of Reason, Justice, Law, Religion, Fortitude* (London: ECCO, n.d., photocopied reproduction of text published in 1730), 4.

10. Ibid., 8–9.

11. Ibid., 6.

12. Ibid., 13, 17.

13. Ibid., 15.

14. Ibid., 17–18.

15. Ibid., 18.

16. Ibid., 30.

17. George Berkeley, *Alciphron; or, The Minute Philosophy: An Apology for the Christian Religion Against Those Who Are Called Freethinkers* (London, 1732), 34.

18. Ibid., 117.

19. David Hume, *Enquiry into Human Understanding* (Chicago: Open Court, 1921), 141.

20. David Hume, *Essays on Suicide and the Immortality of the Soul* (Basil, U.K.: Collection of English Classics, 1799), 10.

21. Ibid., 11, 14.

22. Baron d'Holbach, *The System of Nature*, trans. H. G. Robinson (Boston: Mendum, 1889), 136.

23. Ibid.

24. Ibid.

25. Ibid.

26. Ibid., 138.

27. Ibid., 137.

28. Jeffrey R. Watt, "Suicide, Gender, and Religion," in *From Sin to Insanity: Suicide in Early Modern Europe*, ed. Jeffrey R. Watt (Ithaca, N.Y.: Cornell University Press, 2004), 149.

29. Voltaire, "Cato: On Suicide and the Abbe St. Cyran's Book Legitimating Suicide," *The Works of Voltaire: A Contemporary Version*, trans. William F. Fleming (New York: E. R. DuMont, 1901), 4: 33.

30. Montesquieu, "Sur les causes qui peuvent affecter les esprits et les caractères," in *Oeuvres complete* (Paris: Pléiade), 2: 485–86.

31. Montesquieu, *The Persian Letters*, trans. George R. Heasly (Indianapolis: Bobbs-Merrill, 1964), 129–30.

32. Madame de Staël, "Réflexions sur le suicide," in *Oeuvres completes* (Paris: Firmin Didot Frères, 1861), 3: 179.

33. Johann Wolfgang von Goethe, *The Sufferings of Young Werther*, trans. Elizabeth Mayer and Louise Bogan (New York: Vintage, 1973), 59.

34. Ibid., 61.

35. Michel Foucault, *Histoire de la folie à l'âge classique* (Paris: Gallimard, 1972), 108–9.

36. Michael MacDonald, "The Secularization of Suicide in England, 1660–1800," *Past and Present* 111 (1986): 50–100, 114.

5
The Argument of Community

1. Plato, *Phaedo*, in *The Republic and Other Works*, trans. B. Jowett (New York: Anchor, 1973), 493.

2. Plato, *Crito*, ibid., 481.

3. Plato, *The Republic*, book 10, ibid., 298–99.

4. Aristotle, *Nichomachean Ethics,* trans. Roger Crisp (Cambridge: Cambridge University Press, 2000), 101–2.

5. John Donne, *Devotions upon Emergent Occasions: Together with Death's Duel* (Middlesex, U.K.: The Ecco Library, 2008), 97.

6. Louis Richeome, *L'adieu de l'ame devote laissant le corps* (Lyon, 1590), 50.

7. François de Sales, *Treatise on the Love of God,* trans. John K. Ryan (Rockford, Ill.: Tan, 1975), 2: 226–27.

8. François de Sales, *An Introduction to the Devout Life,* trans. Allan Ross (London, 1937), 261.

9. Nicolas Malebranche, *Traité de morale* (Rotterdam, 1684).

10. Milton uses "talent" in a double sense: as we would use it but also in the sense of the gold coin of Jesus' parable of the talents of Matthew 25:14.

11. Milton, "On His Blindness," in *John Milton: Selected Poems,* ed. Stanley Appelbaum (Mineola, N.Y.: Dover, 1993), 64.

12. Denis Diderot, "Marquise de Claye et le Comte de Saint-Alban," in *Oeuvres completes* (Paris, 1875–77), 2: 522-23; and "Essai sur les règnes de Claude et de Néron," ibid., 3: 244.

13. "Suicide," *The Encyclopedia of Diderot and d'Alembert,* Collaborative Translation Project, trans. Jeffrey Merrick (1765; Ann Arbor: MPublishing, University of Michigan Library, 2003), http://hdl.handle.net/2027/spo.did2222.0000.346.

14. Ibid.

15. Julien Offray de La Mettrie, "Système d' Epicure," in *Oeuvres philosophiques* (London: Jean Nourse, 1751), 2: 37.

16. Jean Jacques Rousseau, *Julie; or, the New Heloise,* trans. Philip Stewart and Jean Vache (Lebanon, N.H.: University Press of New England, 1997), 312.

17. Cited in George Minois, *History of Suicide: Voluntary Death in Western Culture,* trans. Lydia G. Cochrane (Baltimore: Johns Hopkins University Press, 1999), 231.

18. Voltaire, *Précis du siècle de Louis XV,* cited ibid.

19. Voltaire, letter to Mme du Deffand of 21 October 1770, *Correspondence,* 107 vols., ed. Theodore Besterman (Geneva: Institut et musée Voltaire, 1953–65), 77: 34–36, cited ibid., 234.

20. Voltaire, "Lettres à Monsieur de Voltaire sur la Nouvelle Héloïse," in Voltaire, *Mélanges,* ed. Jacques Van den Heuvel (Paris: Gallimard, 1961), 404–5.

21. David Hume, *Essays on Suicide and the Immortality of the Soul,* The Complete 1783 Edition, http://www.anselm.edu/homepage/dbanach/sui-cide.htm/.

22. Denesle, *Les Préjugés du public, sur l'honneur* (Paris, 1766), 3: 425, cited in Minois, *History of Suicide,* 241.

23. Feucher d'Artaize, *Prisme Moral* (Paris, 1809), cited in Minois, *History of Suicide*, 241.

24. Immanuel Kant, *Groundwork of the Metaphysics of Morals*, trans. M. Gregor (Cambridge: Cambridge University Press, 1996), 547.

25. Ibid.

26. Ibid., 31–32.

27. Herman Melville, *Moby-Dick; or, The Whale* (New York: Modern Library, 2000), 4.

28. See, for instance: Jamie Laurentzen, *Sober Cannibals, Drunken Christians: Melville, Kierkegaard, and Tragic Optimism in Polarized Worlds* (Macon, Ga.: Mercer University Press, 2010), 18; and Harold Bloom, *Melville* (New York: Chelsea House, 1986), 132.

29. Victor Hugo, *Les Misérables*, trans. Lee Fahnestock (New York: Signet Classics, 1987), 1183.

30. G. K. Chesterton, *Orthodoxy* (New York: John Lane, 1908), 131–33.

31. Hermann Hesse, *Steppenwolf* (Mattituck, N.Y.: Amereon, 1983), 54.

32. John Berryman, *Dream Songs* (Farrar, Straus and Giroux: New York, 2007), 252.

33. John Berryman, *Collected Poems, 1937–1971*, ed. Charles Thornbury (New York: Farrar, Straus and Giroux, 1989), 206.

34. Kate Miller, "Gray Noise: Walking with the Talking Man in New York," *Io*, n.d., http://www.altx.com/io/gray1.html.

6
Modern Social Science on Community and Influence

1. Amariah Brigham, "Note by the Editor," *American Journal of Insanity* 1 (1845): 232–34, cited in C. Edward Leonard, "Confidential Death to Prevent Suicide Contagion: An Accepted, but Never Implemented, Nineteenth-Century Idea," *Suicide and Life-Threatening Behavior* 31 (2001): 460–66, quotation on 462.

2. J. P. Gray, "Suicide," *American Journal of Insanity* 35 (1878): 37–73, cited ibid.

3. Leonard, "Confidential Death to Prevent Suicide Contagion."

4. Olive Anderson, *Suicide in Victorian and Edwardian England* (Oxford: Clarendon, 1987), 372–73.

5. "Children Who Lose a Parent to Suicide More Likely to Die the Same Way, Study Finds," *Science Daily*, April 21, 2010. Holly C. Wilcox, Satoko J. Kuramoto, Paul Lichtenstein, Niklas Långström, David A. Brent, and Bo Runeson, "Psychiatric Morbidity, Violent Crime, and Suicide Among

Children and Adolescents Exposed to Parental Death," *Journal of the American Academy of Child and Adolescent Psychiatry,* May 2010.

6. Sally Cline, *Lifting the Taboo: Women, Death, and Dying* (London: Abacus, 1996), 273.

7. Fern E. Springs, and William N. Friedrich, "Health Risk Behaviors and Medical Sequelae of Child Sexual Abuse," *Mayo Clinic Proceedings* 67 (1992): 527–32.

8. Loren Coleman, *Suicide Clusters* (Winchester, Mass.: Faber and Faber, 1987), 30–37.

9. Elizabeth Gudrais, "A Tragedy and a Mystery: Understanding Suicide and Self Injury," *Harvard,* January–February 2011, 2.

10. Bill Briggs, "Military Suicide Rate Hit Record High in 2012," NBC News.com, January 14, 2013, http://usnews.nbcnews.com/_news/2013/01/14/16510852-military-suicide-rate-hit-record-high-in-2012?lite; Bill Briggs, "The Enemy Within: Soldier Suicides Outpaced Combat Deaths in 2012," NBCNews.com, January 3, 2013, http://usnews.nbcnews.com/_news/2013/01/03/16309351-the-enemy-within-soldier-suicides-outpaced-combat-deaths-in-2012?lite.

11. Mark Thompson and Nancy Gibbs, "One a Day: Every Day One U.S. Soldier Commits Suicide: Why the Military Can't Defeat Its Most Insidious Enemy," *Time,* July 23, 2012, 22–31.

12. Mark Thompson, "U.S. Military Suicides in 2012: 155 Days, 154 Dead," Time U.S., Battleland, June 8, 2012, http://nation.time.com/2012/06/08/lagging-indicator; Alan Zarembo, "Their Battle Within," *Los Angeles Times,* June 16, 2013.

13. Matthew Nock, "A Soldier's Suicide: Understanding Its Effect on Fellow Soldiers," *Psychiatry* 74 (2011): 107–9.

14. Nock cites J. J. Mann, A. Apter, J. Bertolote, et al., "Suicide Prevention Strategies: A Systematical Review," *Journal of the American Medical Association* 294 (2005), 2064–74; G. A. Bonanno, *The Other Side of Sadness: What the New Science of Bereavement Tells Us About Life After Loss* (New York: Basic, 2010); and H. Hendin, A. Lipschitz, J. T. Maltsberger, et al., "Therapists' Reactions to Patients' Suicides," *American Journal of Psychiatry* 157 (2000), 2017–27.

15. Bryan D. Stice and Silvia Sara Canetto, "Older Adult Suicide: Perceptions of Precipitants and Protective Factors," *Clinical Gerontologist* 4 (2008): 4–30.

16. Maggie Fox, "Middle-Aged Women Drive Rise in U.S. Suicides," Reuters, October 21, 2008, http://www.reuters.com/article/2008/10/21/us-suicide-usa-idUSTRE49K0MY20081021.

17. Rick Nauert, "Middle-Age Suicide on the Rise," PsychCentral, September 28, 2010, http://psychcentral.com/news/2010/09/28/middle-age-suicide-on-the-rise/18824.html.

18. Phillips has also shown a rise in suicides after a suicide on a soap opera; David P. Phillips, "The Influence of Suggestion on Suicide: Substantive and Theoretical Implications of the Werther Effect," *American Sociological Review* 39 (1974): 340–54.

19. T. Taiminen, T. Salmenperä, and K. Lehtinen, "A Suicide Epidemic in a Psychiatric Hospital," *Suicide and Life Threatening Behavior* 22 (1992): 350–63.

20. C. Wilkie, S. Macdonald, and K. Hildahl, "Community Case Study: Suicide Cluster in a Small Manitoba Community," *Canadian Journal of Psychiatry* 43 (1998): 823–28.

21. The authors report eight suicides in a one-year period in a large community in northern Ontario; J. A. Ward and Joseph Fox, "A Suicide Epidemic on an Indian Reserve," *Canadian Psychiatric Association* (1977): 423–26, abstracted in J. McGilvray, *Transcultural Psychiatry* 16 (1979): 216–17.

22. James B. Hittner, "How Robust Is the Werther Effect? A Re-Examination of the Suggestion-Imitation Model of Suicide," *Mortality* 10 (2005): 193–200.

23. D. A. Brent, J. A. Perper, G. Moritz, et al., "Psychiatric Sequelae to the Loss of an Adolescent Peer to Suicide," *Journal of the American Academy of Child and Adolescent Psychiatry* 32 (1993): 509–17.

24. S. Poijula, K. Wahlberg, and A. Dyregrov, "Adolescent Suicide and Suicide Contagion in Three Secondary Schools," *International Journal of Emergency Mental Health* 3 (2001): 163–68.

25. Lars Johansson, Per Lindqvist, and Anders Eriksson, "Teenage Suicide Cluster Formation and Contagion: Implications for Primary Care," *BMC Family Practice* 7 (2006): 32.

26. Frank Zenere, "Pathway of Contagion: The Identification of a Youth Suicide Cluster," *National Association of School Psychologists* 37 (2008): 1, 6–7.

27. David Miller, *Child and Adolescent Suicidal Behavior* (New York: Guilford, 2011), 123.

28. Beth Hawkins, "Bullying Gay and Lesbian Students: How a School District Became a Suicide Contagion Area," MinnPost.com, December 7, 2011, http://www.minnpost.com/politics-policy/2011/12/bullying-gay-and-lesbian-kids-how-school-district-became-suicide-contagion-a.

29. D. Brent, M. Kerr, C. Goldstein, J. Bozigar, M. Wartella, and M. J. Allan, "An Outbreak of Suicide and Suicidal Behavior in High School,"

Journal of the American Academy of Child and Adolescent Psychiatry 6 (1989): 918–24.

30. A. Schmidtke and H. Hafner, "The Werther Effect After Television Films: New Evidence for an Old Hypothesis," *Psychological Medicine* 18 (1988): 665–76.

31. S. Ellis and S. Walsh, "Soap May Seriously Damage Your Health," *Lancet* I 686 (1986), cited ibid.

32. Elmar Etzersdorfer, Gernot Sonneck, and Sibylle Nagel-Kuess, "Newspaper Reports and Suicide," *New England Journal of Medicine* 327 (1992): 502–3.

33. "Suicide Contagion and the Reporting of Suicide: Recommendations from a National Workshop," *Morbidity and Mortality Weekly Report* 43 (1994): 9–18.

34. E. Etzersdorfer, M. Voracek, and G. Sonneck, "A Dose-Response Relationship of Imitational Suicides with Newspaper Distribution," *Australian and New Zealand Journal of Psychiatry* 35 (2001).

35. In March of 2011 the Substance Abuse and Mental Health Services Administration (SAMHSA), a public health agency within the Department of Health and Human Services, issued new recommendations for media reporting on suicide, developed in conjunction with the American Foundation for Suicide Prevention (AFSP), and Suicide Awareness Voices of Education (SAVE), among others. They are available at www.ReportingOnSuicide.org.

36. Madelyn Gould, Patrick Jamieson, and Daniel Romer, "Media Contagion and Suicide Among the Young," *American Behavioral Scientist* 49 (2003): 1269–84.

37. Ibid., citing M. S. Gould, "Suicide Clusters and Media Exposure," in *Suicide over the Life Cycle: Risk Factors, Assessment, and Treatment of Suicidal Patients*, ed. S. J. Blumenthal and D. J. Kupfer (Washington, D.C.: American Psychiatric Press, 1990), 517–32.

38. R. Ostroff, R. Behrends, K. Lee, and J. Oliphant, "Adolescent Suicides Modeled After a Television Movie," *American Journal of Psychiatry* 142 (1985): 989. See also R. Ostroff and J. H. Boyd, "Television and Suicide," *New England Journal of Medicine* 316 (1987): 876–78.

39. Gould, Jamieson, and Romer, "Media Contagion."

40. Frank J. Zenere, "Suicide Clusters and Contagion," Student Services, http://www.nasponline.org/resources/principals/Suicide_Clusters_NASSP_Sept_%2009.pdf.

41. Ibid., citing Madelyn Gould as cited in Julian Joyce, "Unraveling the Suicide Clusters," BBC News, January 24, 2008, http://news.bbc.co.uk/2/hi/uk_news/7205141.stm.

42. Ibid., citing John Henden as cited in A. L. Berman and D. A. Jobes, *Adolescent Suicide Assessment and Intervention* (Washington, D.C.: American Psychological Association, 1994).

43. Ibid., citing Gould as cited by Joyce, "Unraveling the Suicide Clusters."

44. Jessica Hamzelou, "Copycat Suicides Fuelled by Media Reports," *New Scientist*, September 30, 2009.

45. D. A. Jobes, A. L. Berman, P. W. O'Carroll, S. Eastgard, and S. Knickmeyer, "The Kurt Cobain Suicide Crisis: Perspectives from Research, Public Health, and the News Media," *Suicide and Life Threatening Behavior* 26 (1996): 260–69.

46. Ibid.

47. M. Gould and D. Shaffer, "The Impact of Suicide in Television Movies: Evidence of Imitation," *New England Journal of Medicine* 315 (1986): 690–94, cited in Howard S. Sudak and Donna M. Sudak, "The Media and Suicide," *Academic Psychiatry* 29 (2005): 495–99.

48. Matthew Hoffman, "Recognizing the Warning Signs of Suicide," WebMD, 2012, http://www.webmd.com/depression/guide/depression-recog nizing-signs-of-suicide.

49. "U.S.A. Suicide: 2009 Official Final Data," http://www.suicidol ogy.org/c/document_library/get_file?folderId=228&name=DLFE-494.pdf.

50. Alan L. Berman, "Estimating the Population of Survivors of Suicide: Seeking an Evidence Base," *Suicide and Life-Threatening Behavior* 41 (2011): 110–16.

51. A. E. Crosby and J. J. Sacks, "Exposure to Suicide: Incidence and Association with Suicidal Ideation and Behavior—United States, 1994," *Suicide and Life-Threatening Behavior* 32 (2002): 321–28.

7
Hope for Our Future Selves

1. Michel Montaigne, "A Custom of the Island of Cea," *The Complete Essays of Montaigne*, trans. Donald M. Frame (Stanford: Stanford University Press, 1957), 255.

2. Hugo Friedrich, *Montaigne* (Berkeley: University of California Press, 1991), 273.

3. Voltaire, "Cato: On Suicide and the Abbe St. Cyran's Book Legitimating Suicide," *The Works of Voltaire: A Contemporary Version*, trans. William F. Fleming (New York: E. R. DuMont, 1901), 4: 21.

4. John Stuart Mill, *On Liberty* (Boston: Ticknor and Fields, 1863), 23.

5. Ibid., 198–99.

6. Arthur Schopenhauer, *The World as Will and Representation*, 2 vols., trans. E. F. J. Payne (New York: Dover, 1969), 1: 389.

7. Bryan Magee, *The Philosophy of Schopenhauer* (Oxford: Clarendon, 1983), 223.

8. Arthur Schopenhauer, *Parerga and Paralipomena: Short Philosophical Essays*, 2 vols., trans. E. F. J. Payne (Oxford: Clarendon, 1974), 2: 309, 307.

9. Schopenhauer, *The World as Will and Representation*, 1: 280. In Roman mythology, Orcus was a god in the land of the dead.

10. Ibid.

11. Ibid., 2: 399–400.

12. Ibid., 2: 399–400.

13. D. H. Lawrence, "The Ship of Death," *The Complete Poems of D. H. Lawrence* (London: Wordsworth, 1994), 603–4.

14. D. H. Lawrence, "Healing," ibid., 513.

15. Rudyard Kipling, "If," *Kipling: Poems,* ed. Peter Washington (New York: Everyman, 2007), 170–71.

16. Ludwig Wittgenstein, *Notebooks* (Oxford: Blackwell, 1961), 91.

17. Between that confession and his direct reference to suicide are these sentences: "I have been through it several times before: it is the state of not being able to get over a particular fact. It is a pitiable state, I know. But there is only one remedy that I can see, and that is of course to come to terms with that fact. But this is just like what happens when a man who can't swim has fallen into the water and flails about with his hands and feet and feels that he cannot keep his head above water. That is the position I am in now." Ludwig Wittgenstein to Paul Englemann dated 6/21/1920, in Brian McGuinness, *Wittgenstein, A Life: Young Ludwig, 1889–1921* (Berkeley: University of California Press, 1988), 157.

18. Sigmund Freud, "The Psychogenesis of a Case of Homosexuality in a Woman," *The Standard Edition of the Complete Psychological Works of Sigmund Freud,* ed. James Strachey (London: Hogarth, 1958), 18: 162.

19. Emmanuel Levinas, *Totality and Infinity,* trans. Alphonso Lingis (Pittsburgh: Duquesne University Press, 1969), 146.

20. William Shakespeare, *Macbeth,* in *The Arden Shakespeare: Complete Works,* ed. Richard Proudfoot, Ann Thompson, and David Scott Kastan (London: Thomson Learning, 2001), 797.

21. Emmanuel Levinas, *Time and the Other,* trans. Richard Cohen (Pittsburgh: Duquesne University Press, 1987), 73.

22. A. T. Nuyen, "Levinas and the Euthanasia Debate," *Journal of Religious Ethics* 28 (2000): 119–35.

23. Emmanuel Levinas, *Is It Righteous to Be?* cited in *The Cambridge Introduction to Emmanuel Levinas,* ed. Michael Morgan (Cambridge: Cambridge University Press, 2011), 20.

24. *Emmanuel Levinas: Basic Philosophical Writing,* ed. Adriaan T. Peperzak and Simon Critchley (Bloomington: Indiana University Press, 2008), 181, n. 24.

8

The Twentieth Century's Two Major Voices on Suicide

1. Emile Durkheim, *Suicide,* ed. George Simpson, trans. John A. Spaulding and George Simpson (New York: Free Press, 1979), 209.

2. Ibid., 63.

3. Ibid., 389.

4. Ibid., 337.

5. Ibid., 337–38.

6. Albert Camus, "An Absurd Reasoning," in *The Myth of Sisyphus and Other Essays,* trans. Justin O'Brien (New York: Knopf, 1969), 3.

7. Ibid., 8.

8. Ibid.

9. Ibid., 63.

10. Ibid., 62.

11. Ibid., 65.

12. Ibid., 64.

13. Ibid., 54.

14. Ibid., 55.

15. "The Myth of Sisyphus," ibid., 120.

16. Ibid.

17. Ibid., 122.

18. Ibid., 123.

19. Ibid., 123.

20. Jean-Paul Sartre, *Literary and Philosophical Essays* (Paris, 1943), reprinted as Jean-Paul Sartre, "An Explication of *The Stranger,*" in *Modern Critical Interpretations: The Stranger,* ed. Harold Bloom (New York: Infobase, 2001), 6.

21. Denis Diderot, *Lettres à Sophie Volland,* ed. Jean Varloot (Paris: Gallimard, 1994).

22. Arthur Schopenhauer, *The World as Will and Representation,* trans. E. F. J. Payne, 2 vols. (New York: Dover, 1969), 2: 357.

9
Suffering and Happiness

1. John Keats, *The Complete Poetical Works and Letters of John Keats*, ed. Horace E. Scudder (New York: Houghton Mifflin, 1899), 505–6. A hornbook, used by young pupils, was a slab of wood marked with the alphabet and other elementary educational information and protected by a thin sheet of transparent horn.

2. Friedrich Nietzsche, *The Gay Science*, trans. Walter Kaufmann (New York: Vintage, 1974), 269–70.

3. The Nietzsche scholar Cynthia Halpern has made this careful distinction: "The big problem . . . with all arguments that oversimplify the valuation or affirmation of suffering, is not taking seriously Nietzsche's claim that it is not suffering itself, but the meaninglessness of suffering that causes our greatest troubles with it. Any suffering like the suffering of surgery, or athletic training, or psychological therapy is entirely intelligible and purposeful, and therefore it is not harmful in the way Nietzsche wants to warn us against, as causing *ressentiment,* revenge, hatred of ourselves and of life itself"; Cynthia Halpern, *Suffering, Politics, Power: A Genealogy in Modern Political Theory* (New York: State University of New York Press, 2002), 210.

4. Calvin Trillin, *About Alice* (New York: Random House, 2006), 8–9.

5. Erica Jong, "Dear Colette," in *Loveroot* (New York: Holt, Rinehart and Winston, 1975), 3.

6. Kwame Anthony Appiah, *The Honor Code: How Moral Revolutions Happen* (New York: Norton, 2010).

7. Ibid., 203–4.

8. Albert Schweitzer, Speech of December 3, 1935, to the Silcoates School, recorded in "Visit of Dr. Albert Schweitzer," *Silcoatian,* n.s. 25 (1935): 781–86; Eleanor Roosevelt, *This Is My Story* (New York: Dolphin, 1961), 229; Bertrand Russell, *The Conquest of Happiness* (New York: Norton, 1986), 190–91.

9. David Foster Wallace, *The Pale King* (New York: Little, Brown, 2011), 231.

10. Anne Sexton, *Anne Sexton: A Self Portrait in Letters,* ed. Lois Ames (New York: First Mariner, 2004), 251.

11. Tad Friend, "Jumpers: The Fatal Grandeur of the Golden Gate Bridge," *New Yorker,* October 13, 2003, http://www.newyorker.com/archive /2003/10/13/031013fa_fact#ixzz1rNATAJkP.

12. K. Hawton, "United Kingdom Legislation on Pack Sizes of Analgesics: Background, Rationale, and Effect on Suicide and Deliberate Self-Harm," *Suicide and Life-Threatening Behavior* 32 (2002): 223–29.

10

Modern Philosophical Conversations

1. Emile M. Cioran, *The New Gods* (New York: Quadrangle, 1974), 58–59.

2. Zilla Gabrielle Cahn, *Suicide in French Thought from Montesquieu to Cioran* (New York: Peter Lang, 1998), 379.

3. Albert Camus, "An Absurd Reasoning," in *The Myth of Sisyphus and Other Essays,* trans. Justin O'Brien (New York: Knopf, 1969), 7.

4. Michel Foucault, *History of Madness,* trans. Jonathan Murphy (New York: Routledge, 2006), 335–36.

5. According to James Miller, Foucault's longtime companion considered his suicide attempts the product of an anomalous suffering; James Miller, *The Passion of Michel Foucault* (Cambridge: Harvard University Press, 1993), 56.

6. Michel Foucault, *Foucault Live: Interviews, 1961–1984,* ed. Sylvere Lotringer (New York: Semiotex(e), 1996), 295–97. The book contains essays as well as interviews.

7. Thomas Szasz, *The Theology of Medicine* (New York: Harper and Row, 1977), 73; emphasis in the original.

8. R. M. Martin, "Suicide and False Desires," in *Suicide: The Philosophical Issues,* ed. M. Battin and D. Mayo (New York: St. Martin's, 1980); M. Pabst Battin, *The Death Debate: Ethical Issues in Suicide* (Upper Saddle River, N.J.: Prentice-Hall, 1996); M. Cholbi, "Kant and the Irrationality of Suicide," *History of Philosophy Quarterly* 17 (2000): 159–76; M. Cholbi, "Suicide Intervention and Non-Ideal Kantian Theory," *Journal of Applied Philosophy* 19 (2002): 245–59.

9. R. Bruffaerts, K. Demyttenaere, I. Hwang, et al., "Treatment of Suicidal People Around the World," *British Journal of Psychiatry,* January 2011, 1–7.

10. Ibid., 1.

Index